FREE to LOSE

An Introduction to Marxist Economic Philosophy

John E. Roemer

Radius • An imprint of Century Hutchinson Ltd
London • 1988

Radius

An imprint of Century Hutchinson Ltd
62-65 Chandos Place London WC2N 4NW

Century Hutchinson Australia (Pty) Ltd
PO Box 496, 16-22 Church Street, Hawthorn,
Victoria 3122, Australia

Century Hutchinson New Zealand Ltd
PO Box 40-086, Glenfield, Auckland 10, New Zealand

Century Hutchinson South Africa (Pty) Ltd
PO Box 337, Bergvlei 2012, South Africa

British Library Cataloguing in Publication Data

Roemer, John E.
  Free to Lose: an introduction to Marxist economic philosophy

  1. Marxian economics
I. Title.
335.4'092'4   HB97.5
ISBN 0-09-172999-8
ISBN 0-09-172994-7 Pbk

ISA 233

To Sara Margaret and Andrea Rebecca

Preface

Students who wish to learn Marxist economics must, for the most part, master a language that is a century old and not visibly compatible with what they read in contemporary social science. My aim in this book is to present the lasting ideas of Marxist economics in a way that makes them accessible to readers today. But it would be dishonest to say that only the language is new. Many classic Marxist arguments do not appear here, or have been drastically revised, because I believe they are wrong. The theory of the falling rate of profit is a case in point. And the labor theory of value, so important in the classic Marxist account, is unimportant here, for it contributes nothing to our understanding and, even when most charitably interpreted, is at best misleading. It is, indeed, a secondary purpose of this book to show that the conclusions of Marxist analysis do not depend at all on the labor theory of value. The revised Marxism I present is shaped by the insights that the tools of contemporary economics—that is, neoclassical economics—can bring to bear.

In the century since Marx wrote, his ideas have been important in large part because they provide an argument for the immorality of the capitalist system; and my theme is, similarly, to trace the connections between the economic concepts of Marxism and the ethical ideas to which they are related. Whereas contemporary neoclassical economics advertises its moral neutrality, the task of Marxist economics is to challenge the defensibility, from a moral viewpoint, of an economic system based on private ownership of the means of production. The method of economic theory can provide only one kind of argument in this debate, but one that I hope reveals its usefulness, especially in connection with historical, sociological, and philosophical approaches.

The material I present can form the syllabus of an upper division or graduate course in Marxist economic philosophy. I hope the book will be useful to social science and philosophy students and to the social scientist or philosopher who wants an elementary and quite brief presentation of the links between political philosophy and the ideas of exploitation, class, and historical materialism.

I wish to thank my students, whose enthusiasm encouraged me to write this book, and my friends in the September Group ("Marxismus sine stercore tauri"), who have met annually in London for the better part of a decade to argue about what Marxism has to offer to the social science of our day. This book reflects what I have taken from those discussions. I am especially grateful for the comradeship of G. A. Cohen and David Donaldson, who read the manuscript and commented on it in a degree of detail far beyond what duty required. Finally, I am indebted to Jodi Simpson of Harvard University Press for her incisive editorial work.

Contents

Free to Lose

1

Introduction

Marxism is a set of ideas from which sprang particular approaches to economics, sociology, anthropology, political theory, literature, art, philosophy, and history. Some Marxist ideas have been so successful that they are no longer regarded as Marxist; they have become absorbed by social science, or historical analysis. (An example of such an idea in economics is the two-factor growth model, which focuses on the contributions of labor and capital. Prior to Marx, land had been viewed as an equal contributor, with labor and capital, to growth.) Alfred North Whitehead said that any science that hesitates to forget its founder will soon die. One does not refer to contemporary microeconomics as Smithian—although it was inspired by Adam Smith—because his insights were so pervasive that they came to dominate the whole field. (To call oneself a Smithian would presuppose the existence of non-Smithians.) Marxism, in some parts of the world, has achieved this kind of intellectual hegemony. At least one third of the world's population lives in states founded mainly on principles resulting from the Marxist analysis of capitalism. Although many, perhaps most, of the people in these states do not call themselves Marxist, just as most Americans do not call themselves Lockean or Hobbesian or Rousseauian, the worldview of Marxism—based on class, exploitation, and historical materialism—is pervasive in those societies. I say this with an appreciation of the degree to which many are politically opposed to the regimes in which they live.

Even within social science as it is practiced in the capitalist world, some Marxist ideas have occasionally become so powerful that everyone is a Marxist in some dimensions. History and sociology show this assimilation most; political theory and economics least. Perhaps

Marxism is less influential in economics because economic theory in the West is so closely tied to rationalizing the capitalist order. But Marxism may be uninfluential in economics for another reason: some of the key economic models and theories that Marxism champions, such as the labor theory of value and the falling rate of profit, are simply wrong. The labor theory of value claims that market prices should be proportional to the labor time required to produce commodities, but this is simply not the case. The theory of the falling rate of profit claims that competitive technical innovations by rational capitalists will lead to a capital intensity of technology that will cause the competitive rate of profit to fall. Again, just the opposite is true in the standard competitive model, which was not available in Marx's time. When economists use these famous theories to test the validity of Marxism, they find it lacking; so it is not surprising that they do not take Marxism seriously.

Although these particular Marxist claims are wrong as theoretical and abstract statements about capitalism, the insights that they were intended to emphasize are nevertheless powerful, and frequently those insights can be salvaged, or at least examined and treated seriously, by using methods of contemporary economic theory. For example, the labor theory of value was intended to emphasize the fact that capitalists exploit workers in a capitalist system. Although the labor theory of value is false, I think the conclusion is true. Similarly, although the theory of the falling rate of profit is false as an economic theory, capitalism is subject to recurrent crises that create massive unemployment, which is what that theory intended to show.

The strategy of this book will be to study a few of the central ideas of Marxism by using the tools of contemporary economics. Those central ideas are exploitation and class, the understanding of which are important for the applications of Marxism to sociology, history, ethics, and political theory.

1.1 The Private Property System

Marxist economics is not the economics of socialism; it is one analysis of the economics of capitalism. The main difference between Smithian and Marxist analyses of capitalism is this: Smith argued that the individual's pursuit of self-interest would lead to an outcome

disorder, confusion, absence of gov't or control to society

beneficial to all, whereas Marx argued that the pursuit of self-interest would lead to anarchy, crisis, and the dissolution of the private property-based system itself. Thus, for Smith the aggregation of self-interested actions taken by members of a society is socially optimal, whereas for Marx it is suboptimal. Smith spoke of the invisible hand guiding individual, self-interested agents to perform those actions that would be, despite their lack of concern for such an outcome, socially optimal; for Marxism the simile is the iron fist of competition, pulverizing the workers and making them worse off than they would be in another feasible system, namely, one based on the social or public ownership of property.

Private ownership of property, more specifically the alienable means of production, is attacked in two general ways in Marxism: on grounds of efficiency and on grounds of equity. To claim that the capitalist system is *inefficient* means that there is some alternative system that would be better for all. The private ownership of the capital stock holds back social development, the development of society and of individuals. To claim that the private ownership of property is *inequitable* means that it is unfair to some, although it might be very good for others.

This book will concentrate almost entirely on the inequity of capitalism, not on its inefficiency. Can a system based on the private ownership of the means of production be just and fair, or at least as just and fair as some alternative system that does not allow that form of property? I have chosen to concentrate on the equity issue, at the expense of an analysis of efficiency, because I believe it is perceptions and ideas about justice that are at the root of people's support for or opposition to an economic system. When people support capitalism as a system, it is, I think, not only because they believe capitalism delivers the goods better than other systems, but also because they believe that in a capitalist system people deserve what they get. Similarly, even when socialism works reasonably well in delivering the goods, as it does for some kinds of goods and in some socialist societies, the opposition that most who live in capitalist democracies have to it is based on ideas about freedom—that people do not get what they deserve because of their lack of what is conceived of as economic freedom, namely, the right to accumulate private property. Fundamentally, what is at issue is the moral legitimacy of private property in the means of production.

1.2 Exploitation

Exploitation is the concept around which the Marxist condemnation of capitalism is organized. But the term *exploitation* has two nontechnical meanings: to make use of a thing, as in "to exploit a resource," and to take unfair advantage of someone, as in "to exploit one's wife." The feature of capitalism (according to Marxism) that explains both its ability to expand—by accumulation of capital—and its inequity is the exploitation of workers by capitalists. Capitalists make use of workers and exploit their labor, as miners exploit a natural resource. This process permits accumulation and economic growth. But workers are, in the same process, unfairly treated, and this unfair treatment constitutes the essential inequity of a system based on the private ownership of the means of production.

A good fraction of this book deals with the concept of exploitation. The economic models I present will clarify the concept, so that I may then ask whether, in fact, there is anything wrong with exploitation, as Marxists define it. It is essential to separate the nontechnical concept of exploitation (taking unfair advantage) from its technical definition (see Chapter 2). This distinction quickly leads to questions of political philosophy. Attitudes toward private property are at the heart of the matter: but those attitudes depend on even more fundamental viewpoints, such as those about the rights of individuals to benefit from the skills and traits they have been born with or have acquired.

Does a woman have the right to benefit by virtue of being born into a family that owns a valuable piece of land that passes to her? That is, does anybody have a right to inherit property? If not, does a man have a right to benefit by virtue of being born with a talent that makes him able to earn a large income, say, while expending much less effort than others? What is the essential difference, from a moral point of view, between the inheritance of a talent, by genes or luck, and the inheritance of a fertile piece of land or a big bank account? From a moral point of view, does one deserve to benefit by virtue of being born in the United States instead of in Calcutta? Although it is too ambitious a task to answer these questions definitively in such a short book—questions that are at the heart of contemporary moral and political philosophy—my purpose is to show how the Marxist view of the injustice of capitalist society is predicated on quite reasonable answers to these questions. Furthermore, it will become apparent that the Marxist condemnation of the injustice of capitalism is not so different from the conclusion that other apparently less radical and contemporary theories of political philosophy reach, albeit in language less flamboyant than Marxism's.

1.3 Classes

A second concept central to Marxist discussions is class. *A class is a group of people who all relate to the labor process in a similar way.* For instance, all those who sell their labor for a living form a class; and all those who hire labor form a class; and those who work for themselves and neither hire nor sell labor form a third class. Things get much more complicated when one considers the fact that people have widely differing skills. But in the simplest schematic model of capitalism, these are the three principal classes, and Marxism argues that much can be explained about the evolution of society based on the struggle between classes so defined. The class that sells its labor power is engaged in a more or less constant struggle with the class that hires labor.

Sometimes a class is defined as a group of people who all have approximately the same wealth. This definition of class with reference to wealth is not the same as my definition, although a relationship between class and wealth will be deduced later.

I will not spend much time discussing the history of class struggle, but will concentrate on presenting microeconomic models of exploitation and class and applying them to political philosophy. With a formal economic model, I will show how classes emerge in a systematic way in capitalist society.

1.4 Historical Materialism

Marxism does not take a myopic view of capitalist society; it recognizes that a capitalist system is only one phase of class society— perhaps the last one, but certainly not the first. Whereas Adam Smith considered it natural for men to "truck and barter," and for private property to emerge as an institution, the historical analysis associated with Marxism opposes this view. It claims that a system of production and exchange based on the private ownership of the means of production and on the separation of the vast majority of people from the means of production is just one relatively recent way of organizing an economy.

The theory of historical materialism claims that societies evolve through class struggle and that West European society has evolved in an explicable fashion from systems based on slavery, to feudalism, and then to capitalism. Society will in the future continue its evolution, perhaps in the direction of socialism and, finally, communism. The mechanism that brings about this evolution is class struggle: the struggle of the exploited against the exploiters, of those dispossessed of property against those who own it. But, according to historical materialism, the reason such an evolution occurs lies somewhat deeper: evolution occurs because *the level of development of the technology outgrows the particular form of social organization, which comes to constrain and fetter it.* This theory is perhaps the most famous and important part of Marxism.

1.5 Capitalism and Freedom

Capitalism is championed by those who profit from it, and even by many others, as the system that gives to each his just deserts and allows each the freedom to accomplish what he will. Historical research reveals that this attitude toward the predominant system is not so new: slave systems and feudalism had their contemporary advocates as well. Indeed, Aristotle argued that each soul has his particular role to play—the self-realization of a slave involved fulfilling his slaveness properly. Christianity recapitulated this theme in the Middle Ages by teaching people to be content with their lot, as they were but small cogs in God's universal wheel. Now laissez-faire economists and philosophers maintain that an unfettered capitalism is the system that maximizes individual freedom and the opportunities of each.

Marxism is much more skeptical. It does not claim that any social system—slavery, feudalism, or capitalism—is particularly virtuous in terms of the freedom accorded its members. Rather, it claims that such systems evolve, like organisms, in a more or less adaptive way as a consequence of the internal and external pressures they confront. Private property and untrammeled free trade do not make for the best of all possible worlds, although the results are probably better for most people than systems based on explicit bondage. Whether they are better than what can be achieved with the abolition of private property is a pivotal question of our century. Because we are just at the beginning of the period of the transition to socialism, the question cannot be finally answered. But it is possible to think about it.

Before thinking about an alternative to capitalism in which the means of production are not held as private property, it is important to construct a challenge to private property. Classical Marxism made that challenge over a century ago; to many it seems antiquated, a dusty chapter in nineteenth-century intellectual thought. I will rephrase the challenge in language that I hope is comfortable for contemporary students of these questions, so that they will not have to battle with the linguistic and logical oddities of Marxist discourse. It is unfortunate, I think, that these oddities are preserved in much modern Marxist debate, because they unnecessarily dissuade those who do not already share the ideas from becoming acquainted with them.

1.6 Method

My approach to Marxism is that of a contemporary student of economics and political philosophy. I wish to study the logic of the ideas and the internal coherence of the claims. Focusing on those aspects of Marxism that bear on the legitimacy of private property from the ethical point of view enables one to evaluate the cogency of the claim that capitalism is an exploitative and unfair system. It is of utmost importance to study this claim, for contemporary liberal capitalist thought makes the opposite claim. I do not take a historical approach or an empirical one. In one sense that is a shame, for abstract arguments are often less convincing than palpable evidence. Concrete cases of the genesis of private property in blood and slavery often do more to convince people of its moral illegitimacy than do the abstract and theoretical arguments given here. The revelation that Ferdinand Marcos accumulated billions of dollars in twenty years as the president of a country that paid him an annual salary of $4000 is a particularly lurid case of the kind of "primitive accumulation" of capital that Marxism claims characterizes the history of capital formation more generally in many parts of the world. If this is in fact the case, there is a strong argument for abolishing private property in the means of production simply so that people cannot amass vast economic and political power over others by virtue of accumulating it in such obviously immoral ways.

Because the approach I take here is not historical, it does not lead to a result as clear-cut as that of the Marcos story. It involves, instead, tying one hand behind one's back, and asking whether a system based on private property should be viewed as a good one, or a necessary one, even if property is accumulated in more honest ways. What are the moral antecedents of private property, and what are its economic consequences?

1.7 A Preview

According to Marxism, the consequence of private property is exploitation—by those who have it against those who do not. In Chapter 2 I present a simple two-good model to illustrate the main themes of the next three chapters. The Marxist definition of exploitation is presented with this model, which also shows how exploitation, class, and accumulation emerge with private ownership of the means of production. The approach taken in Chapter 2 is certainly not the standard approach to defining exploitation: the classical notions of circulating capital, variable capital, the value of labor power and surplus value, with which Marxists have been brought up, do not appear. Instead I try to make the principles of exploitation clear in a standard microeconomic equilibrium model, in which competition and market-clearing prices and wage rates determine an outcome at which some people are exploited and others are exploiters.

The models of Chapter 2 show that exploitation, as Marxists define it, emerges under conditions that include the relative scarcity of capital compared with the labor available for it to employ, and the unequal distribution of ownership of that capital. Chapter 3 compares the exploitation that emerges under capitalism—through the market where no agent is compelled in the usual sense to engage in economic activity—with the forcible extraction of the economic surplus under feudalism, from serfs by lords. Indeed, the economic puzzle Marx wrestled with was explaining how wealth, or economic surplus, could accumulate in the hands of a small class under capitalism when no extraeconomic coercion was involved.

Chapter 4 is a more formal and largely algebraic presentation of the ideas presented in Chapter 2. A definition of exploitation more general than that in the earlier chapter is provided, the concepts of embodied labor and profit rate are defined, and the relationship between exploitation and profits is described. I also show how the social division of labor can obscure the perception of exploitation by those who are exploited in a commodity-producing society. This is one of the ways in which capitalism is traditionally distinguished from feudalism—by virtue of the "veil" that commodity relations place on social relations. In Chapter 4 the labor theory of value is only briefly discussed, because I think it is wrong and because the arguments about private property and exploitation can be made completely independently of it. Indeed, one purpose of my analysis is to show that those who are interested in the political and social ideas that Marxism stresses should not take the circuitous and misleading route of the labor theory of value to those ends.

Chapter 5 asks a question that is far too often lost in the mass of details in Marxist discussions. What is wrong with exploitation, technically defined in the Marxist way? There is, of course, the nontechnical usage of exploitation that I have referred to; but in what sense does Marxist exploitation correspond to or reflect taking unfair advantage of a person? Five possible explanations are presented for the evolution of differential ownership of assets in the external world, the inequality that in turn leads to exploitation. Three of these explanations are robbery and plunder, entrepreneurship, and the willingness to take risks. The first of these is clearly morally condemnable, whereas the second and third are not. The story becomes even more complicated when the nonviolent causes of unequal wealth are considered. One essential issue is self-ownership: Does a person have an unfettered right to the income stream flowing from an attribute associated with his person that, in the last analysis, it was his (genetic) luck to acquire? I certainly have not resolved the controversy surrounding this issue in Chapter 5, but some of the main questions are posed and the link between self-ownership and exploitation is discussed.

Whereas Chapter 5 addresses mainly philosophical concerns, Chapter 6 returns to economic analysis and shows how, in the standard model of corn and labor introduced in Chapter 4, a class structure of agents in an economy with private ownership emerges as a result of self-interested economic activity. The main purpose is to show that a person's class is not something that should be taken as a given before the person begins economic activity; it is an economic characteristic that emerges from market activity. A person acquires membership in a certain class by virtue of rational activity on her part, by virtue of choosing the best option available subject to the constraints she faces, which are determined by the value of the property she owns. Two theorems are presented: the Class–Wealth Correspondence and the Class–Exploitation Correspondence. The first of these shows that a person's wealth is related in a systematic way to his class position; the second theorem shows that persons who optimize by hiring others belong to a class of exploiters and persons who optimize by selling labor to others belong to a class of exploited persons.

Chapter 6 provides microfoundations for claims that are elsewhere treated as postulates in Marxist social science. I show that both the class position of a person and his status as exploited agent or exploiter emerge from rational, optimizing activity in which the principal distinguishing feature of agents is their wealth. Traditional Marxist analysts postulate that those who hire are the exploiters and those who are hired are exploited. Hence, the analysis of Chapter 6 reduces what was a postulate to a theorem, and thus enriches our understanding of exploitation and class, in the sense of providing a prior determination of the phenomena.

Classical Marxists view exploitation as intimately related to the labor theory of value and to transactions that take place in the labor market. One theme developed in Chapters 2 through 6 is that exploitation has much more to do with property relations than with the labor market—and that Marxists' focus on the labor market has been excessive and has given rise to their own fetishism of labor. In Chapter 7 this theme is pursued more vigorously. I show that the phenomena of exploitation and class that are fully developed with a labor market in Chapters 2 and 6 can be just as fully developed in a model of an economy in which no labor market exists—where agents borrow and lend capital to each other, but where the hiring and selling of labor does not occur. The driving factor of exploitation and class that emerges in Chapter 7, on what I call Capital Market Island, is just the same as before: differential ownership of the capital stock. But I emphasize the point that it is wrong to focus on the labor market if one's concerns are the ethical ones that an interest in exploitation implies. In Chapter 7 I also show that exploitation can emerge without a market for either labor or capital—all that is needed is the exchange of commodities of the usual sort, excluding labor and finance capital.

Given this result, the question that naturally emerges is, Why has capitalism historically utilized labor markets, rather than capital markets, to organize economic transactions between those with wealth and those without it? Why does labor not hire capital instead of capital hiring labor?

Although it is difficult to summarize the topic of historical materialism in one short chapter, I have attempted to do so in Chapter 8, for it is necessary to put into perspective the discussion of private property. For this purpose, I rely almost entirely on G. A. Cohen's summary of the interpretation of historical materialism, an interpretation many view as a particularly deterministic form of historical materialism. I contrast Cohen's view of historical materialism with another Marxist view, that of Robert Brenner, which puts more emphasis on the determination of historical change by class struggle than does Cohen's reading. This discussion should serve as a brief introduction to some of the exciting work being done in philosophy and history by those who view their tradition as Marxist. But the main point of the chapter is to explain the emphasis that Marxism places on the evolution of forms of property. The private property system is just one possible way of organizing economic activity; it may have been the best way for a certain period but is probably not the best way today, nor will it be in the future.

Chapter 9 builds on the view of evolving property relations presented in historical materialism by proposing a hierarchy of forms of exploitation, each based on different forms in which property might exist: slave property, feudal property (serfs), capitalist property (means of production), and socialist property (skills and perhaps status). The claim is made that forms of property tend to be abolished over time, and that those forms which in the past were viewed as legitimate eventually come to be viewed as illegitimate. Associated with each form of property is a characteristic form of exploitation; the focus of this book, exploitation as defined by Marxist theory, is in fact the particular form of exploitation associated with capitalist property, with unequal ownership of assets (excluding skills and other people) that are useful as means of production. In Chapter 9, I discard entirely the classic Marxist definition of exploitation in terms of surplus labor, which was developed earlier, and propose a definition of exploitation in terms of property relations. Essentially, the exploitation associated with a particular economic structure or mode of production is defined as that inequality of outcome associated with the unequal ownership of that property which is the characteristic property form of that mode of production. (For example, feudal exploitation is that inequality associated with the unequal holdings of property rights in the labor of other people.) In Chapter 9, as well as discarding the traditional Marxist view of exploitation, I replace it with a more general conception that fits into the panorama of economic structures highlighted by historical materialism. A concern with exploitation is now viewed, more fully, as a concern with inequality in access to property and the consequences thereof: what evolves through history are the types of property whose unequal distribution characterizes economic structures, and upon which it is essential to concentrate.

If exploitation is the consequence of unequal ownership of a certain kind of property, then why not end it by redistributing that property so that everyone owns an equal share? Socialists advocate abolition, not just of the unequal distribution of property in the means of production, but also of the property form itself. No one should be allowed to hold any property in alienable means of production, which under socialism are to be held publicly. This question of why property forms are abolished does not apply only to the transition from capitalism to socialism, for in previous periods, forms of property were abolished as well. The great revolutionary transitions all are characterized by abolition of forms of property (such as serfs and slaves). Thus far I have not addressed this question of why socialization of the alienable means of production is the answer to capitalist exploitation, rather than syndicalization, which is a kind of people's capitalism in which everyone would own an equal share but markets would continue to operate in the usual way. In Chapter 10, I propose several reasons why Marxists advocate the abolition of the property form in alienable assets.

Chapter 10 concludes with the most tentative part of the argument, because it represents work in progress. What does public ownership of the means of production mean? Suppose one wishes to socialize ownership of productive assets in the external world but wishes to allow people to retain property rights over their internal productive assets, that is, their skills and talents. What kind of distributions of income, or of final welfare, will respect these two kinds of property rights: private ownership of self and its skills, and public or joint ownership of the productive assets in the external world? On the basis of the history of capitalist societies, one has a good idea of what private ownership of assets means. (I doubt that our ideas would have been so clear in feudal times, when, for example, various rights that different people had in a given parcel of land were complex and incomprehensible by modern standards.) The final sections of Chapter 10 take an axiomatic approach to designing an economic constitution that respects both public ownership by persons of the external world and some limited private ownership (at least) of their own skills. Are there any such constitutions, and what sort of inequality of final outcome will they permit? The approach taken here is a far cry from a historical one to the question of public ownership, which would of necessity be limited to studying the experience of various states in which property has been nationalized during the last sixty years. It is, instead, an attempt to outline in an abstract way what public ownership of the external world in conjunction with protection of property rights in skills might entail. The motivation for this attempt is philosophical, but the tools for solving the problem are economic.

Finally, let me amplify my reasons for limiting the discussion of issues of incentives associated with private property, which are so much the province of economic thinking on the subject. (Incentive issues are briefly discussed in Chapters 5 and 9.) I think that ethical considerations are to an extent independent of incentive problems. It could be argued that the criticisms of private property, and even of self-ownership, which are occasionally made, are wishful thinking and continue a long Marxist tradition of utopianism. But I do not believe that to be the case. I think the timelessness of incentive problems is exaggerated by contemporary economic theory, in the sense that the behavior and preferences of individuals are to a large extent determined by the property forms that exist in the societies in which they live. Indeed, the incentives and remuneration that people expect depend in large part on what they think they deserve, and therefore on *their* assessment of ethical considerations. Were some kind of socialism universally established, by which I mean that private property in the means of production would become as scarce as slavery is today, I think people would compete, excel, and realize themselves in ways other than the accumulation of material wealth. In fact, they already do. But this is a hackneyed theme, which I shall not pursue further.

2

The Origin of Exploitation

Exploitation has a technical definition that must be distinguished from its colloquial one. When Marxists say that workers are exploited by capitalists, they mean—colloquially—that an economic relation of exploitation exists between workers and capitalists (that workers are used by capitalists) and that capitalists take unfair advantage of workers (that workers are used by capitalists in an ethically indefensible way). In this chapter I will define exploitation in a technical sense, using a simple model of an economy that produces only one good. In Chapter 5, I will discuss when technical exploitation should be considered as unfair treatment of workers by capitalists.

2.1 An Egalitarian Distribution of Capital

Imagine a society consisting of 1,000 members. There is one produced good, corn, which all like to consume. Corn is produced from inputs of labor and seed corn. All members of this society are equally skilled and productive, and all have knowledge of the technologies that exist for producing corn. Each person is assumed to have *subsistence preferences*: each needs to consume 1 unit of corn per week (to survive, let us say); after having done so he prefers to take leisure rather than to work more and consume more corn. There is one additional condition: each agent desires to reproduce the stock of seed corn, if any, with which he began. He does not want to begin the next week with a smaller corn stock, which is the only kind of capital in this model. Thus, a person's utility, or welfare level, is a function of corn consumed and labor expended—or corn consumed and leisure consumed. The particular preferences I have posited are easy to analyze, because the trade-offs between corn and leisure are very simple: to get 1 unit of corn, a person is willing to do anything, and after that he is willing to do nothing.

Suppose there is a total initial capital stock of 500 units of corn ($K = 500$). Further, assume that in this society there are two ways of producing corn, or two techniques of production, which are called the Farm and the Factory:

Farm   3 days labor
            + 0 units of seed corn $\rightarrow$ 1 unit of corn

Factory   1 day labor $\rightarrow$ 2 units of corn, gross,
            + 1 unit of seed corn   or 1 unit of corn, net

The production period for both the Farm and the Factory techniques is 1 week (7 days); that is, seed corn is tied up in the ground that long before it produces a harvest, even though it may take only 1 day to plant, as in the Factory technology.

Thus far, no distribution of the means of production, or of the capital stock, which in this model is just seed corn, has been assumed. Now assume that there is an egalitarian distribution of capital stock. Each agent owns ½ unit of corn—the aggregate capital stock is divided equally among all. Given the technologies described, the preferences of the agents, and the distribution of assets, what is the equilibrium in this economy?

The equilibrium solution is that each agent works a total of 2 days: ½ day in the Factory and 1½ days on the Farm. Assume that a person can switch costlessly and instantaneously between one technology and the other. In the ½ day a woman works in the Factory technology, she plants her ½ unit of seed corn, which at the end of the week will yield for her 1 unit of corn, gross. Her capital stock is tied up in the ground for that week. The 1 unit of corn, gross, she gets in this process is sufficient to replace her original seed corn stock and leave her ½ unit of corn to consume. She must somewhere produce another ½ unit of corn for consumption; and to do so she moves to the Farm, where in 1½ days she can produce ½ unit of corn, with no capital stock.

One might ask what type of technology can produce corn using labor alone. Perhaps the Farm technology involves going to the forest and hunting around for wild corn, which grows there: this labor-intensive process yields corn but requires much more labor than is needed to produce an equivalent amount of corn using the Factory process. But the specific technologies of production are irrelevant. The important assumption is that there are two ways of surviving in the economy. One way is to engage in a production process that uses capital, that is, some scarce nonlabor input, which in this model is seed corn. The alternative way is one everyone can engage in whether or not he has access to capital—in this model, the Farm technology.

The solution I have outlined is autarkic—there is no trade. Each person works only for herself; she neither sells nor hires labor, nor does anyone sell corn to anyone else. The solution is clearly egalitarian. Each person works 2 days and consumes 1 unit of corn. No one can do any better, and the corn stock is reproduced for the beginning of the next week. A careful definition of the term *equilibrium* is not necessary; simply notice that this is the natural solution to the problem that people face in this economy—of producing the corn they require subject to the constraints determined by their capital stock and the technology. Given the subsistence preferences that have been posited, no one will work any longer, for after consuming 1 unit of corn, these people prefer only to take leisure.

From this solution I can define the *socially necessary labor time* (SNLT) for this society to reproduce itself. Given the technologies, the capital stock, and the consumption requirement, the socially necessary labor time required to produce 1,000 units of corn is 2,000 days; or, from the vantage point of an individual, the labor socially necessary to produce 1 unit of corn is 2 days. Each producer works, in this equilibrium, precisely socially necessary labor time. More generally, the labor time socially necessary to produce a certain amount of corn is the amount of labor that is needed to produce that corn and to reproduce the seed corn used up in the process. Society will use all its capital stock first in the Factory process, which in 1 week will produce 500 units of corn, net, with 500 days of labor; in the meantime the remaining 500 units of corn will be produced by working a total of 1,500 days on the Farm.

Suppose that instead of requiring 1 unit of corn per week for consumption, each person requires 2 units of corn per week. Then the total weekly requirement for this society would be 2,000 units of corn. It would still be true that 500 units of corn, net, can be produced using the Factory in 500 days. To produce the additional 1,500 units of corn required would now necessitate expending 4,500 days of labor on the Farm; and the socially necessary labor time for producing 2,000 units of corn would be 5,000 days. Or, from the point of view of the individual, 1 unit of corn would require 2½ days of labor. Thus, the amount of time socially necessary to produce a unit of corn depends on the total corn production required and on the fraction of that production that must be carried out using the inferior (Farm) technology.

If, in a third model society, people only required ½ unit of corn per week for consumption, then the total corn requirement of this society would be 500 units of corn per week, all of which could be produced using the Factory technology alone. No one would use the Farm, and the labor time socially necessary to produce 1 unit of corn would fall to just 1 day.

Return, now, to the initial subsistence preferences, in which each person needs or wants to consume 1 unit of corn per week, in which case the amount of labor time socially necessary to produce society's requirement is 2 days per unit of corn per individual (or 2,000 days in total). I can also say that 2 days is the labor embodied in 1 unit of corn. In other words, the *labor embodied* in a unit of corn is the amount of labor required to produce that commodity and to reproduce the inputs used in producing it, given the technologies and capital stock available. Socially necessary labor time is the labor embodied in the corn consumption bundle required by the population.

There is, however, an ambiguity in this definition that I wish to point out. If I ask, Given the technologies, how much labor is required to produce 1 unit of corn, net? the answer is 1 day. (Just use 1 unit of seed corn in the Factory.) This, however, cannot be done on an economy-wide scale—that is, this society cannot produce 1,000 units of corn in 1,000 days. When I speak of the labor embodied in a unit of corn, that should be understood to mean the average amount of social labor time required to produce that unit, given the total amount of corn produced. Thus, the labor embodied in 1 unit of corn is 2 days in this economy, because at equilibrium 1,000 units of corn, net, are produced with 2,000 days of labor.

The particular equilibrium solution I have discussed above is autarkic, but there are other ways of arranging an equilibrium in this economy that do involve trading among members—in particular, when some persons hire the labor of others. Suppose there are two groups of agents, called H (for hirers of labor) and S (for sellers of labor). Any 750 agents may constitute the H group and the remaining 250 will constitute the S group. Those in the S group are going to sell their labor for a wage to those in the H group. Each person in the S group first works up her own capital stock using the Factory technology. That requires ½ day of labor and generates for her ½ unit of corn, net, by the end of the week. She needs to earn another ½ unit of corn to consume. Instead of going to the Farm to produce that corn, she offers to sell her labor to someone, or to several members, of the H group. What real wage will prevail in this economy to make this offer of labor attractive to both hirers and sellers on the labor market?

The answer is that members of H will offer to hire members of S to work on their (H's) capital stock at a wage rate of 3 days labor for 1 unit of corn, or a real wage of ⅓ unit of corn per day's labor. Why? First, observe that at this wage rate a member of S can work up the capital stock of 3 members of H, expending a total of 1½ days of labor, and she will earn as a total wage precisely ½ unit of corn. Combining the labor traded with that she has already done for herself, she will have worked a total of 2 days—partly for herself and mainly for others—earned exactly 1 unit of corn, and reproduced her original seed stock, as required. So a member of S is willing to accept this wage: she is indifferent between this proposal and working autarkically in the Factory and then on the Farm, as in the first equilibrium solution described. Now from the viewpoint of a member of H, he will have his ½ unit of corn capital worked up by some member of S, producing 1 unit of corn, gross. Out of that, ½ unit reproduces his capital and he pays a wage of ⅓ unit of corn/day × ½ day = ⅙ unit of corn, which leaves a profit for him of ⅓ unit of corn. He must go elsewhere to produce the other ⅔ units of corn he needs, for his capital stock is tied up. To earn the additional corn he requires, he uses the Farm technology and works for 2 days, producing ⅔ units of corn. Thus, he, too, ends up working exactly 2 days, reproducing his capital stock and having 1 unit of corn left for consumption.

The second equilibrium is exactly the same with regard to the labor–corn allocation as the first one. Each person works 2 days, reproduces his or her capital stock, and consumes 1 unit of corn. But the *class structure* differs from that of the first equilibrium. Every producer just works for himself in the first equilibrium; there is only one class of self-employed producers and no division of labor. In the second equilibrium there are two classes—H and S—and there is a complete *social division of labor*. Some work only on the Farm and some only in the Factory.

What is a *class*? That is best seen from the model. It is a group of people, all of whom relate to the labor market in the same way. In the first equilibrium each person is a self-employed peasant, or artisan. In the second equilibrium 250 people are sellers of labor power (and also work for themselves part time) and 750 people are hirers of labor power (and also work for themselves part time). A more precise definition of class will be given in Chapter 4.

Note that in both of these equilibria each person works just socially necessary labor time. Indeed, given the preferences of agents in this model, no one has any reason to prefer one equilibrium over the other. For in each equilibrium each person works 2 days and consumes 1 unit of corn. This indifference between the equilibria follows because the only arguments of the utility function of people in this society are leisure and corn. No person has any preference for rural life over urban life or vice versa. Nor does anyone care whether she works for herself or for a boss. But suppose that working for a boss is a source of disutility; that is, labor performed for hire is more unpleasant than labor performed for oneself. In that case it would no longer be correct to say people cared just about corn and leisure: they would care about corn and the various types of labor they expend—labor expended on one's own account being of a different type from labor expended for someone else. Were this the case, the second equilibrium outlined would not be an equilibrium, because members of S would prefer to work autarkically, as in the first equilibrium, rather than work for a boss. Given this preference, would it still be possible to arrange an equilibrium involving the two classes H and S? The wage rate would have to be higher than ⅓ unit of corn per day to compensate a member of S for expending labor under a boss, an activity that she now finds relatively distasteful. But if that were so, the hirer's profits would fall, and he would have to work longer than 2 days on the Farm to get all the corn he needs. What would entice him to do that? Nothing—unless, perversely, he receives utility from being a boss over someone, or unless he has a preference for rural life over urban life. If hirers have preferences of this sort, then indeed one could have an equilibrium with a complete social division of labor, but with slightly different outcomes than those described in the second equilibrium above.

Conditions other than disutilities involving types of labor expended can motivate a social division of labor. Suppose there are *set-up costs* in moving from the Farm to the Factory, because it takes time to move. Then, in fact, the autarkic equilibrium discussed above is not achievable, for when each person moves from Farm to Factory, he uses up some time. It would require 2 days plus set-up time to produce 1 unit of corn by oneself. If these set-up costs exist, it would be to the advantage of society to minimize them, by having one group work only in the Factory and the other only on the Farm. This is, in fact, what the second equilibrium accomplishes. With set-up costs, one would observe *only* the second equilibrium, because the autarkic solution would not be Pareto optimal: everyone could be rendered better off by the social division of labor, because only by specializing could each person acquire 1 unit of corn for consumption for 2 days of labor. Thus, despite the class structure of this equilibrium, the result is completely egalitarian in terms of the corn consumed and the labor expended by members of the society. So a class structure is not ipso facto associated with inequality of final welfare.

2.2 The Technical Definition of Exploitation

Exploitation is said to exist if in a given economy some agents must work more time than is socially necessary (longer than the socially necessary labor time) to earn their consumption bundles and others work less time than is socially necessary to earn their bundles. Exploitation does not exist in the economy described in Section 2.1, because everyone works precisely socially necessary labor time. Nevertheless, it is noteworthy that *class differentiation* can emerge without exploitation, at least at this level of theoretical abstraction. That is the lesson of the second equilibrium, which has the two classes H and S. However, without the kind of set-up costs referred to above, the class structure is rather ephemeral: it is not forced into existence, for society could just as well organize itself as it does in the autarkic equilibrium, that is, in an undifferentiated way. Class structure becomes interesting, and conforms more to Marxist expectation, when there is no other way for society to organize itself to achieve an equilibrium.

2.3 Unequal Ownership of the Capital Stock

What happens when a society is organized with unequal ownership of the capital stock (in this model, capital stock is the seed corn)? Instead of the equal distribution posited in Section 2.1, suppose that each of 10 agents (call them rich agents 1, 2, 3, . . . , 10) owns 50 units of corn and the other 990 own none. The only productive asset these last own is their labor power, the capacity to work. This economy also differs from that described in Section 2.1 in another way, namely, that each person's utility function is strictly increasing in corn. In other words, if he can get more corn without expending additional labor, then he wishes to do so. A person having subsistence preferences is not indifferent to getting more than 1 unit of corn, he simply is not willing to expend more of his own time to get more corn. Should more corn come his way for nothing, he is happy to accept it. Otherwise, all features of the economy (preferences for leisure time and technologies) are the same as before.

What is the equilibrium in this economy with the skewed initial distribution of seed corn? First I will try the obvious autarkic arrangement. Each of the propertyless agents (I will call them peasants) works 3 days on the Farm, to get 1 unit of corn. Each of the propertied agents works up 1 unit of corn of his capital stock, producing 1 unit of corn, net, at the end of the week, which he consumes. Thus, each of the rich agents 1, 2, . . . , 10 works 1 day and each of the other 990 agents works 3 days. This arrangement would be a case of exploitation, but it is not an equilibrium. There is exploitation in this society because the socially necessary labor time for this society is 2 days of labor. That calculation does not change as the distribution of corn changes, because the calculation of socially necessary labor time is independent of the distribution of assets. It depends only on total consumption, technology, and the total amount of capital and labor available. (If the needs of people, or their demands, were to change with the redistribution of wealth, the story would be more complicated.)

But this arrangement is not an equilibrium. The rich agents can do better for themselves, without the poor ones doing any worse. Using a labor market, a deal can be struck. Each rich agent can become a capitalist and offer to hire labor. As before, the rich agents constitute the class H. Each rich agent has a lot of unused seed corn in the preceding solution. Suppose each rich person offers to hire peasants to work up his capital stock in the Factory technology—at a wage rate of 2 days of labor for 1 unit of corn (that is, ½ unit of corn per day). Then all 990 peasants will flock to the Factory gates to work, for that is a better deal than working on the Farm, at a rate of 3 days of labor for 1 unit of corn. Each peasant will wish to supply 2 days of labor (and thereby earn his needed 1 unit of corn). But, to put this supply of labor to work in the Factory requires 2 × 990 = 1,980 units of seed corn, an amount that is not available. Thus, at the wage rate just proposed, the supply of labor far exceeds the demand for the labor by the capitalists. Hence, ½ unit of corn per day is not an equilibrium wage. The capitalists can lower the wage from ½ unit of corn per day, because the supply of labor exceeds the demand for labor at that proposed wage.

How far will they lower it? The alternative for a peasant is to work at a real wage of ⅓ unit of corn per day on the Farm. So long as the Factory wage is higher than that, all peasants will flock to the Factory. But there is not enough capital stock to produce the subsistence needs of this population using only the Factory. Therefore, no wage higher than ⅓ unit of corn per day can be sustained. Furthermore, no wage lower than ⅓ unit of corn per day can be sustained, for at a wage lower than ⅓ unit of corn per day no labor will be offered; all peasants will prefer to stay peasants, earning their livelihood on the Farm. Hence, the only possible wage that can clear the labor market is ⅓ unit of corn per day (3 days of labor for 1 unit of corn).

At this wage each peasant is indifferent to working on the Farm or in the Factory, because the real wage is the same in both places. Hence, the labor supplied at the wage ⅓ unit of corn per day is anything between 0 days and 3 × 990 = 2,970 days. That is, each peasant, and there are 990 of them, is willing to work any amount of labor from 0 to 3 days for a capitalist at the wage of ⅓ unit of corn per day. Figure 2.1 shows the supply and demand curves of labor in this economy. An equilibrium can be arranged as follows. The capitalists hire exactly the number of peasants required to utilize fully their capital stock. This requires 500 days of labor, or 500/3 peasants, each of whom becomes a "factory worker" and earns 1 unit of corn for 3 days of labor. The other 823.33 (990 − 500/3) peasants stay as peasants on the Farm and earn their subsistence bundle of corn there. The capitalists, as a class, work 0 days; the workers in their factories produce 1,000 units of corn, of which 500 units replace the seed stock, 500/3 units is paid out as wages, and the remaining ⅔ × 500 = 333.33 units of corn are profits. Thus, each capitalist gets 33.3 units of corn as profit in this equilibrium, and does not work at all. He can certainly consume his needed 1 unit of corn, or even much more than that. Or he can accumulate corn.

In the equilibrium in this model, there are three classes: capitalists, who do not work but only hire others and reap profits; workers, who

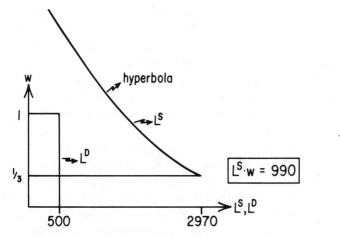

Figure 2.1 Equilibrium in the peasant economy. L^S, labor supply (days); L^D, labor demand (days); w, wage (units of corn per day).

work for capitalists and earn a subsistence wage; and peasants, who do not work for capitalists and earn a subsistence wage. Each worker and peasant works for 3 days to earn 1 unit of corn. But I concluded earlier that the amount of *labor embodied* in 1 unit of corn is 2 days, given the demands of this society. So exploitation has emerged in this model, because capitalists work less than socially necessary labor time, whereas the workers and the peasants work more than socially necessary labor time.

2.4 The Causes of Exploitation

What are the features of the economy described in the preceding section that have caused exploitation to emerge? Two are worthy of mention: the scarcity of capital relative to the labor available for it to employ; and differential ownership of the capital stock. The second feature has already been emphasized by the comparison of the models of Sections 2.1 and 2.3; exploitation has emerged with the differential ownership of the capital stock. But what effect does scarcity of capital have?

Capital is relatively scarce in the economy described in Section 2.3. By this I mean that it is impossible for the society to "reproduce itself economically" (that is, to produce 1,000 units of corn, net, in a week) using only the Factory technology, because it lacks the necessary capital stock to do so. Suppose, on the other hand, that capital is abundant—say, the total endowment of capital is 5,000 units of corn instead of 500, and that each capitalist owns 500 units of seed corn. What would happen when the wage rate offered is 3 days of labor for 1 unit of corn? I have computed that at most $3 \times 990 = 2,970$ days of labor will be offered, which can be used in conjunction with 2,970 units of seed corn in the Factory, but there is much more seed corn lying around. Capitalists will start to compete with each other; one thinks that if he raises the real wage a bit, he will attract more labor, thereby using all his capital stock and reaping much more profit than he currently gets. Hence, the real wage rate will rise, essentially to the point where profits are zero. It will rise to the rate of 1 unit of corn per day's labor, at which rate the capitalists make zero profits, and no one works on the Farm. (In fact, this is a simplification; it will rise to some value a bit less than 1 unit of corn per day, so that the capitalists can earn at least some of their own consumption bundle. But this is a detail that is not important for my story.)

If capital is sufficiently abundant relative to the labor available for it to employ, then the profit rate drops and exploitation virtually disappears. Of course, socially necessary labor time decreases in this economy as the capital to labor ratio rises, because it becomes possible to produce 1,000 units of corn with much less labor. With $K = 5,000$, socially necessary labor time per individual is 1 day of labor, because society does not need to use the Farm at all.

The essential aspect of capital is that it is an input to production that cannot be instantaneously produced. It must already exist in order for it to be used in the present. Thus, either it was produced in the past (as I assumed the seed corn was) or it is a nonproduced factor (like land or some natural resource). (The incomes that accrue to owners of capital that was produced in the past are often called profits, whereas the incomes to owners of natural resources that were never produced are called rents.) When capital (whether it was produced in the past or is an appropriated natural resource) becomes private property and is distributed in an inegalitarian manner, differentiation and exploitation arise, through the market process.

Recall that the sense in which the exploitation that occurs here is a technical, but not obviously an ethical, one. It is not clear that the factory workers who are exploited in the equilibrium described in this section are being unfairly taken advantage of (or being exploited in the colloquial sense) unless one had some reason to believe that the initial unequal distribution of the capital stock that gave rise to that exploitation is unfair.

2.5 The Industrial Reserve Army

In Marxist parlance, the excess of labor relative to capital is supplied by what is called the *industrial reserve army*. That army consists of the people who are potentially in the work force and can be employed by capital but are working "on the Farm," that is, on the margins of the capitalist sector. It is their existence that, in this story, keeps the wage rate down to its subsistence level—and profits at a maximum. The most proximate source of this industrial reserve army is the unemployed, and for this reason, Marxism views unemployment as a necessary condition for maintaining a "good investment climate," that is, a profit rate sufficiently high to induce capitalists to invest.

Many Marxists have claimed that, because it is in the interests of the capitalist class to have an industrial reserve army, capitalism creates such an army, that is, that it deliberately maintains unemployment. Perhaps it does through monetary and fiscal policies. If so, those policies must be policies of the state. Whether maintenance of a pool of unemployed workers is a deliberate policy of the capitalist state is a subject of research and contention.

A second source of the industrial reserve army is a pool of migrant workers. If the labor market becomes international and workers can move across borders in search of employment, then capitalists can hold down the real wage by importing workers from other countries, from what has been called the agricultural periphery. Or, alternatively, capital can move to where the workers are. Capital movement has become a very real phenomenon in the United States during the past twenty years as industry formerly located in the United States has moved to Southeast Asia, an area with cheap labor. The effect of this movement has been a reduction of the real wage of workers in the United States. This is not necessarily a bad thing: Do workers in the United States have any more right of access to the capital stock, and employment, than workers in Southeast Asia who were otherwise (perhaps at best) employed on subsistence "farms"?

The hypocrisy of capitalists with respect to "illegal aliens" is explained by the effect these workers have as an industrial reserve army. On the one hand, capitalists do not want the supply of such workers cut off; on the other hand, it is in their interest for the workers to be maintained in an illegal status, for that tends to keep them subservient on the job. The optimal policy for capitalists is therefore to maintain a pool of illegal workers and to have the illegality only mildly enforced. An example of this policy in action is provided by an article by Robert Pear in the *New York Times* (January 23, 1986) headlined "Reagan's advisers say bill on aliens can hurt economy." The Council on Economic Advisers reported to Reagan that punishing employers for hiring illegal aliens would have adverse effects on the nation's economy. The report says that the presence of low-skilled foreign workers in the United States "enables domestic business enterprises to produce goods profitably that would not otherwise have been produced here."

2.6 Concluding Comments

One might ask how realistic the models of Sections 2.1 and 2.3 are as schemata approximating capitalism. For instance, it does not seem as if there are two technologies today. Do people have an alternative like the Farm, where they can go to produce their consumption needs outside of the capitalist sector? There might be several approximations to the Farm, or institutions that take the place of the Farm, in modern capitalism. Some of these are associated with the state: unemployment insurance and welfare assistance may provide the alternative that sets a lower bound on the real wage. But the image of a Farm to return to, as an alternative, is not a real one in modern capitalist society, and the real wage must indeed be set by some procedure more complicated than the one in these models.

Before discussing the exploitation that has emerged in the society in Section 2.3, and whether or not it is a bad thing, I want to point out that the phenomenon is one that can exist in a perfectly competitive situation. First of all, there is no cheating or coercion in the model. Nor is there any collusion on the part of capitalists. In this sense, exploitation in the technical sense—that some live off the labor of others by virtue of their possession of capital—is a phenomenon that emerges in a model with competitive markets. For Marx, it was important to explain this feature of capitalism. How could accumulation take place and capital be concentrated systematically in the hands of a small class without cheating or coercion, or in what one would today call a regime of perfect competition? The question becomes interesting when one observes that the concentration of wealth in the hands of the landed gentry under feudalism was accomplished only with coercion. Notice, as well, that in this model exploitation and the unequal distribution of income are not the consequence of people having different preferences: everyone has the same preferences. This may not be an accurate depiction of the world; the point is, exploitation and inequality result even under that stringent assumption. Thus, exploitation in this model cannot be explained by the existence of different kinds of people—unless it is the differences between people, unalluded to here, that explain why they started off with different amounts of capital. The internal differences between people that might explain differential wealth will be the topic of Chapter 5.

Finally, I want to point out the differences between the equilibria of the models of Sections 2.1 and 2.3. The first difference is in the initial distribution of the capital stock. In the model of Section 2.1 there is no essential class distinction, whereas in the model of Section 2.3 there are three distinct classes, defined in terms of how they relate to the selling and hiring of labor. In the model of Section 2.1 there is no exploitation at equilibrium, whereas in the model of Section 2.3 there is. Finally, and this is a point I have not emphasized until now, in the model of Section 2.1 there is no accumulation of capital, whereas in the model of Section 2.3 there is. Thus, in the model of Section 2.1 precisely the consumption needs of the population are produced at equilibrium, and the society ends up at the beginning of the next week in exactly the same situation as that at the beginning of the first week. In the model of Section 2.3, however, each capitalist makes 33.3 units of corn profits. If I assume that he consumes just 1 unit of corn, then he begins the second week, not with 50 units of corn, but with 82.3 units of corn. Thus, there are three essential consequences of the differential ownership of the capital stock: the emergence of exploitation, class, and accumulation.

3

Feudalism and Capitalism

Adam Smith and David Ricardo were, with others, champions of and intellectual impresarios for capitalism. They constructed economic interpretations of capitalism emphasizing the aspects of capitalism that made it appear to be more progressive than feudalism, or any aristocratic system in which the form of income of the propertied class was rent from land. Capitalists were pictured as progressive because they created industry and physical capital in the process of competition with each other, whereas landed rentiers were parasites who did nothing of social value. These distinctions between capital and land are not present in the models of Chapter 2, although one can construct other models to emphasize that difference. The purpose of the models of Chapter 2 is to focus on the emergence of classes, accumulation, and the highly unequal distribution of income that emerges as the consequence of private and unequal ownership of the means of production (whether these means are capital stock, like seed corn, or land).

3.1 A Brief Account of Feudalism

I will characterize feudalism in a fairly simple way, omitting many nuances for the sake of simplicity. A lord owned a large amount of land and had the rights to certain amounts of labor provided by serfs or peasants who lived on the estate. Each serf family had its family plot of land, on which it produced its subsistence needs. In addition to working on the family plot, the serf was required to provide labor to the lord: corvée and demesne labor—working a certain number of days a year on the lord's land, building roads to keep up the manor, participating in the activities of the armed forces of the lord. The quid pro quo between serfs and lords was complicated, in the sense that the property rights of the peasant plot were not well-defined from the modern point of view. (For a study of the incredible intricacy of feudal property rights, see Milsom, 1981.) As a rule, the lord could not expel the peasant family from its plot of land. (Sometimes this could happen at the time of death of the head of the peasant household.) Nor, on the other hand, could the serf decide to leave, to go to a town, for example, to work as an artisan or laborer. If he did, he would be hunted down by the lord, returned to the manor, and punished. Thus, the serf and his family had certain rights to the family plot and to the grain he could produce there, and the lord had certain rights to the serf's labor.

Feudalism was a coercive system; force against the peasantry was needed to extract the corvée and demesne labor that, under feudal rights, were owed to the lord. Such coercion was necessary, because the peasant family had access to its own means of reproduction, by virtue of its tenure on the family plot. Furthermore, the peasant could not, according to the above description, be removed from the plot if he failed to perform his duties to the lord. Hence, it was necessary for the lord to use *extraeconomic coercion* to extract serf labor for the manor. The coercion is called extraeconomic because it dispenses with the institution of the market. Serfs were forced to work not for a wage, but because their access to the family plot meant they did not need a wage.

From the economic viewpoint, there were two classes under feudalism: lords, who had property rights in land and in the labor of serfs who lived on their manors; and serfs, who had certain property rights in family plots (of a muddy sort) and some property in their own labor. The surplus above subsistence consumption was produced by serfs, and almost entirely during the time when they worked for the lord, doing corvée and demesne labor. The huge castles in which the lords lived and the extravagant consumption they enjoyed were the product of serf labor, and it is difficult to view those things as not being part of the economic surplus, that part of the product above subsistence needs. Indeed, the Marxist characterization of feudalism incorporates this idea: a large class of serfs produced the feudal surplus product, which was the property of a small class of lords. The initial property rights that gave rise to this transfer of the surplus from those who produced it to those who owned it were property rights over a certain fraction of resident serf labor and were established by feudal law.

The labor expended in the production of the surplus I will call *surplus labor*. Under feudalism, the performance of surplus labor was transparent to the serf: his week (or year) was divided into two parts, one in which he worked to reproduce himself on the family plot, and another in which he performed corvée and demesne labor for the lord. It would have been difficult to obscure these class relations and to claim that the serf was working for himself the whole time. Justifying feudalism required justifying feudal property rights and teaching the serf that his duty lay in providing surplus labor for the lord, because the lord was a vassal to another lord, who was in turn vassal to the king, who was the representative of God. Feudal property rights thus descended in a tree originating with the king; and if the king represented God, then to challenge these property rights involved taking on a much bigger challenge. So, ultimately, religious ideology was used to justify feudal property rights, to the extent that such a justification was attempted.

There were hundreds of peasant rebellions against feudalism, and these rebellions, in conjunction with a vital capitalism that was associated with an emerging merchant class in towns, eventually contributed to the demise of the feudal system. As the rebellions demonstrated, feudal ideology was not entirely successful in convincing serfs of the righteousness of feudalism. In England in 1381, for example, there was a peasant uprising in which 100,000 peasants formed an army, slaughtered lords, and marched on London. Their goal was to see the king, whom they believed to represent God, and who would therefore right the wrongs perpetrated upon them by the lords. The king agreed to meet with their leaders, whom he promptly executed, displaying the head of one Wat Tyler on a lance. Although this ended the rebellion, the incident sounded the death knell of English feudalism. The class consciousness of some of the participants in this rebellion is indicated in a sermon delivered by one of its leaders, the priest John Ball (Dobson, 1983, p. 374). The sermon began:

> When Adam delved and Eve span
> Who was then a gentleman?

The Marxist interpretation of feudalism mentioned earlier has been challenged by some contemporary neoclassical economists (North and Thomas), who maintain that it is incorrect to view the feudal surplus as an unearned return accruing to feudal lords by virtue of their property rights in serf labor. Their argument is that lords performed certain socially necessary functions in organizing life on the manor; their income, in compensation for these functions, was what I have called the feudal surplus product. Chief among these functions was the provision of defense of the serfs and the manor against invasion by bandits and, perhaps (in some countries where feudal law was not well established), by other lords. The provision of defense is a public good, and there is a free-rider problem in the provision of public goods. In other words, no serf would voluntarily join the manor's army, for the costs to him of so doing were greater than the marginal benefits that he derived, and whether or not an effective army existed would be unaffected by whether or not he joined. So coercion was necessary to create this public good, and the lord was the agent whose role it was to provide such coercion. The same could be said for the building of roads and the provision of an infrastructure on the manor. Feudalism, according to this account, is a system of exchange in which each factor or agent receives a return that is necessary for that factor or agent to supply its services. Were lords not to receive lordly income, they would not take on the onerous entrepreneurial, and coercive, task of manor organization, which was socially necessary. Even the amount of the lord's income could be viewed as emerging from an implicit contract between the serfs and the lord. And even the coercion of the serfs could be viewed as the outcome of a prior implicit contract between serfs and lords in which the serfs agreed to be coerced by the lord, knowing that in their myopic self-interest they would otherwise act as free riders, and ultimately deprive themselves of the public goods they needed. Serfs, like Ulysses in his attempt to avoid the sirens, agreed to have themselves chained to the mast for fear of otherwise acting in self-destructive ways.

This account does not explain why the particular men who were lords occupied that role. One might speculate that the lords were those who possessed the entrepreneurial talent to take on these organizational tasks. They were the risk lovers and the adventurers who were capable of doing grand things. Or, more realistically, one could maintain that to a large extent lordliness was inherited. It was not so crucial who the lord was, it was only necessary that someone take on the responsibility of being the lord. According to this second proposal, the feudal class system was socially necessary, although it would be inappropriate to view any particular lord as deserving his income, in the sense of his having exceptional capacities for the provision of lordly services. According to the first proposal (lords as adventurers), there is an even stronger argument for lordly income being a "return to scarce talents," in line with the general neoclassical explanation of income distribution.

Deciding whether the Marxist or the neoclassical account of feudal class relations and power and income distribution is more accurate is largely a historical matter. Both views are probably internally consistent accounts, although I believe historical evidence makes it clear that the neoclassical implicit-contract account of feudalism is a fairy tale. One of the authors of the neoclassical account I have summarized appears to have retracted his belief in it (see North, 1982)—which does not, of course, establish that it is wrong. For some rebuttal of the neoclassical account by a Marxist historian, see the article by Brenner (1977).

3.2 A Difference between Capitalism and Feudalism

In a capitalist system no one is coerced (in any normal sense of the word) to sell his labor power. If coercion was the driving force behind the production of the feudal surplus, then what is the driving force behind the production of the capitalist surplus? How does it come about that, in a system with no cheating and no coercion, a surplus materializes in the hands of a small class of capitalists and a large class of workers remains at a level of relative subsistence?

This question was, for Marx, essentially economic. The problem was exacerbated by the apparent lack of surplus labor performed by the workers. Although it was clear under feudalism when the surplus labor was performed, such is not the case under capitalism. A particular worker does not divide his week up between production of his subsistence needs and production of a surplus that is appropriated by capitalists. Instead, he might stamp out auto fenders all day, every day. Furthermore, he is not coerced to do so; he bargains with the capitalist for his wage and is free to take his labor elsewhere if he chooses.

Some, although not all, of the explanation for the emergence of a surplus appropriated by capitalists can be seen in the model of Section 2.3. Because workers are deprived of the ownership of the capital stock (the seed corn), they are willing to sell their labor power to capitalists who own capital and can put them to work on it. In both models of Chapter 2, workers still have the equivalent of a subsistence plot to return to, although that is not an essential part of the story. One can substitute for the Farm technology in those models the statement that workers simply cannot live if they receive a wage lower than ⅓ units of corn per day. In the models in Chapter 2 a worker did not work more than 3 days per week, and he needed 1 unit of corn per week to survive. To be more consistent with my statement above, let me stipulate that a worker must consume 2 units of corn per week to survive; production of this consumption bundle requires 6 days of work per week on the Farm. This stipulation changes the equilibrium in the models of Chapter 2, because people must work longer. Then a wage of ⅓ unit of corn per day would be a subsistence wage and must be paid by the capitalist, even in the absence of a Farm technology, if he is to have a steady pool of workers (I should say, a pool of steady workers). Any lower wage would not allow workers to meet their own consumption requirements while working for the capitalist, assuming 6 days is the maximum work week. The only productive asset the workers own is labor power, the capacity to work, and this they agree to sell to those who own the means of production, as the only way to gain an income with which to live. The wage workers receive is bid down to the subsistence wage, or to their next best alternative wage (which they earn on the Farm), because of the abundance of labor relative to capital.

The Marxist expression is that workers are "free in a double sense": free to sell their labor power and move around (unlike serfs) and freed from access to the means of their economic reproduction (also unlike serfs). Because workers are separated from the means of reproduction, capitalism can operate without extraeconomic coercion; workers will willingly offer their labor power for sale, because capitalists have something they need. Despite the lack of extraeconomic coercion, a surplus does emerge, because the wage rate that equilibrates the labor market is sufficiently low to produce a profit. This outcome was demonstrated in Chapter 2—and profits emerged even without postulating that capitalists had a strong desire to accumulate. Of course, real capitalists do not have the subsistence preferences assumed in the models of Chapter 2, so it becomes even easier to see how profits emerge in a real economy.

From the viewpoint of the worker, capitalist property relations obscure the nature of surplus appropriation. Whereas the serf could see that he was expending surplus labor for the lord, because of the physical division of his time between work for his own economic reproduction and work for the lord, the proletarian has no such vision. (In some cases, feudal dues were a portion of the product from the serf's plot, a kind of extraction by the lord also highly visible to the serf.) The proletarian, in contrast, stamps out auto fenders all week long and uses his wage to buy other goods that he does not make. The social division of labor under capitalism makes it impossible for any worker to see clearly that the amount of labor he expends during the week is greater than the amount of labor that is socially necessary to produce the wage goods that he consumes. The model in Section 2.3 was a bit too simple to make this point well, because only corn was produced there. A demonstration of how capitalist property relations obscure, from the worker's viewpoint, the expenditure of surplus labor, requires a model with at least two goods (besides leisure), a model in which a worker might work in one industry yet consume goods from several. (This model will be presented in the next chapter.) Nevertheless, even in the model in Section 2.3 the worker can be mystified by capitalist property relations with respect to the expenditure of surplus labor. If I were to ask either a worker or a peasant in that model, "How long must you work to earn enough corn to live?" he would reply, "Three days." But if I were to ask a serf the same question, he would reply, "I only have to work two days on my family plot, but then the lord forces me to provide an extra day of labor for him." (If he is a class-conscious serf, he will not mince his words this way.) For the proletarian, there is no clear separation between surplus labor and labor necessarily expended for his own economic reproduction.

It might be more clear to the proletarian that he is providing surplus labor if he were to see the capitalists lazily collecting profits without working. In fact, the real world is more complicated: first of all, real entrepreneurs do work hard; and, second, capitalist firms are owned, not by their managers, but by stockholders who are quite invisible to the worker. Third, although many people own some stock, they are not capitalists. The big stockholders are often financial institutions, and therefore the identity of capitalists is difficult to trace. (It is perhaps more accurate to say that, because of the role of financial institutions in the stock market and on the boards of corporations, it is the agents of capital owners who become important.) The essential point, however, is that a surplus far above the present consumption needs of a capitalist society emerges, and in the Marxist analysis, this is due to the abundance of labor relative to capital, which serves to bid down the wage to a level permitting profits.

These are appropriated by the owners of capital, the relatively scarce factor of production.

The purpose of the Marxist economic analysis of a capitalist economy, or at least that dimension of the analysis discussed here, is to point out that the class of agents who are separated from the means of production produce not only their own subsistence needs but also the entire surplus that becomes the property of capital owners as a consequence of competition. Competition under capitalism replaces coercion under feudalism, but beneath the surface the story is the same in this regard: a small, propertied class appropriates the surplus produced by a large, unpropertied one. So long as capitalist property relations obscure this appropriation, religious ideology and direct coercion are not so important as they were under feudalism. It is much easier to maintain the belief that each person is receiving his just deserts under capitalism, for there is no extraeconomic coercion and workers are free to leave or to start businesses and become capitalists themselves. Some even succeed in doing so.

There are various ways in which these claims are simplifications of reality, or are false. First of all, there *is* extraeconomic coercion under capitalism, chiefly in two places: on the job, and in the protection of property rights. The police and judicial power of the state protect capitalist property rights, and capitalists exert coercion on the job in the form of authority that is not mediated through markets. When workers go on strike, state power is often used to help the capitalists in a one-sided way. Nevertheless, the extraeconomic coercion under capitalism is less proximate than it is under feudalism.

Second, I have not yet argued that the distribution of income—profits and wages—under capitalism is unjust, as Marxism claims it is under feudalism. I have established that workers produce the surplus product as the consequence of a series of market bargains emanating from an initial unequal ownership of the means of production. But is there anything wrong with that income distribution? To establish that would seem to require an argument for the injustice of the initial distribution of the means of production. And although the argument that feudal lords earned the property rights that gave rise to their wealth is incredible, an analogous argument with regard to capitalism is not. If capitalists came to own their capital by virtue of working harder or more skillfully in the past than those who are now proletarians, is it wrong to deprive them of the profits that emerge from voluntary trades with proletarians on the labor market? I will pursue this question in later chapters.

4

Exploitation and Profits

This chapter presents a simple, algebraic model that formalizes some of the concepts presented in the models of Chapter 2. I will define embodied labor value, exploitation, and the profit rate and then investigate the relationship between exploitation and profits.

4.1 Embodied Labor and Exploitation

Imagine a corn economy with just one technology, that called the Factory in Chapter 2. One unit of corn, gross, can be produced using a units of corn as input and L days of labor. Thus, the technology can be summarized

$$\{a,L\} \to 1,$$

or, in terms of net corn production,

$$\{a,L\} \to 1 - a.$$

Clearly, for this technology to be productive, a must be less than 1. Otherwise, stocks would dwindle to zero.

The *labor embodied in a unit of corn* is defined as the amount of labor that is necessary to produce 1 unit of corn, including the labor needed to reproduce the corn input used in the process. To derive this quantity, let x be the amount of corn that would have to be produced in order to end up with 1 unit of corn after replacing the corn input used in the production of x. Because the technology is assumed to exhibit constant returns to scale, the production of x units of corn requires an input of ax; to end up with 1 unit of corn, net, x must satisfy

$$x = ax + 1. \tag{4.1}$$

Equation (4.1) can be read as "gross output = input used + net output." Solving (4.1) for x gives

$$x = \frac{1}{1 - a}.$$

The amount of labor needed to produce this amount of corn is, therefore,

$$\frac{L}{1 - a} \equiv \lambda. \tag{4.2}$$

λ is the labor embodied in a unit of corn.

There is a useful interpretation of (4.2). Because $a < 1$, we can expand the expression $L/(1 - a)$ as a geometric series:

$$\lambda = L + La + La^2 + La^3 + \cdots \tag{4.3}$$

In (4.3), the first term L is the direct, live labor expended today to produce 1 unit of corn, gross. But we must replace the seed corn, used in amount a. The labor that had to be expended last week to produce a unit of seed corn for use this week was La, the second term. But, how much seed input was needed two weeks ago, to plant then, so as to have a units of corn available last week? Precisely a^2 units of corn, and that required expending, two weeks ago, La^2 units of direct labor. In this way, the expression (4.3) decomposes the labor embodied in a unit of corn into the direct labor expended at various times in the past to produce the inputs needed to produce the inputs needed to produce the inputs needed, and so on forever back into the past, to produce the corn today.

There is another useful derivation of the labor embodied in a unit of corn. The embodied labor value of a good is the sum of live labor expended during the current production period to produce the good, plus the labor already embodied in the inputs used in production. Let λ stand for the embodied labor value in a unit of corn. The labor expended today in producing corn is L, and the labor embodied in the a units of corn used as an input in corn's production is, by definition, λa, because λ is the labor content of 1 unit of corn. Thus, by the second sentence of this paragraph,

$$\lambda = L + \lambda a. \tag{4.4}$$

Solving Equation (4.4) for λ yields, again, Equation (4.2).

The expression (4.2) looks very much like the multiplier in macro-economics, and this is no accident. Recall that

$Y = C + I$ (gross output = consumption + investment)

$C = aY + d$ (consumption function).

Combining these two equations yields

$$Y = \frac{d + I}{1 - a}.$$

The interpretation is the same as that given for expression (4.2). An increase in investment from I to $I + \Delta I$ increases national income, not by ΔI, but by $\Delta I/(1 - a)$, where a is the propensity to consume. An increase in investment of ΔI leads to an increased consumption of $a\Delta I$; in turn, those consumption expenditures generate additional incomes of $a\Delta I$, and people receiving that income increase their consumption by $a^2\Delta I$, and so on into the future. Thus, the decomposition

$$\frac{\Delta I}{1 - a} = \Delta I + a\Delta I + a^2\Delta I + \cdots$$

has the same sort of interpretation, going into the future, as the decomposition of Equation (4.3) does going into the past.

Socially necessary labor time is defined as the amount of labor embodied in the bundle that the worker consumes, a bundle that he purchases with his wage. Suppose that the daily subsistence amount of corn that a worker consumes in this economy is b units of corn. If the wage is a subsistence wage, then his entire wage is spent on purchasing this amount of corn. Thus, socially necessary labor time is defined as

$$\text{SNLT} \equiv \lambda b = \frac{bL}{1 - a}. \tag{4.5}$$

Notice that this definition is slightly different from that in Chapter 2, where the total capital stock available was considered and socially necessary labor time was an appropriate average of labor time expended in the Factory and Farm sectors. In this model, which has no Farm sector, I do not have that option. Although the definitions are different, the end result will be about the same, and one should not worry about this detail, except to acknowledge its existence.

Suppose labor time is denominated in days of labor. There is some fixed length of the working day, by hypothesis; and, by definition, the worker works for 1 day in order to receive his wage, which is w. The wage can be paid in either corn or money. The worker is said to be exploited if the amount of corn he can purchase with his daily wage embodies less than 1 day, the amount of time the worker toiled to earn the wage. If the daily wage just suffices to purchase corn in amount b, then the worker is exploited if

$$\lambda b < 1.$$

The *rate of exploitation* is defined as

$$e = \frac{1 - \lambda b}{\lambda b}. \tag{4.6}$$

In other words, e is the ratio of surplus labor time expended by the worker to socially necessary labor time. The *surplus labor time* is that portion of the daily labor that the worker expends above that embodied in the corn he is paid. It becomes embodied in corn that ends up as profits for the capitalist, as I will show in the next section.

4.2 Prices and the Profit Rate

Suppose a unit of corn sells for a price of p, denominated in some currency. Then the fact that the wage in this model is a subsistence one is summarized by

$$pb = w. \tag{4.7}$$

The amount the worker must pay to buy his corn bundle is just his wage.

For each unit of corn the capitalist produces, she must pay $pa + wL$ for her inputs of corn and labor. I assume she pays the wage at the beginning of the production period (which may not be realistic), so wage costs are considered to be part of her investment costs. (But nothing of significance changes if the capitalist pays the workers at the end of the production period.) Then the profits per unit of corn that a capitalist makes, because I assume she is able to sell her corn at the going price, are

$$p - (pa + wL) = \text{unit profits.}$$

The *profit rate*, π, is defined as the rate at which her investment grows; it is the ratio of profits to investment. Thus,

$$\pi = \frac{p - (pa + wL)}{pa + wL}. \tag{4.8}$$

Rewriting (4.8) in a more convenient form yields

$$p = (1 + \pi)(pa + wL). \tag{4.9}$$

The capitalist in this model wishes to expand her stock of capital. She is not the same sort of subsistence agent discussed in Chapter 2. Her preferences, for whatever reason, are for accumulation and dictate that she expand her capital stock as rapidly as possible. I will not inquire into what social norms or other constraints or forces give rise to these preferences in capitalists. Suffice it to say that competition among capitalists forces each to expand as rapidly as possible in order to have the funds to innovate and not be driven out of the market altogether. So in this model I will simply assume that capitalists strive to accumulate. The measure of the rate of the capitalist's accumulation is π, the profit rate. It is the rate at which investment capital expands from one period to the next.

In summary, the data of the model are $\{a, L, b\}$. These are given, exogenous magnitudes. The endogenous variables, determined by the data, are e, λ, p, and π. Notice that I have left out w. There is one degree of freedom in the model, because there are more unknowns than equations. Equation (4.2) defines λ from the data and Equation (4.6) defines e. I am left with Equations (4.7) and (4.9) to determine p, w, and π. This cannot be done uniquely, because only relative prices matter. I therefore have the liberty to set either p or w at some arbitrary level, and I have chosen to set $w = 1$. Hence, the price p is the price of corn relative to the wage, or the wage-price of corn.

4.3 The Relationship between Exploitation and Profits

One can solve for the rate of profit in terms of the data. Substituting from Equation (4.7) into (4.9) and dividing through by p yields

$$\frac{1}{1 + \pi} = a + bL. \tag{4.10}$$

The expression $a + bL$ is called the *augmented input coefficient*. The first term, a, is the amount of corn that must be planted in the ground to yield 1 unit of corn. The second term, bL, is the amount of corn that must be fed into the worker to yield 1 unit of corn. Hence, from a technological point of view, $a + bL$ is the amount of corn that must be used as input, in one way or another, in the production of 1 unit of corn. If there are to be any profits, this augmented input coefficient had better be less than the amount of corn produced,

$$a + bL < 1. \tag{4.11}$$

And from (4.10), this is just the condition necessary to generate a positive value for the rate of profit, π.

Thus, the condition summarized by inequality (4.11) is required for generating a positive rate of profit. What is the condition for generating a positive rate of exploitation? It is, by reference to the definition of e in Equation (4.6),

$$\lambda b < 1. \tag{4.12}$$

But by the derivation of the formula (4.5) for socially necessary labor time, (4.12) is equivalent to

$$\frac{bL}{1 - a} < 1 \quad \text{or} \quad a + bL < 1,$$

which is just condition (4.11), the necessary and sufficient condition for a positive rate of profit. Thus, condition (4.11) is necessary and sufficient both for the rate of profit to be positive and for the rate of exploitation to be positive. This is summarized by the following theorem.

Theorem 4.1 $\pi > 0$ if and only if $e > 0$.

In other words, the necessary and sufficient condition for the existence of a positive profit rate is that labor be exploited. Some writers have called this the fundamental Marxian theorem (Morishima, 1973). (I do not think it is really so fundamental, for reasons I will mention later.) The theorem verifies the intuition, mentioned earlier, that surplus labor becomes embodied as profits. It is only by virtue of the fact that workers are paid a wage enabling them to buy only an amount of corn embodying less labor than they expended in production that some corn is left over for capitalists. Whether the capitalists consume this surplus, or sell it to buyers other than workers, or invest it, is not my present concern.

Theorem 4.1 shows that profits are positive if and only if workers are exploited. But what makes it possible for capitalists to exploit workers? Why should the corn wage, b, not rise until the profit rate falls to zero? The answer to this question is provided in Chapter 2. Capitalists own scarce capital—in this case, seed corn—which is needed for production. Recall that the technology $\{a,L\}$ in this model is like the Factory technology of Chapter 2. Because of the scarcity of seed corn (which is owned by the capitalists) relative to the labor available for hire, workers compete for access to the technology, a situation keeping their wage low enough to maintain a positive rate of profit. In other words, the wage is bid down to just the amount required by the worker as a consequence of competition among the workers for employment on the scarce capital stock. Nothing in the story requires that the corn wage of workers be a subsistence wage in any biological sense. As long as labor is sufficiently abundant relative to the capital that is available to employ it, the wage rate will settle at some level that permits a positive rate of profit. At any such wage rate, exploitation occurs.

4.4 An Economy with Many Produced Goods

One weakness of the model presented thus far is that it does not provide for a division of labor among workers. Everybody produces only corn and consumes only corn. The social division of labor can be exhibited only in a model in which many goods are produced. To analyze such a model requires some linear algebra. But, in the final analysis, the result is just the same as Theorem 4.1: profits exist if and only if there is exploitation.

Assume that there are n goods and that x represents a vector in R^n of levels of production of these n goods. The technology is summarized by the data $\{A,L\}$, where A is an $n \times n$ input coefficient matrix. The jth column of A, A_j, lists the amounts of the n goods needed as inputs into the production of 1 unit of the jth good. Thus, in the matrix $A = \langle a_{ij} \rangle$, a_{ij} is the amount of the ith good used as input in production of 1 unit of the jth good. L is a row vector of n components, $L = \langle L_j \rangle$, where L_j is the amount of direct labor needed as input in producing 1 unit of good j.

4.4.1 The Vector of Embodied Labor Values

Let the subsistence vector of consumption be the n-vector b. No longer do people consume just corn. Then the labor embodied in b is the amount of labor necessary to produce b as a net output. Thus, using reasoning similar to the reasoning prior to Equation (4.1), I search for the vector of gross outputs x that will produce b as its net output,

$$x = Ax + b. \tag{4.13}$$

(If x is the vector of gross output, then Ax is the vector of inputs consumed in the process and b is the vector of net output. Equation (4.13) is of the form, gross output = input + final demand.)

Let I be the $n \times n$ identity matrix. If $(I - A)$ is invertible, then the solution to (4.13) is

$$x = (I - A)^{-1}b. \tag{4.14}$$

Indeed, a well-known theorem of linear algebra states that $(I - A)$ is invertible and its inverse is a nonnegative matrix if A is a productive matrix. A *productive matrix* is one capable of producing a vector of positive net outputs. This is an eminently reasonable economic condition to require of A. The amount of labor that must be expended to produce x (namely, Lx, the scalar product of L and x) is just

$$\text{SNLT}(b) = L(I - A)^{-1}b, \tag{4.15}$$

or the socially necessary labor time.

Equation (4.15) is the vector analogue of Equation (4.5). As one might guess, the expression $L(I - A)^{-1}$, which is a row vector with n components, is the expression for the vector of embodied labor values, Λ, embodied in the n commodities in the economy; and Equation (4.15) can be written as

$$\text{SNLT}(b) = \Lambda b, \tag{4.16}$$

which looks like the first part of Equation (4.5).

Indeed, this expression can be derived for the vector of embodied labor values in commodities, Λ, by an argument like the one leading to Equation (4.4). Let Λ be the vector of embodied labor, or labor values. Then a typical component Λ_j of Λ is the sum of labor expended in the present production period in the production of commodity j, and labor embodied in the inputs manufactured in the past, but used today, in the production of commodity j. The first term of direct labor is the component L_j of L; the expression for labor embodied in the inputs used to produce commodity j is

$$\Lambda_1 a_{1j} + \Lambda_2 a_{2j} + \cdots + \Lambda_n a_{nj},$$

which is the scalar product of Λ with A_j, the jth column of A. Thus,

$$\Lambda_j = L_j + \Lambda A_j. \tag{4.17}$$

Writing Equation (4.17) as a vector equation, for all j, gives

$$\Lambda = L + \Lambda A. \tag{4.18}$$

Equation (4.18) is the vector analogue of Equation (4.4). It can be solved for Λ by inverting the matrix $(I - A)$. Hence,

$$\Lambda = L(I - A)^{-1}$$

as conjectured. It follows that Equation (4.16) is another way of writing Equation (4.15).

As in the corn model, an agent is defined as exploited if socially necessary labor time is less than the amount of time he works, assuming his daily wage only allows him to purchase the vector of consumption b. The labor embodied in the vector b is

$$\Lambda_1 b_1 + \Lambda_2 b_2 + \cdots + \Lambda_n b_n = \Lambda b,$$

and so the condition for exploitation of the worker is

$$\Lambda b < 1. \tag{4.19}$$

The rate of exploitation is defined as before,

$$e = \frac{1 - \Lambda b}{\Lambda b},$$

and has the same interpretation, namely, the ratio of surplus labor time in the working day to the labor embodied in the worker's daily consumption bundle.

4.4.2 Prices

The derivation of prices in the multidimensional model requires an additional argument: I must invoke the fact that capitalists compete. There are now n possible sectors to invest in, but a capitalist will only invest in lines of production that achieve the maximal profit rate, for no other line will expand his capital so rapidly. Let p be the n-dimensional row vector of prices of goods. (Recall that in Section 4.1 the daily wage was set at 1 and that A_j is the jth column of A.) Then the cost of inputs and labor to produce 1 unit of good j is

$$pA_j + L_j,$$

and hence the profit rate, at prices p, of producing good j is

$$\pi_j \equiv \frac{p_j - (pA_j + L_j)}{pA_j + L_j}. \tag{4.20}$$

I have argued that only those processes that achieve the maximal profit rate will be operated. Suppose that in this economy all the sectors must operate (perhaps in order to produce the subsistence requirements and the inputs required for that purpose). Then the economy cannot be considered to be in a long-run equilibrium unless prices are such that *all* sectors generate the maximal profit rate and all goods are produced. Hence, at such an equilibrium, the profit rates are equalized across all sectors; I will call that uniform profit rate π. The price equation can be deduced from (4.20):

$$p = (1 + \pi)(pA + L), \tag{4.21}$$

which is a vector equation stating that the vector p is proportional in its components to the vector $(pA + L)$, with a constant of proportionality $(1 + \pi)$.

As before, the subsistence wage equation can be written as

$$pb = 1, \tag{4.22}$$

which states that workers must expend their entire daily wage to purchase the daily subsistence requirement b. Substituting from (4.22) into (4.21) and factoring p out of the right-hand side yields

$$p = (1 + \pi)p(A + bL), \tag{4.23}$$

where $A + bL$ is the *augmented input coefficient matrix*. Note that bL is the product of a column vector with a row vector, each of length n; so it is an $n \times n$ matrix. Indeed the ijth component of $A + bL$, which is $a_{ij} + b_iL_j$, is just the total amount of good i that enters into production of good j when one considers not only the factor input that occurs directly (a_{ij}), but also the input of good i that enters indirectly into good j through the worker's consumption. This last amount is b_iL_j and is called the *labor-feeding input coefficient*.

A theorem of linear algebra known as the Frobenius–Perron theorem asserts that if the matrix $(A + bL)$ is productive, in the sense defined earlier, then a unique nonnegative price vector p and an associated profit rate π that solve Equation (4.23) exist. Thus, prices capable of reproducing this economy exist, so long as the technological and subsistence data $\{A,L,b\}$ render the augmented technology $(A + bL)$ capable of producing a surplus.

4.4.3 Exploitation and Profits in a Multidimensional Model

Equation (4.15) and the definition of the rate of exploitation yield the condition for a positive rate of exploitation:

$$L(I - A)^{-1}b < 1. \tag{4.24}$$

I have remarked that p and π are uniquely determined, given A, b, and L, by Equation (4.23). Hence it should be possible to investigate whether there is a relationship between the condition for a positive rate of exploitation, as given by (4.24), and the existence of a positive rate of profit. Indeed, using the Frobenius–Perron theorem one can prove the following theorem.

Theorem 4.2 In the n-dimensional model, $\pi > 0$ if and only if $e > 0$.

The result is the same as that of the simple corn model. A positive rate of profit is sustainable in a reproducible economic system if and only if workers are exploited, in the sense that the labor embodied in the goods they can purchase with their wage is less than the labor they expend. The proof of Theorem 4.2 is given in the Appendix.

4.5 The Social Division of Labor and the Perception of Exploitation

In Chapter 3 I presented the notion that capitalism and feudalism share a common trait, namely, the extraction of a surplus by a small class of property owners from a large class of direct producers. This view is verified by Theorems 4.1 and 4.2 of the last two sections. According to these theorems, profits exist because workers only spend part of the working day working for themselves; the rest of the day they work to produce the profits of the capitalist. Under feudalism this separation of work time between necessary and surplus time was observable by the producer, but such is not the case under capitalism, because of the social division of labor and the production of commodities.

A worker does not actually produce the goods b that he consumes. Suppose that he produces auto fenders all day long. Further suppose that the auto worker works 40 hours a week producing fenders, but the wages he is paid enable him to buy consumption goods embodying only 20 hours of labor (expended mostly by other workers). Because of the social division of labor, he has no clear conception of the amount of labor that is necessary to produce the goods he consumes. For the auto worker, the division of his labor time is not apparent. For the serf under feudalism, however, the work week, or work year, was clearly divided into labor time expended in the production of his subsistence commodities and labor time expended directly for the lord. Thus, the social division of labor—the arrangement by which no worker in modern capitalism produces all the goods that make up his consumption bundle—obscures the relation of exploitation between capitalist and worker.

A commodity is defined as a good produced for exchange, not for the producer's own use. Capitalist production, unlike most production under feudalism, is commodity production. And commodity production is clearly related to the existence of the social division of labor. It could therefore be said that the system of commodity production is responsible for obscuring the nature of exploitation in a capitalist economy.

4.6 The Labor Theory of Value

Associated with the classical economists Smith and Ricardo, and also with Marx, is the claim that prices in a market economy are a reflection of the embodied labor values of commodities. In its starkest form this assertion is interpreted to mean that prices are proportional to labor values; that is, that the vector p is proportional to the vector Λ. In fact, Marx did not assert this "labor theory of value." Rather he used it as an approximation to simplify his arguments about exploitation, because he (rightly) believed that the deviations of prices from embodied labor values were not relevant to his theory of exploitation. The price vector p that solves Equation (4.23) is not proportional to the vector Λ that solves Equation (4.18), except in certain unusual circumstances (either when the profit rate is zero, or when the technology exhibits a singular property known as equal "organic compositions of capital"). Nevertheless, as I have shown in this chapter, the relationship between exploitation and profits does not depend on the proportionality of labor values to prices, and so nothing of substance is lost by acknowledging that the labor theory of value is false.

Then why did classical economists put some stock in the claim that exchange values, or prices, would be proportional to labor values?

Imagine a society that produces deer and beaver, as in Adam Smith's example. In this society everyone needs or wants to consume the same consumption bundle of venison and beaver pelts—say, 1 unit of venison and 1 beaver pelt. Suppose that it takes 6 days to hunt a deer and produce 1 unit of venison ready for trade or consumption and 3 days to produce 1 beaver pelt. Suppose that all labor is equally skilled at either occupation and can move freely between the venison and beaver pelt industries. But suppose further that set-up costs are such that there is a social division of labor, so people must trade with one another to end up with their desired consumption bundle. Suppose that people have subsistence preferences and want to minimize their labor expended in hunting. What will the equilibrium price ratio be between venison and beaver pelts?

It will be 2. At that price ratio, each person, regardless of occupation, will spend 9 days hunting, and each will end up with his desired consumption bundle. If the price ratio were higher than 2 everyone would want to move into the venison industry, in an attempt to reduce their hunting times. More realistically, some beaver trappers would start to move into the venison industry, thereby producing an oversupply of venison and driving down its price. If the price ratio were less than 2, producers would move into the beaver pelt industry. Thus, the only price ratio that can support the production of both venison and beaver pelts is 2. Note that 2 is also the ratio of the embodied labor of venison to the embodied labor of beaver pelts, because those labor times are 6 days and 3 days, respectively. Thus, equilibrium prices are proportional to embodied labor values.

In the deer–beaver model, the labor theory of value is true. It fails to be true, however, once capital stock is introduced into the economy—so long as the capital stock is scarce relative to the hunters who would use it. Suppose that hunting a beaver requires traps and that hunting a deer requires bows and arrows and that these implements take a fairly long time to make. A hunter who does not already own traps or bows cannot devote time to making them, because it takes so long to do so that he would not have time to earn his consumption bundle and would starve. Now, suppose that there is a capital stock of bows and traps owned by a class of agents who had them made in the past, from their accumulated surpluses. These capitalists today will hire trappers to use the traps and bows to hunt beaver and deer and will pay them wages in return. If there is a scarcity of traps and bows relative to the trappers who would use them, then the wage of trappers will be bid down to that amount needed to purchase only their "subsistence" bundle of 1 beaver pelt and 1 unit of venison. The embodied labor of both beaver pelts and venison must now include an element that takes into account the depreciation of the traps and bows incurred when they are used to hunt the deer and beaver. Moreover, the prices of venison and beaver pelts will include an element of profit that the owners of the implements are able to charge by virtue of the scarcity of their capital stock. When the prices of beaver pelts, venison, and traps and bows equilibrate to a level at which trappers can purchase their consumption bundle with the wage and at which profit rates in the various lines of production are equalized so that all goods will be produced, it will no longer be true that equilibrium prices of beaver pelts and venison are proportional to the embodied labor values of beaver pelts and venison.

The deer–beaver model without capital shows why classical economists believed there was some tendency for market prices to be proportional to embodied labor values of commodities. This relation does exist so long as all goods are produced without scarce capital and so long as there are no naturally scarce and nonproduced inputs (like land) that will command a rent, which will be a component of the price.

Marxists also adhere to a labor theory of value because of their belief that the real source of all value is labor. Marx argued that the one property that all commodities had in common was their production by "abstract labor." It is hard to see why this should be regarded as the *one* property that all produced commodities have in common. They also share the property of being desired by people; and that property gives rise to a welfare-based theory of value (which is reflected in the statement occurring in neoclassical economic theory that prices are proportional to marginal utilities). In fact, the labor theory of value is a supply-side theory, in which prices are thought to be determined entirely by their labor costs; in contrast, emphasizing the importance of the degree to which a commodity fulfills desires or needs or welfare in determining its price is the demand side. The correct theory of market price must take both supply and demand into account. There are some special cases in which demand will not affect price, which is technologically determined, but recourse to those cases should not be sought in an attempt to defend the labor theory of value.

I will present one more example in order to emphasize the point that the existence of exploitation, in the Marxist sense, has nothing to do with the proportionality of labor values to prices. Imagine that

Andrea planted grape vines on scarce land several years ago and that the grapes are now ready to harvest. Bob would like to consume the wine that can be made from the grapes. Andrea expended very little labor in planting the vines—as little as you please. (Imagine that she only had to press a button some years ago to start the grape-growing process.) Furthermore, assume that no more labor is needed to make the grapes into wine today. Bob produces bread today, which requires a good deal of current labor. He wants to trade some of his bread for Andrea's wine, and Andrea does not want to drink her wine on an empty stomach, so she also wants to trade. After the trade has taken place, Bob will be consuming a bundle of bread and wine, which together embody less labor than he expended—for, by hypothesis, the wine embodies almost no labor. Andrea, in contrast, worked hardly at all and consumes wine and bread that embodies a good deal of Bob's labor. The prices at which bread and wine exchange do not reflect the amounts of labor embodied in the two commodities. Andrea's wine may command quite a high price relative to Bob's bread, because no other source of wine is available for Bob, but Andrea could produce her own daily bread by expending the appropriate labor. One might wish to argue that Andrea is exploiting Bob, because some of his labor has been transferred to her (embodied in the bread), whereas he gets virtually none of her labor in return.

In this case, the time elapsed between the planting of the grapes and the present is like capital: although wine can be produced, it cannot be produced quickly, and this is reflected in the price of wine. Or, perhaps more to the point, Andrea but not Bob owns scarce land, a circumstance that explains why Bob did not plant vines some time ago. Note that this example is especially simple, because neither Andrea nor Bob hires the other. Nevertheless, Andrea exploits Bob, in the technical sense, because he expended more labor than is embodied in the bundle of bread and wine he ends up possessing and consuming, and she expended less labor than that embodied in what she consumes. The transfer of labor from Bob to Andrea occurs in an indirect fashion—through the trade of the commodities they produce—because the prices of those commodities are not proportional to the labor embodied in them. One might view the Andrea–Bob economy as a precapitalist one, because the relationship of wage labor has not yet been established. Nevertheless, the divergence of commodity prices from labor values has emerged, because there is an element of capital involved in the production of some goods. As long as there is differential ownership of the capital stock used in producing goods for consumption today, commodity prices will not generally be proportional to labor values, and some producers will work more hours than the hours embodied in the goods they consume while others work fewer.

Even though Marx understood that equilibrium prices were not generally proportional to embodied labor values in a market economy, he made many calculations in an attempt to elucidate how labor values could be "transformed" mathematically into equilibrium prices. One might view this algebraic transformation problem as an attempt to mirror the transformation of economies from simple deer–beaver economies in which prices are proportional to labor values to capitalist economies in which they are not. However, this line of inquiry is not fruitful. The insights from Marxist analysis that remain useful do not require reference to the labor theory of value, or to a special Marxist theory of price determination. Prices are determined by market-clearing (equilibrium) requirements, by the equating of supply and demand.

I have referred to a stark form of the labor theory of value, which maintains that prices are proportional to embodied labor values. There is a looser claim advocated by some, namely, that the labor theory of value means that embodied labor values determine equilibrium prices, though not proportionally. Although it is hard to evaluate such a claim, because "determination" is not as clear a relationship as "proportionality" is, there is no interesting sense in which this claim is true. Indeed, there is a sense in which the direction of determination is the other way, that prices determine labor values. Further references on this matter are given in the Bibliographical Notes for this chapter.

Although I have verified the claim that exploitation of workers is necessary and sufficient for positive profits, no further headway has been made toward understanding what might be morally wrong with exploitation. Until one can pass judgment on the morality of differential ownership of the capital stock, it is difficult to form an opinion about the exploitation that is its consequence. This is why I remarked earlier that the theorems of this chapter are not so fundamental. To make headway toward understanding the essential ethical question requires some analysis of the conditions that lead to the exploitation of workers, and this is the topic of the next chapter.

5

The Morality of Exploitation

The worker is exploited because the consumption bundle she can purchase with her wage embodies less labor than she expended, and the capitalist is an exploiter because the goods he can purchase with his profits (or the goods that accrue to him as profits) embody more labor than he expended. Even if the capitalist works hard, this will usually be the case.

Why is this accounting of socially embodied labor against labor expended interesting? And to what uses might one put measurements of exploitation? Marxists use exploitation as a statistic for both positive and normative ends. In its positive use, the exploitation of workers is said to explain profits. In its normative use, exploitation is said to indicate unjust treatment of workers by capitalists. In this chapter, I will begin an evaluation of the usefulness of exploitation as a statistic in these roles.

5.1 Exploitation as the Source of Profits

The "fundamental Marxian theorem" (Theorem 4.1) provides the basis for the claim that the exploitation of workers is the condition that explains profits. Although Marx did not prove this theorem in the way it has been presented here, he did reach the conclusions embodied in the theorem, and he believed that he had uncovered the explanation of how profits could emerge in a system of noncoercive exchanges where, on every market, equal value exchanges for equal value. Under the hypothesis of the ubiquitous exchange of equals on competitive markets, how could a surplus systematically emerge in the hands of capitalists? Only if, Marx thought, there is a commodity or factor capable of contributing more value in the production process than it itself had. Marx argued that labor power is that commodity. The worker receives as a daily wage an amount of corn that costs less, in terms of labor, than the amount of labor the worker can expend in a day. The commodity sold by the worker and purchased by the capitalist is *labor power*—the capacity to perform labor—and a day's labor power can release more labor than is embodied in the goods necessary to reproduce that labor power. This is the source of profits and, Marx believed, uniquely so.

I have assigned to labor power the "property of exploitability," because one unit of it can be socially reproduced with less than one unit of labor. Labor power, however, is not the only productive factor that possesses the property of exploitability. I could, in fact, take corn as the numeraire commodity with respect to which embodied values should be defined. Consider the economy of Chapter 4, in which the technology for producing corn is $\{a,L\}$ and the subsistence bundle per day of labor is b. How much corn is embodied in a unit of corn? To produce 1 unit of corn requires the planting of a units of seed, and it requires the consumption of bL units of corn by the laborer to produce the labor used as an input in the corn production process. The total amount of corn embodied in 1 unit of corn is therefore $a + bL$. I noted that the necessary and sufficient condition for profits to exist is that

$$a + bL < 1.$$

But this is precisely the statement that 1 unit of corn be socially reproduced with less than 1 unit of corn. That is, corn possesses the property of exploitability as well. Indeed, a necessary and sufficient condition for the existence of profits is that corn possess the property of exploitability.

This statement generalizes to an economy with n goods. One can adopt any good as the value numeraire and prove a Generalized Commodity Exploitation Theorem, which states that profits exist if and only if each produced commodity possesses the property of exploitability when it is taken as the numeraire for calculating embodied value. This conclusion is not surprising, because the rate of exploitability can be viewed as a measure of the productive efficiency of a factor. The *rate of exploitability of labor power* is the ratio of the surplus labor that can be squeezed out of a unit of labor power to the amount of labor required to reproduce that unit from a social point of view.

The *corn rate of exploitability* is the ratio of the surplus corn that can be squeezed out of a unit of corn to the amount of corn required to reproduce that unit of corn. Every produced commodity used in production must be capable of giving up such a surplus, when measured this way, for any social net surplus (that is, profits) to be forthcoming.

Marx was wrong in thinking that he had discovered the unique source of profits in the exploitability of labor power. What distinguishes the exploitability of labor power from that of corn? One identifies the exploitability of labor power with the exploitation of the worker. Some have argued that the exploitability of labor power is different because the extraction of labor from labor power can only be performed with the conscious and cooperative participation of the worker, whereas the productive powers of corn can be harnessed without such intimate participation of a human agent. The capitalist must design ways of organizing the manufacturing process to ensure that the worker works—methods of supervision, technologies that lend themselves to controlling the rate of labor extraction (such as assembly lines), and methods of reward that either give workers the right incentives or constrain them in ways that assure that labor will be forthcoming. But, if labor and corn differ by virtue of the ability of workers to resist providing labor, that difference is not elucidated by looking at rates of exploitation. One should, instead, study the methods capitalists have used to extract labor, as Marxist social science has done. The seminal work in this area of recent years is the book by Braverman (1974).

5.2 The Initial Distribution

If the exploitation of the worker is an important concept, it is so for normative reasons—because it is indicative of some injustice and not because the exploitability of labor power is the unique source of profits. In the model in Section 2.3, exploitation emerged because of the inequality of ownership of the capital stock. If the exploitation of the worker seems unfair, it is because one thinks the initial distribution of capital stock, which gives rise to it, is unfair.

I will elucidate this claim. Imagine the following situation, in which exploitation emerges as a consequence of an initial distribution of resources that one thinks of as fair. (Note that I use the term *exploitation* in its technical sense throughout this chapter.) Suppose that there are two agents, Adam and Karl. They have different preferences for corn and leisure and will live for many weeks. Assume that a week is the length of time required for corn to grow and that Karl and Adam have available the same technologies used in the models of Chapter 2:

| Farm | 3 days labor | → 1 unit of corn |
| Factory | 1 day labor
+ 1 unit of corn | → 2 units of corn, gross |

Adam and Karl each start with ½ unit of corn. Karl is highly averse to performing work in the present: he desires only to consume 1 unit of corn per week, subject to the requirement that he not run down his seed stock. In the first week, he therefore works ½ day in the Factory (fully utilizing his seed corn) and 1½ days on the Farm, producing a total of 1½ units of corn, 1 of which he consumes at harvest time, leaving him with ½ unit to start with in week 2. Adam accumulates during the first week; he works ½ day in the Factory, utilizing his seed corn, and 4½ days on the Farm, producing 2½ units of corn, gross. After consuming 1 unit of corn, he has 1½ units left with which to start week 2. In week 2, Karl works up his own seed stock in ½ day in the Factory, producing 1 unit of corn; then, instead of going to the Farm, Karl borrows or rents Adam's 1½ units of seed corn and works it up in the Factory. This takes Karl precisely 1½ days and he produces 3 units of corn, gross, in the process. Of the 3 units of corn, he keeps ½ unit of corn and returns 2½ units of corn to Adam (Adam's principal of 1½ units of corn plus interest of 1 unit of corn). Indeed, Karl is quite content with this arrangement, for he has worked for a total of 2 days and received 1½ units of corn, just as in week 1, when he had to use the inferior Farm technology. This means the rate of interest that Adam has charged him (66.6%) is just the rate at which he is indifferent between borrowing from Adam and working on the Farm. (One can see that if there are many people like Karl and only a few like Adam, then competition will drive the interest rate to this value. Thus, the competitors for access to Adam's capital will have bid away any advantage they might have derived from borrowing from Adam rather than working on the Farm. The equilibrium interest rate is the competitive interest rate in a world where there are many people with Karl's preferences and relatively few with Adam's.) Adam, on the other hand, receives a profit of 1 unit of corn from Karl's labor, which he consumes, and is left again to begin week

3 with 1½ units of corn. He has not worked at all in week 2. This arrangement can continue forever, with Karl working 2 days and consuming 1 unit of corn each week, and Adam consuming 1 unit of corn each week but working 5 days during the first week and 0 days thereafter (Table 5.1).

Clearly there is exploitation in all weeks after the first in this arrangement. Adam does not work but lives off the interest he receives from lending his capital to Karl. Alternatively, I could have had Adam hire Karl to work on his capital stock in the Factory, paying him a wage of ⅓ unit of corn per day. The interest rate, like the wage that Karl will settle for, is determined by his next best opportunity on the Farm, and if there are many Karls and a few Adams, the competitive wage is ⅓ unit of corn per day.

But is there anything wrong with this exploitation? Karl and Adam (or the Karls and the Adams) started out with equal endowments of corn. Is there any sense in which Adam has taken unfair advantage of Karl? None is apparent, unless one views Karl's preference for leisure today as a kind of handicap, which gives him the right to some kind of protection from Adam's offer. Or, perhaps, Karl (but not Adam) was incapacitated in some way and thereby prevented from working more than 3 days a week. In this case one might decide that they faced unequal opportunities at the beginning, which would surely prejudice the judgment that the outcome was fair.

Karl is said to have a high rate of time preference, as he is relatively unwilling to forestall present consumption for the sake of greater consumption in the future. Adam has a low rate of time preference. In this case, the commodity whose consumption over time is at issue is leisure. Suppose Karl's high rate of time preference is due to impa-

Table 5.1 Work patterns of Karl and Adam

Week	Amount of Adam's labor expended (days)	Amount of Karl's labor expended (days)	Units of corn consumed by each individual
1	5	2	1
2	0	2	1
3	0	2	1
4	0	2	1

tience rather than to some physical handicap that prevents him from working as long as Adam does during the first week. If one were to forbid transactions of lending or hiring between Adam and Karl, then Karl still would be no better off (he would continue to work, as he did in week 1, in both Factory and Farm for a total of 2 days to produce his 1 unit of corn, net), but Adam would be worse off. Would it not, therefore, be spiteful to forbid these trades between them? Forbidding these transactions would only give rise to a Pareto suboptimal allocation of streams of corn and leisure over the lives of Adam and Karl. If Adam could not deal with Karl, then he would have to work every period himself, while Karl would work no less. Now suppose— to make the argument stronger—that there are set-up costs in moving from the Factory to the Farm. Then, when Karl works in both places, as in week 1, he would have to expend more than 2 days of labor to get 1 unit of corn. In week 2, when he borrows from Adam, he uses only the Factory, and so he works just the 2 days. Thus, with set-up costs, both Karl and Adam strictly gain by virtue of Adam's accumulation in week 1. (It is not clear precisely how the interest rate would be set when set-up costs exist, but that is a matter of second-order concern.) For a socialist society to prevent such exploitation, it "would have to forbid capitalist acts between consenting adults" (Nozick, 1974, p. 163).

There may be reasons to forbid such transactions, but they are not visible at the level of simplicity of this model. Yet even at this level exploitation unquestionably obtains. The conclusion to be drawn from the example, then, is this: when exploitation is an injustice, it is not because it is exploitation as such, but because the distribution of labor expended and income received in an exploitative situation are consequences of an initial distribution of assets that is unjust. The injustice of an exploitative allocation depends upon the injustice of the initial distribution. In the example, the initial distribution of equal seed corn endowment was taken to be just, and I was consequently hard put to identify the ensuing exploitation as evidence of anything nasty.

What, then, might be the causes of a highly unequal initial distribution of the means of production, and what are our attitudes toward such causes? Should the exploitation that will arise from an unequal distribution, variously caused, in a system of private property be considered morally bad?

5.2.1 Robbery and Plunder

If the initial distribution is highly unequal because some agents robbed and plundered, then clearly there are grounds for viewing the ensuing exploitation as bad. This is the case Marx made against European capitalism, particularly English capitalism. Part VIII of the first volume of *Capital* is entitled "The So-Called Primitive Accumulation." In this section Marx relates the history of the concentration of wealth by the English gentry through the enclosure movement and other forms of robbery. The appropriate folk rhyme, popular at the time is (Cheyney, 1923, p. 188):

> The law locks up the man or woman
> Who steals the goose from off the common,
> But leaves the greater villain loose
> Who steals the common from the goose.

The unequal distribution of land that the enclosure movement accomplished not only created a wealthy class but also created a potential proletariat by disenfranchising peasants of all means of production except their labor power. Before the enclosure movement the yeoman peasant had access to the commons and a small herd, and perhaps a small plot of land of his own; therefore, he had no need to sell his labor power to survive. The enclosure movement made it impossible for large numbers of disenfranchised peasants to survive without selling labor power. Thus, proletarianization of a population is often a by-product, intended or otherwise, of the concentration of land or capital. The newly formed class of propertied agents thus becomes wealthy, not only by virtue of the land it has acquired, but also because, in the process of that acquisition, it has "liberated" a mass of producers from their means of production, thus making them available as a labor force for hire. Without the existence of a class willing to sell its labor power (or to be enslaved or enserfed), large land holdings would do their owners no good.

In the Marxist account, the enclosure movement in England was a clear case of robbery and plunder, although that interpretation is not unchallenged. A contemporary analogue to enclosure was accomplished in the mid-twentieth century by the green revolution, during which new varieties of seed (for example, wheat) that were vastly more productive than old varieties were developed. Use of the new seed, however, required capital investment in irrigation, insecticides, and fertilizers (as well as knowledge), which small peasants could not undertake. Large landholders, by virtue of their wealth, were able to make the transition to the new technology, which created an increase in wheat yield and a decrease in the price of wheat. Small peasants who had survived by selling wheat on the market could no longer survive under these competitive pressures. They had to sell their land and become either landless laborers or urban proletarians. (The amount they could get for their small plots was too little to enable them to become petty capitalists, in part because the big landlord to whom a peasant sold his land was in a monopsonistic position.) It is argued that this process of proletarianization contributed to the rapid growth of Mexico City and the massive unemployment accompanying it. Even though the long-term consequence of technological change has been to increase the income of society, including that of its proletarians, in the short-run technological changes of certain kinds, like the green revolution, can proletarianize large masses of people, who become unemployed and poor. This example is not precisely a case of robbery or plunder, but it underscores the point that the concentration of capital (a process leading to unequal distribution of capital) is often accompanied by the proletarianization of a mass of people, and, hence, benefits the propertied class in a double sense. (For further discussion of the green revolution, see the book by Hewitt de Alcantara [1976].)

It is often difficult to decide when an act that leads to the concentration of wealth constitutes robbery. When the American Indians voluntarily agreed to sell Manhattan Island to the Dutch for $24, was that robbery? One might argue that if full information concerning a trader's alternatives is not available, then the trade is immoral, with one side taking unfair advantage of the other. Fairness involves not simply a gain to both sides from a trade but also an equitable division of the gains.

Most historical episodes of rapid concentration of land in the hands of a few are accomplished either by direct force or at least by deals in which political power is used in unprincipled ways. The history of capitalism is replete with examples of the accumulation of wealth through clearly unethical means, so it is not very difficult, on these grounds, to condemn the present distribution of wealth. But the question I am investigating is whether all possible causes of an unequal distribution of capital are condemnable.

5.2.2 *Differential Rates of Time Preference*

If agents have differential rates of time preference, then exploitation will quickly be generated, as it was in the story of Karl and Adam. Whether one views such exploitation as bad depends upon the view one takes toward the genesis of the different rates of time preference of these agents. Suppose the different rates came about as a consequence of exposure to different environments—say, families with different habits and different wealths. Adam, with a low rate of time preference, learned to save because he grew up in a well-off family that taught him the virtues of delayed gratification, whereas Karl's impatient preferences are the consequence of never having been taught by his parents to think about tomorrow. Perhaps, in such a situation, one could say that the differential rates of time preference that brought about the exploitation were themselves the consequence of a prior injustice—the different wealths of Karl's and Adam's families, which gave rise to their attitudes. More generally, the different attitudes toward saving of Karl and Adam may be the consequence of different external opportunities that one deems to be unfair.

Suppose, on the other hand, that Karl's and Adam's external opportunities were identical but that they were born with different rates of time preference. To condemn the ensuing exploitation, in this case, involves construing a high rate of time preference as a handicap. (This is the kind of value judgment that economists are loath to make.) Even if Karl's rate of time preference is so high that he does not take proper care of himself, does one have some objective basis for interfering with the deals he might make? (One might want to interfere because Karl's behavior eventually imposes costs on the minimally benevolent society that insists upon hospitalizing him, and paying for it, when he deteriorates as a result of his own neglect. But that is an issue quite different from the one of exploitation, which I am currently discussing.)

Suppose that Karl and Adam have different rates of time preference because of their prior exposure to different external opportunities. It is not necessarily the case that the preferences either one of them has are irrational. In fact, it may be that their rates of time preference are adapted to the environments in which they expect to live. Suppose that there are many Karls, each of whom expects to live only two weeks, and a small number of Adams, each of whom expects to live for many weeks. Except insofar as their different expectations about the lengths of their lives may influence their choices, the Karls and Adams all have the same attitudes about consumption of corn and leisure over time. If a Karl only expects to live two weeks, it is rational for him to enjoy life this week, as well as next week; and so he chooses to work, each week, just long enough to produce his subsistence requirement (and not run down his stock of corn, which he wants to pass on to his child, who will survive him). An Adam, however, is willing to work exceedingly hard during the first week, knowing that he can reap the benefits of leisure postponed to later periods by hiring the Karl types, an option that Karl does not have. Hence, to say that Karl and Adam have different rates of time preference by virtue of their different environments does not imply that one of them is behaving irrationally—against his self-interest, calculated by his best estimate. Each chooses a pattern of work and consumption based on his life expectancy. In this case, one might have grounds to condemn the exploitation of Karl by Adam, not because of the exploitation as such, but because the cause of their differential life expectancies may be proximately related to an injustice. One cannot, in this example, say that the cause of Karl's low life expectancy is his poverty, because by assumption Karl and Adam each began with the same wealth in corn. But perhaps Karl came from a poor family or a poor country (whereas Adam did not) and his attitudes about life expectancy were formed in that environment.

It might seem silly to discuss these possibilities, but an important justification for capitalism, which Marx attacked, was the theory that capital was the reward for abstinence from consumption: some people abstain from present consumption and provide a benefit to everyone as a consequence, as does Adam in the example. The "surplus labor" that others perform is the premium they pay to those who provide the socially useful function of abstinence from present consumption of leisure or corn, which produces a capital stock for tomorrow. Marx's answer to the abstinence defense of capitalist inequality was that the primitive accumulation of capital did not come about that way. Doubtless that is true. The original capitalists, by and large, both saved and consumed at prodigious rates. Nevertheless, even in modern capitalism, it is quite clear that some people become moderately well-off by virtue of extremely hard but unskilled work, such as small shopkeepers who are willing to work 80 to 90 hours a week. The argument, for example, is made that in England East Indians are willing to set up shops and work those hours; eventually, they become moderately well-off, in consequence of having chosen a path the native English worker is unwilling to take, even though the capital requirements and skills are within his means. East Indian immigrants have created, for the first time, a British dream.

Although one does observe different rates of time preference, it is a mistake to consider those differences to be a consequence of autonomous choices that people have made. Neoclassical economists tend to treat the rate of time preference as an aspect of a person's nature, something that the person should therefore bear the consequences of. But I think this is a myopic view. Attitudes toward saving are shaped by culture, and cultures are formed by the objective conditions that their populations face. If the East Indians work hard and build up small businesses while the native British workers do not, then that outcome is due to the history of the societies in which those populations formerly lived, societies that inculcated them with different values. Their differential success in capitalist enterprise is itself a consequence of past experience with capitalism, which in the one case demoralized the worker and in the other engendered in him a certain degree of ambition. When one sees patterns of behavior that characterize whole populations or classes, one must look for factors of social origin. If there is very little movement out of the working class in Britain, but more in the United States, that difference is due not to an innate enterprising spirit among American workers but to the differences between institutions and cultures in the two countries.

Marxists and left-liberals view rates of time preference as socially determined. Therefore in their view it is not possible to justify exploitation and inequality by appealing to differential rates of time preference, for those differences arose from prior conditions of inequality and oppression. Conservatives generally view the rate of time preference as innate. But even if one grants that the trait is innate, it does not follow that a person should bear the responsibility for that trait. In the 1960s, a number of conservative writers, such as Arthur Jensen and Richard Herrnstein, argued that blacks were innately inferior to whites, as measured by IQ tests, and that a high rate of time preference was linked to low intelligence. The evidence for an innate difference in IQs between blacks and whites has now been thoroughly discredited, but in the mid-1980s a new version of the argument surfaced. James Q. Wilson and Richard Herrnstein argue that the consumption of tobacco and alcohol by poor and, particularly, black pregnant women creates brain damage in fetuses and results in a population of black children who lack the capacity to think about tomorrow. In their provocatively titled book, *Crime and Human Nature*, they claim that much inner city crime is explained by this population of black youth with pathologically high rates of time preference. The evidence for this position has been sharply challenged by Leon Kamin, the same psychologist who exposed the concocted data that was used to advance the racist IQ theories of the 1960s.

Thus, ideological positions are fought over in an apparently scientific way. The origin of differential rates of time preference is an important case in point, because the view that wealth is a return to abstinence and saving has a long history. If people can be shown to "deserve" their rates of time preference, perhaps because a preference for planning and saving is a constituent of a person's personality or character, then an argument will have been established to justify inequality. It is important to recall the structure of the counterargument. First, the initial conditions of differential ownership were established, in all capitalist societies, by processes of theft and brute power. Second, to the extent that people do have different rates of time preference, and succeed differentially in capitalist society on that account, those differences are largely due to the process by which they are formed, namely, as a reaction to conditions of inequality and oppression. It is incorrect to argue that differential rates of time preference are the primal cause of unequal wealths if the genesis of those differences is due to a prior history of inequality. Third, even if there are some genetic or innate differences in rates of time preference, why should people benefit or lose on that account? If having a high rate of time preference is a handicap in a society with minimal social insurance, then should not those with that handicap receive social compensation?

5.2.3 Entrepreneurship

It is often argued in defense of capitalist inequality that profits are a return to entrepreneurial ability. People with this ability see ways of organizing labor and producing commodities that others do not see, and this scarce factor is rewarded with profits. Entrepreneurial ability plays the role in this explanation that a low rate of time preference played in the explanation in Section 5.2.2. Two questions concerning entrepreneurial ability can be raised: Is it a factor that is necessarily scarce, or is it scarce because most people in a capitalist system do not have the opportunities to develop their entrepreneurial abilities? Even if entrepreneurial ability is really scarce, is it appropriate for it to be rewarded as it is, with the accumulation of capital? I cannot answer the first question. With respect to the second, the argument can be made that entrepreneurs will continue to exercise their scarce talents even without the tremendous rewards that accrue to them in a capitalist system, so the capital stock that they (under assumption) accumulate need not be personally accumulated by them in order for their talents to be available to society. Perhaps the salary society would have to pay an entrepreneur is considerably less than he gets in a free enterprise system. By virtue of the private property rights, the entrepreneur who organizes and hires other factors of production is the claimant who gets what is left after wages and other costs are paid. But one can argue that a good part of that residual is a surplus that the entrepreneur neither needs (to perform his productive function) nor is entitled to.

Why might he not be entitled to it? Because his entrepreneurial skill could be considered to be the consequence of environmental or genetic factors from which he does not deserve to benefit. Suppose, to invoke an example already given, he acquired those entrepreneurial skills by virtue of growing up in a family in which he learned them by example. The proletarian had no such luck. The advantage accruing to the entrepreneur over that accruing to the proletarian is then a consequence of an unequal opportunity and is perhaps one a society committed to equality of opportunity should not condone. Granted, the entrepreneur performs a socially beneficial function, but in this case he should be paid only what is required to get him to do so. Indeed, various capitalist societies do take this position to different degrees, because they tax profits and managerial salaries at very different rates. In Japan the managers of big corporations are paid much less than their counterparts in the United States. But apparently they perform their entrepreneurial and organizational functions at least as well. Some argue that managers are not entrepreneurs but hired labor. But many entrepreneurial functions are performed by managers, and the popular justification of high managerial salaries in the United States is based on a belief in the scarcity of entrepreneurial talent.

Suppose that entrepreneurs do not learn their talents but are born with them, or, more realistically, that some people are born with the capacity to acquire entrepreneurial skills and others are not. In this case, people face different opportunities, but of a genetic sort. There may appear to be more reason to allow these natural entrepreneurs to keep the capital they accumulate, if one holds to a principle of *self-ownership*, which claims that a person ought to be entitled to the income that can be earned by the traits coming with his person. This principle can be challenged. First, do not such genetic dispositions constitute unequal opportunities, and what is our attitude toward such inequality? Perhaps the entrepreneur will derive sufficient pleasure from exercising his entrepreneurship, a pleasure unexperienced by the ordinary person, to draw forth his scarce talent. Is it necessarily the case that he should be repaid, as well, with the accumulation of a large capital stock? Even if one endorses self-ownership, it does not obviously require that degree of accumulation. Second, the entrepreneur may be perfectly willing to exercise his organizational talent without the accumulation of capital that attends its exercise under capitalism. In that case, there would be no reason from a social point of view to reward him in this way.

Thus far, I have taken the position that entrepreneurship is a talent. In reality, much of that "talent" may consist in having the right connections, something that is clearly associated with growing up with a certain class background. There may be an element of the feudal lord in the modern entrepreneur: somebody has to be one, but almost anyone could be, and so the positions go to those with family connections. Joseph Schumpeter argued that in early capitalism entrepreneurship was scarce and that capitalism served the function of bringing it to the fore. But now the requisite entrepreneurial skill can be taught to managers of socialist enterprises in business schools. It is available to many, regardless of connections and background.

Neoclassical economists tend to argue, in various ways, that each factor receives its appropriate return. Sometimes, in cruder versions of the neoclassical theory, appropriate return is translated as "just return." But, usually, appropriate return is taken to mean "that return required to make the factor contribute its services." This hardly seems to be the case, however, given the large variation in remuneration to talent that exists in different capitalist societies. The Marxist position is that each factor requires some remuneration to be reproduced and for it to be offered for productive service. What is left over after the payment of these necessary remunerations is an economic surplus, and there is considerable leeway in the manner in which society may distribute this surplus. In a laissez-faire system, there is some bargaining over the surplus (between workers and capitalists, for example), but there is no guarantee that the agreement reached is just or that it reflects a socially necessary pattern of remuneration. Thus, one need not deny the existence of a scarce talent called entrepreneurship to deny the justice of the vast inequalities that may be attributable to it in a capitalist system. Moreover, it is incorrect to assume that entrepreneurship is a resource that would only be forthcoming in a private property system. Even without the remuneration to entrepreneurship available in a capitalist system, there would in all likelihood be many people who would learn and would like to exercise the entrepreneurial skill that society needs.

5.2.4 Risk Propensity

The third category of scarce and valuable attributes that capitalism rightly (it is said) remunerates with profits is the willingness to take risks. This factor, again, is not captured in the models presented thus far. In reality investment is a risky business. Suppose there are two kinds of people: those willing to take risks and those not willing to take risks. Among the risk takers, many go bankrupt (and perhaps become proletarians or people of modest income) and some become capitalists. Proletarians are those who are not willing to take risks or those who have taken them and failed. Their surplus labor, accruing to the capitalists as profits, is the insurance premium they pay to capitalists to take risks for them. The worker is guaranteed his steady wage and sleeps well at night, paying the capitalist to gamble for him.

I find this story extremely implausible. I believe that many workers would like to have the opportunity to become capitalists; they would love to take those risks. But they cannot, either because of lack of access to capital markets or because of lack of some aspect of entrepreneurial ability (which might include having the right connections). Second, it cannot be seriously maintained that a worker's life involves less risk than a capitalist's. Workers face the risk of occupational disease, unemployment, and an impoverished retirement, which capitalists and managers do not face. Failing as a capitalist does not usually mean becoming destitute. I do not know of any sociological studies that verify my belief, but I think that the "American dream" encourages most young American white workers to try to escape from the working class, in one way or another, by taking various kinds of financial risks. If they fail, it is not for lack of trying but for lack of something else, most likely access to capital of a sufficient amount to escape the perils of small business.

5.2.5 *Luck*

Some argue (for example, Robert Nozick, 1974) that luck is a legitimate means of acquiring assets and that this factor could justify an initial distribution of capital that is highly unequal. Here I am not referring to luck that is the consequence of having taken a gamble: that would be covered under risk propensity. The kind of luck I am referring to is that which is not the outcome of choice under uncertainty on the part of the agent but is completely unanticipated; it is sometimes called brute luck. Perhaps the most important kind of luck by which people may acquire differential ownership of capital stock is inheritance.

Inheritance can be looked at from the point of view of the giver or the receiver. If one agrees that the giver has property rights in the wealth that she has legitimately earned and saved by virtue of her labor, skills, rate of time preference, and propensity toward risk, then it would seem that she should be entitled to dispose of that wealth as she pleases, and that would include giving it away to whatever heir she chooses. But from the point of view of the next generation—the group of potential receivers—inheritance constitutes perhaps the grossest of unequal opportunities. Does not everyone in the next generation have the right to begin with the same opportunities, including those determined by access to capital? This, after all, is a particularly easy kind of opportunity to equalize, unlike the differential opportunities that exist naturally by virtue of the fact that people grow up in different families.

Rights must be circumscribed in many ways, because a complete set of rights one might like to specify cannot simultaneously be satisfied. It seems to me that the right of the generation of givers must be constrained by the unequal opportunities it creates for the receivers. From an ethical viewpoint, I do not think it is so difficult to argue against the right to inheritance. But there is an efficiency issue that must be faced in advocating stiff inheritance taxes, and it is of the same nature as the efficiency question discussed under entrepreneurship. If inheritance of physical assets is forbidden, will that restriction act as a disincentive for people to save? The answer to this question is unclear; we do not have enough experience with the enforcement of stiff inheritance taxes in capitalist countries to know. Alfred Nobel created the trust that finances the prizes bearing his name instead of giving his accumulated wealth to his children, for he felt that they should earn it the hard way, as he did. One might allow an estate to escape taxes if the donor gave it for some specific purpose, such as building a hospital, or buying a piece of land for a park, or financing an opera company, each of which could bear her name. Means by which her contribution to society would be publicly recognized could easily be created. These alternatives to passing wealth down to individuals might both be socially more useful than the individual alternative and create as much incentive to save as the present inheritance laws do. The efficiency argument for individualized inheritance is not convincing; such a claim would have to be established empirically.

In a recent paper, D. W. Haslett argues for purifying capitalism, a system that he otherwise likes, by abolishing inheritance. He regards inheritance as an institution inconsistent with the equality of opportunity that capitalism champions. Haslett, like Alfred Nobel, believes that virtuous incentive effects would be generated by abolishing inheritance. He offers the following analogy. If two runners start a race with one far behind the other, will the second runner try hard to win? Indeed, how fast will the leader run? Contrast this with how hard each of them will run if they begin the race together. The analogy implies that everyone will work harder if the members of each generation begin with the same level of wealth, assuming people have the usual desires to excel materialistically.

It is worth noting the degree to which inheritance is responsible for differential wealth in the United States. The wealthiest 1 to 2% of American families own 20 to 30% of the net family wealth in the United States. The wealthiest 20% own 80% of the wealth, whereas the poorest 20% own just 0.2% of the wealth. Inequality of wealth is far more severe than inequality of income: the top 20% of families in the income distribution earned 57% of the total family income in the mid-1970s. In a study published in 1978, John Brittain showed that 67% of the large fortunes in the United States are derived from inheritance, not present earnings. Even while nominal inheritance taxes were fairly high (before 1981, when the Reagan administration started reducing them), the actual taxes paid on large estates were incredibly small. The average tax rate on estates was 0.2%, and on estates of over $500,000 it was a mere 0.8%. Thus it is said that the inheritance tax is a voluntary one, or a tax on poor planning. Given these facts about the origins of current American wealth, it is hard to countenance the conservative position that the position of people in American society is due to their hard or skillful work. The family into which a person is born is much more important in determining her fortune than are any voluntary choices she makes.

On grounds of equal opportunity, I think there is a strong argument against luck as a legitimate means for acquiring material assets. One might better argue that those assets which materialize because of luck belong to everyone, not to the person on whom they just happen to fall. Why should the point in time at which opportunities are declared to be equal be before Lady Luck has thrown the dice, and not after? After all, by definition, no one has done anything to earn the fruits of luck, and the motivation for equality of opportunity is that each is entitled to what he earns from a starting point of equality. (This statement applies to luck that is not the outcome of a calculated gamble, which, as I said, is a case excluded here but included under considerations of the rights to earn differentially from differential risk propensities.)

Whether the argument of the preceding paragraph also makes a case against allowing individuals to reap the fruits of genetic luck is a more difficult question. Do I have the moral right to the income stream that my inborn talent enables me to earn?

5.3 Justification of Unequal Distribution

A normative justification for measuring exploitation lies in the meaning of the colloquial definition of exploitation: "to take unfair advantage of." Because exploitation is the consequence of inequality in the initial distribution of physical assets, it would seem that its existence indicates unfairness only if the initial unequal distribution of assets is unfair. Marxists argue that all capitalist societies established the take-off point of unequal capital ownership by processes akin to robbery, slavery, and plunder. If this argument is accepted, the case for unfairness is then clearly made, the unfair nature of the exploitative allocation being inherited, as it were, from the initial unjust distribution. But ideologues of capitalism have argued that the initial distribution of unequal ownership could have arisen (even if actually it did not) in morally respectable ways: as a result of differences in the rates of time preference, or in risk propensities, or in entrepreneurial abilities and skills, or as a result of unanticipated luck. Such a clean beginning would establish the cogency of capitalism as a system against which there is, so they say, no principled ethical argument—although there may be specific arguments against specific historical instances of capitalism. Capitalist ideologues argue from two fronts: that it is necessary to recognize and reward these differential attributes of people differentially in order for the good attributes to emerge and be available for society, and that the holders of these attributes deserve the fruits that thereby accrue to them in a private ownership system. These arguments are not consistent either with economic theory or with the history of developed capitalism, a history replete with the establishment of fortunes by wars, or through the exercise of monopoly power, or as the consequence of market imperfections.

At the most general level, neoclassical economists maintain that (at least in a certain class of economies) all income generated can be viewed as the return to some factor. But it is unclear whether return means an income which that factor must receive to continue to offer its services, or an income that *should*, on ethical grounds, go to that factor. There is, furthermore, the distinction, not usually made in neoclassical analysis, between the factor and its owner. One cannot in general divide the pie produced by capital goods and labor up into two parts, one of which was produced by labor and one by capital. Nor, even if one could, is it clear that the part produced by the capital should go to the capitalist and the part produced by labor should go to the laborer. The Marxist analysis avoids the notion of returns and argues instead that the cooperation of labor and physical capital and land produces an income that is larger than the income needed to reproduce the factors used up, and is even larger than the income needed to get people to offer those factors for use. There is a genuine surplus, and society must adopt some rules for distributing it. Under capitalism, the distribution of the surplus is decided on the basis of property rights in the ownership of the initial factors. Workers and capitalists may bargain over the property rights in the surplus to which their factor contribution entitles them. The state takes some of the surplus through taxation; and the tax laws may also be the consequence of interclass bargaining, the state acting as an agent representing one of the classes, or perhaps as an independent agent with its own interests. But the deep justification of capitalism must be based on a justification, either on pragmatic (efficiency) grounds or on ethical grounds, of the initial distribution of ownership in the means of production, a distribution that sets the initial conditions for interclass bargaining over the surplus.

There is one particularly opportunistic argument that defenders of unequal ownership make: "What's good for General Motors is good for the country." In other words, capitalists must have the prospect of a sufficiently high profit rate in order to invest (rather than to consume, presumably, or to take their capital elsewhere). So for workers to have jobs it is necessary that profits exist and be high. Neither liberals nor conservatives have a principled disagreement with this statement; they disagree, instead, over the rate at which capital can be taxed before it "goes on strike." Conservatives say, Not very much, and liberals say, Quite a lot. Both of these non-Marxist political viewpoints accept the necessity of returns to capitalists in principle. But the Marxist position need not argue that taxes on profits or wages can be increased substantially under capitalism; it need not favor policies that would lower the rate of profit and cloud an otherwise good investment climate. It can accept the necessity of high profits for the viability of capitalism and use that to argue against the suitability of an economic system based on private ownership of the means of production. If those who control the capital stock have to be bribed in order to make it available to society, is that an argument for bribing them or an argument against the system that makes such bribes necessary?

6

The Emergence of Class

In the models of Chapter 2, classes emerged, first, in an inessential way when wealth was equally distributed, but then in an essential way when the capital stock was unequally owned. In the second model of that chapter (Section 2.3), three classes existed: capitalists, proletarians, and peasants. In this chapter, I will elaborate more formally on the emergence of class as a consequence of the unequal ownership of the means of production, and I will discuss the relationship of class to both exploitation and wealth. In the interest of simplicity, I will use the one-dimensional corn model introduced in Chapter 3. Finally, I will evaluate what the description of an agent's class adds to our understanding of positive and normative issues.

6.1 A Definition of Equilibrium for a Corn Model with Assets

Consider an economy that consists, as before, of N agents and a technology for producing corn, $\{a,L\}$. This model, unlike previous models, contains an explicit specification of the initial corn endowment of the ith agent. This endowment, ω^i, varies from agent to agent. Each agent, as before, is endowed with 1 unit of leisure, which can be converted into labor. And each agent has subsistence preferences: each wishes to work only so long as is necessary to produce an income sufficient to purchase an amount b of corn, which I will take to be his subsistence requirement. He will not allow himself to deplete his initial corn stock of ω^i. Under what conditions will this economy reproduce itself and satisfy each agent's needs?

Suppose there is a labor market. Because only relative prices matter, the wage is normalized at 1, and the price of corn is p. An agent can engage in three kinds of activities: she can work up her own corn stock, using her own labor to produce corn; she can hire others to work up her corn stock, paying them wages; or she can sell her labor power to others at the going wage and work up their corn stock. For agent i, let x^i be the amount of corn she produces by working up her own seed corn; let y^i be the amount of corn produced by those whom she hires to work up her seed corn; and let z^i be the amount of labor she sells on the labor market. Then her total net revenues will be

$$(p - pa)x^i + [p - (pa + L)]y^i + z^i.$$

The first term is equal to the net revenues she receives from operating the corn activity herself; that is, revenues remaining after paying for the corn input she uses. The second term is the net revenues she receives from hiring labor; that is, revenues remaining after paying wages and paying for the capital stock used in the process. The third term is her wage income. The subsistence requirement is that agent i earn sufficient net revenues to purchase her corn consumption bundle, that is,

$$(p - pa)x^i + [p - (pa + L)]y^i + z^i \geq pb. \tag{6.1}$$

What constraint does the agent's initial ownership of the capital stock place on her? Assume that there is a labor market in this economy, but no capital market. No agent can borrow, although she can sell her labor power. Thus, agent i is constrained to choose levels of corn production that can be supported by the capital she has available to advance, given her initial stock. I will assume that she need not advance the wage payments to the labor she hires at the beginning of the period—instead, they are paid at the end of the period out of revenues. (This assumption differs from the one I made in Chapter 4, and I make it here only because it simplifies some of the calculations.) Under this assumption, the amount of finance capital agent i must have in order to operate corn production at level x^i herself and hire others to operate it at level y^i is $pax^i + pay^i$. Her capital constraint is

$$pax^i + pay^i \leq p\omega^i. \tag{6.2}$$

Furthermore, agent i is constrained not to use more labor than she possesses:

$$Lx^i + z^i \leq 1. \tag{6.3}$$

The first term in (6.3) is the amount of labor agent i expends on her own corn stock, and the second term is the amount of labor she sells on the labor market. The right-hand side of (6.3) is her labor endowment.

The goal of agent i is to minimize the labor she expends subject to producing a subsistence income and subject to satisfying her capital constraint (6.2) and labor constraint (6.3). Her utility maximization problem can therefore be written as, choose x^i, y^i, and z^i to

minimize $Lx^i + z^i$

$$
\begin{array}{lll}
\text{subject to} & (p - pa)x^i + [p - (pa + L)]y^i + z^i \geq pb & (6.1) \\
& pax^i + pay^i \leq p\omega^i & (6.2) \quad (P^i) \\
& Lx^i + z^i \leq 1 & (6.3)
\end{array}
$$

and subject to the constraint that the variables x^i, y^i, and z^i are nonnegative.

Call this optimization problem for the agent i, (P^i).

In this economy there are N agents, each of whom is trying to solve a program of the type (P^i). Such an economy is in equilibrium if the markets clear. In other words, a wage-price of corn, p, will equilibrate the economy if it allows the markets to clear. There are two markets: one for corn and one for labor. The corn market clears if the net amount of corn produced suffices to meet the demand for corn, which is Nb; and the labor market clears if the total supply of labor offered for sale by the N agents equals the total demand for hired labor by the N agents.

To represent these conditions, it is first convenient to define

$$
x \equiv \sum x^i, \qquad y \equiv \sum y^i, \qquad z \equiv \sum z^i,
$$

where x is the total amount of corn, gross, produced by agents working for themselves, y is the total amount of corn produced by agents who are working as hired labor, and z is the total labor supplied on the labor market. The total amount of corn produced in this economy, without taking account of replacing the seed stock, is $(x + y)$; the net corn production is $(1 - a)(x + y)$. Hence, the requirement that the supply of corn, net of replacement, meet the demand for corn is

$$
(1 - a)(x + y) \geq Nb. \tag{6.4}
$$

As defined above, the total supply of labor offered for sale is z; and the total demand for labor by hirers is Ly. Thus, the labor market clears if

$$Ly = z. \tag{6.5}$$

Finally, the production plan of this economy must be feasible, which is to say that the total inputs society has available, $\omega \equiv \Sigma\omega^i$, suffice to supply the inputs for the outputs generated; that is,

$$a(x + y) \leq \omega. \tag{6.6}$$

Definition 6.1 Reproducible Equilibrium A price for corn of p(and a wage of 1) will be said to be a reproducible equilibrium for this economy if the solutions $\{\langle x^i,y^i,z^i\rangle\}$ to the individual optimization programs (P^i) generated by this price are such that the aggregate quantities x, y, and z satisfy Equations (6.4), (6.5), and (6.6).

To summarize, each agent begins with some initial endowment of seed corn. There is a corn market and a labor market. Facing a price for corn and a wage, each agent decides on his best strategy, which will enable him to earn the income necessary for purchasing his required corn consumption while not running down his seed corn stock. This strategy is his labor-minimizing one, because I have assumed that the agents have subsistence preferences. An equilibrium is a price of corn, relative to the wage, having the property that, if each agent pursues his self-interest in this way, markets clear; every individual plan can be realized, and society can reproduce its capital stock.

6.2 Class Formation

As a consequence of their optimizing behavior and their initial endowments, agents end up in different class positions. Hence, by this mechanism, classes are formed.

Facing a price of corn p, an agent solves his program (P^i) with a solution $\langle x^i,y^i,z^i\rangle$. Suppose, for example, that for him the optimum involves setting $x^i = 0 = z^i$ (neither does he himself work up any of his seed corn, nor does he sell labor power) but $y^i > 0$ (he hires labor power to work up his seed capital). He can be represented as having a solution vector of the form $\langle 0,+,0 \rangle$, where a "0" in a certain place indicates that he does not engage in that kind of activity and a "+" indicates that he does. The agent in this example is a pure capitalist, because he optimizes by hiring labor power only; he neither sells labor power nor works for himself. Suppose that another agent's solution to his program involves setting $x^i = 0 = y^i$, but $z^i > 0$. Such a person is represented as having a solution $\langle 0,0,+ \rangle$: he is a proletarian, who optimizes by selling labor power only—he neither works for himself nor hires labor power.

Definition 6.2 Class Position   The class position of an agent is defined by the particular array of 0's and +'s in the optimal solution $\langle x^i, y^i, z^i \rangle$ to his program (P^i) at a reproducible equilibrium.

In principle, there are eight possible ways of arranging 0's and +'s in the three positions of $\langle x,y,z \rangle$. But one of them can be ruled out immediately: everyone must earn some income to purchase his consumption bundle in this economy, because no one is willing to eat into his capital stock; so the class position $\langle 0,0,0 \rangle$ will never occur as a solution. Furthermore, it is not difficult to show that no agent will ever be required both to sell labor and to hire labor at the same time in order to optimize—every agent has an optimal solution in which he does not trade as both a supplier and a demander of labor. This rules out the class positions $\langle 0,+,+ \rangle$ and $\langle +,+,+ \rangle$ as redundant in a parsimonious representation of the class structure of this economy. There remain five possible class positions; and they all can occur and should be named (Table 6.1). I have assigned both industrial and agricultural names to these classes, for the value these may have as historical mnemonics. The reader should verify that each of these class positions corresponds naturally to the name that identifies it.

Table 6.1   Class positions in a corn economy

Class position $\langle x^i, y^i, z^i \rangle$	Class name in an industrial economy	Class name in an agricultural economy
$\langle 0, +, 0 \rangle$	Pure capitalist	Landlord
$\langle +, +, 0 \rangle$	Small capitalist	Rich peasant
$\langle +, 0, 0 \rangle$	Petty bourgeois artisan	Middle peasant
$\langle +, 0, + \rangle$	Semiproletarian	Poor peasant
$\langle 0, 0, + \rangle$	Proletarian	Landless laborer

How is an agent's class position related to his wealth and how is it related to his being either exploited or exploiting? The important idea to keep in mind during the following analysis is that a person's class position is not exogenously given. Rather, it emerges as a consequence of his optimizing procedure, which is to maximize his utility (in this case, minimize labor expended subject to a subsistence constraint) given his initial endowment. Classes emerge endogenously as a characteristic of agents in the equilibrium of the economy.

6.3 Class and Wealth

In this economy wages are paid at the end of the period, so the capital advanced to produce 1 unit of corn is just pa. The equation defining the profit rate is

$$\pi = \frac{p - (pa + wL)}{pa},$$

or

$$p = (1 + \pi)pa + wL. \tag{6.7}$$

Equation (6.7) differs from the formulation of the profit rate in Chapter 4 only in that investment capital does not include wages advanced. As I mentioned there, it is a matter of convention whether one chooses to view wages as paid in advance out of capital or at the end of the production period out of revenues, for the results with which I am concerned do not change.

Class is related to wealth in the way one might conjecture: the greater an agent's initial endowment of corn, the higher he is on the class hierarchy listed in Section 6.2. The richest agents become pure capitalists and the poorest become proletarians.

Theorem 6.1 Class–Wealth Correspondence   The greater an agent's initial endowment of corn, the "higher" he is on the class hierarchy of Table 6.1.

Proof.

1. Let the profit rate, which I assume is positive, be π. At the price p, the value of an agent's initial wealth is

$$p\omega^i \equiv W^i. \tag{6.8}$$

If an agent is sufficiently wealthy, then he clearly can generate enough revenue, simply from hiring others to work for him, to end up with profits of at least pb, which is what he requires. Thus, all those whose wealth is sufficiently great will only hire others; they will be in the class of pure capitalists, as they will neither sell labor power nor work for themselves. This establishes that those at the top of the wealth hierarchy belong to the class $\langle 0,+,0 \rangle$, as Theorem 6.1 claims.

2. It is similarly clear that the agents who are pure proletarians are precisely those who own zero corn at the beginning. For if an agent had some initial wealth, he could derive profits of πW^i from hiring others to work it, thus reducing his own necessary work time. It would be wasteful not to use capital he owned. No such agent would, therefore, be a proletarian. Conversely, if an agent owns no corn but only labor power, then his only source of revenues is to sell his labor power; and he optimizes by taking the class position $\langle 0,0,+ \rangle$. Hence, those in the class position $\langle 0,0,+ \rangle$ are precisely those with zero wealth.

3. It remains to rank by wealth agents who optimize by becoming members of the three "middle classes." These are agents who have some wealth. Let an optimal solution for such an agent i be $\langle x^i,y^i,z^i \rangle$. An agent with some wealth, but not enough to be a pure capitalist, must necessarily engage all his capital in production to optimize, for otherwise he would make more revenue by hiring some labor to operate his unused capital, because $\pi > 0$. Therefore, constraint (6.2) of the agent's program is an equality, and dividing through by pa yields

$$x^i + y^i = \frac{\omega^i}{a}. \tag{6.9}$$

4. Constraint (6.1) of agent i's program can be rewritten as

$$p(1 - a)(x^i + y^i) + (z^i - Ly^i) = pb. \tag{6.1'}$$

Substituting from (6.9) into (6.1') yields

$$\frac{p(1 - a)\omega^i}{a} + (z^i - Ly^i) = pb. \tag{6.10}$$

From (6.10), a rearrangement of terms gives

$$z^i - Ly^i = p\left[b - \frac{(1 - a)\omega^i}{a} \right], \tag{6.9'}$$

from which it follows that

$$z^i - Ly^i < 0 \quad \text{if and only if} \quad \omega^i > \frac{ba}{1-a} \tag{6.11a}$$

$$z^i - Ly^i = 0 \quad \text{if and only if} \quad \omega^i = \frac{ba}{1-a} \tag{6.11b}$$

$$z^i - Ly^i > 0 \quad \text{if and only if} \quad \omega^i < \frac{ba}{1-a} \tag{6.11c}$$

5. From the inequalities of (6.11), the rest of the Class–Wealth Correspondence can be derived. Suppose $z^i - Ly^i = 0$; that is, agent i optimizes by selling exactly as much labor power as he hires to work on his own capital stock. Now observe that he could fire all his hired labor and instead work up the capital they were using himself in the same amount of time (by hypothesis), and he would just break even. He would save wages paid out in amount Ly^i by firing them, and he would lose wages paid to him in amount z^i by taking himself off the labor market; and these two amounts are equal, by the supposition of this paragraph. Thus, he could just as well operate all his capital himself, neither hiring nor selling labor; and he would make the same revenues for the same amount of labor expended. This shows that if

$$\omega^i = \frac{ba}{1-a}, \tag{6.12}$$

then agent i is a petty bourgeois artisan; he has a solution to his program of the form $\langle +,0,0 \rangle$. And, according to (6.11b), the wealth given by (6.12) is precisely the wealth associated with $z^i - Ly^i = 0$.

6. Now suppose $z^i - Ly^i < 0$. Then agent i is hiring more labor power than he expends on the labor market. He cannot, therefore, fire all his hired labor and simply replace them with his own labor in the same amount. If he takes himself off the labor market, he can fire some of his hired labor, but to break even in terms of labor expended and revenues earned he must continue to hire labor in the amount $(Ly^i - z^i)$. Therefore, such an agent is in the class $\langle +,+,0 \rangle$—he can optimize by working on his own capital stock and hiring others. According to (6.11a), this agent has a wealth

$$\omega^i > \frac{ba}{1-a}. \tag{6.13}$$

7. Finally, there is the agent whose optimal solution is characterized by $z^i - Ly^i > 0$. Such an agent can fire all his workers and can

himself work up the capital stock they were employed upon, but he must still supply wage labor to earn the revenues he was making before. He must continue to sell some of his labor power on the labor market, and his class position is therefore $\langle +, 0, + \rangle$. According to (6.11c), this agent has wealth

$$\omega^i < \frac{ba}{1 - a}. \tag{6.14}$$

8. The arguments in paragraphs 5, 6, and 7 establish that agents in the three middle classes are ranked according to their wealths; only agents with wealth exactly equal to $ba/(1 - a)$ are petty bourgeois artisans, and those with higher wealth must hire labor to optimize while those with lower wealth must sell labor to optimize. This demonstration establishes the Class–Wealth Correspondence. ∎

Table 6.2 summarizes the relationships between class and wealth given in the proof of Theorem 6.1. Thus, only the proletarian has nothing to sell but his labor power—and nothing to lose but his chains.

I must reiterate that this relationship between class and wealth is not one that is postulated initially; it emerges as a consequence of economic activity. Agents *choose their own class position*—not willingly, but under constraint, as a consequence of optimizing, given their initial endowments. Theorem 6.1 demonstrates that the relationship between class and wealth need not be postulated—it can be derived under the assumption that maximizing agents confront one another

Table 6.2 Class–Wealth Correspondence

Class position $\langle x^i, y^i, z^i \rangle$	Name	Wealth
$\langle 0, +, 0 \rangle$	Pure capitalist	$\omega^i \geq \dfrac{b}{\pi}$
$\langle +, +, 0 \rangle$	Small capitalist	$\dfrac{b}{\pi} > \omega^i > \dfrac{ba}{1 - a}$
$\langle +, 0, 0 \rangle$	Petty bourgeois artisan	$\omega^i = \dfrac{ba}{1 - a}$
$\langle +, 0, + \rangle$	Semiproletarian	$\dfrac{ba}{1 - a} > \omega^i > 0$
$\langle 0, 0, + \rangle$	Proletarian	$\omega^i = 0$

in a system of private property and markets. The phenomena of class and exploitation are not residues of market imperfections but are the consequences of a "perfect" market system, where agents are free to choose, constrained by their initial endowments of wealth and labor power.

As a historical note, it is worth mentioning that when Lenin wrote *The Development of Capitalism in Russia* he discussed the class structure in the Russian countryside:

> In the peasant mass of 97 million, however, one must distinguish three main groups: the bottom group—the proletarian and semi-proletarian strata of the population; the middle—the poor small peasant farmers; and the top group—the well-to-do small peasant farmers. We have analyzed above the main economic features of these groups as distinct *class* elements. The bottom group is the propertyless population, which earns its livelihood mainly, or half of it, by the *sale of labour power*. The middle group comprises the poor small peasant farmers, for the middle peasant in the best of years just barely manages to make ends meet, but the *principal* means of livelihood of this group is "independent" (supposedly independent, of course) *small-scale farming*. Finally, the top group consists of the well-to-do small peasant farmers, who exploit more or less considerable numbers of allotment-holding farm labourers and day labourers and all sorts of wage-labourers in general. (Lenin, 1899 [1974, p. 508])

Richer than all these peasants, and not discussed in this paragraph from Lenin, were the landlords, who did not work at all by virtue of owning so much land.

Similarly, Mao Zedong, in his pamphlet "Analysis of the Classes in Chinese Society," wrote:

> Although both the overwhelming majority of the semi-owner peasants and the poor peasants belong to the semi-proletariat, they may be further divided into three smaller categories, upper, middle and lower, according to their economic condition. The semi-owner peasants are worse off than the owner-peasants because every year they are short of about half the food they need, and have to make up this deficit by renting land from others, selling part of their labor power, or engaging in petty trading. In late spring and early summer when the crop is still in the blade and the old stock is consumed, they borrow at exorbitant rates of interest and buy grain at high prices; their plight is naturally harder than that of the owner-peasants who need no help from others, but they are better off than the poor peas-

ants. For the poor peasants own no land, and receive only half the harvest or even less for their year's toil, while the semi-owner peasants, though receiving only half or less than half the harvest of land rented from others, can keep the entire crop from the land they own. The semi-owner peasants are therefore more revolutionary than the owner-peasants, but less revolutionary than the poor peasants. (Mao, 1926 [1974, pp. 16–17])

Mao refers to borrowing and lending, which is not part of the model of this chapter—but I will show later that his identification of borrowing with the selling of labor power and lending with the hiring of labor power is borne out. Moreover, he makes some sociological observations about the revolutionary nature of the peasantry as a function of their wealth, a topic that I have not discussed. The salient point is that the model of this chapter seems to capture aspects of historical observation. Textual analysis of Lenin's statement reveals that he is discussing the lower four classes in the five-class hierarchy of my model, whereas Mao discusses only the bottom three. He does not make explicit mention of rich peasants who systematically hire labor, or lend money, or rent land to others.

6.4 Class and Exploitation

I have identified class position with wealth in an unambiguous way. But how is class position related to exploitation?

Theorem 6.2 Class–Exploitation Correspondence   Agents who optimize by placing themselves in a labor-hiring class are exploiters, and agents who optimize by selling labor are exploited.

Proof. Consider the agent who has wealth that puts him in the petty bourgeois artisan class; his wealth (Equation 6.12) is $\omega^i = ba/(1 - a)$. He must utilize all his capital, for otherwise he could earn more revenue by hiring some labor to use his excessive capital and thereby reduce his own work time further. Therefore, if his optimal solution is $\langle x^i, 0, 0 \rangle$, it must be the case that

$$ax^i = \omega^i = \frac{ba}{1 - a}, \quad \text{or} \tag{6.15}$$

$$x^i = \frac{b}{1 - a}.$$ (6.15′)

Hence, the amount of time he works is

$$Lx^i = \frac{bL}{1 - a} = \lambda b = \text{SNLT},$$ (6.16)

the last equation following because the labor value of corn, λ, is equal to $L/(1 - a)$. Equation (6.16) says that agent i works just socially necessary labor time.

Now consider an agent j, who is richer than agent i. By Theorem 6.1, agent j must be in a labor-hiring class; and an agent who is richer than agent i will work less time than i works, because his object is to minimize time worked subject only to his wealth constraint and the subsistence constraint. Thus, agent j works less time than λb and is consequently an exploiter. Similarly, consider an agent k, who is poorer than agent i; agent k will be in a labor-selling class, by Theorem 6.1, and will work more time than λb. Hence, k is exploited. Thus, every agent in a labor-hiring class works less than the socially necessary labor time, and every agent in a labor-selling class works longer than the socially necessary labor time. This establishes Theorem 6.2. ∎

Both the exploitation and class status of an agent emerge as endogenous characteristics of agents in the equilibrium of this economy; they are not postulated from the start. Hence, the Class–Exploitation Correspondence is not an obvious fact, because it relates two properties of an individual, both of which emerge as the consequence of economic activity. In the one-good model, Theorem 6.2 is very easy to prove; in a model with many goods, it remains true but is more difficult to prove. Furthermore, the characterization is not quite so neat. In a model with many goods (like the one of Section 4.3), there is a range of wealths associated with being in the class $\langle +,0,0 \rangle$, not just one number, as there is here. The generalization of Theorem 6.2 to many goods states that any agent in the top two classes is an exploiter and any agent in the bottom two classes is exploited, but it is not the case that all agents in the middle artisan class are exploitation-neutral, as in the one-good model. The *precise* identification of exploitation status with class status, as shown here, is an artifact of the one-good model.

With Theorems 6.1 and 6.2 I have established a wealth–exploitation correspondence. Table 6.2 shows that any agent whose wealth is greater than a certain amount $[\omega^i > ba/(1 - a)]$ is an exploiter and any agent whose wealth is less than a certain amount $[\omega^i < ba/(1 - a)]$ is exploited.

In this chapter I have adopted two major simplifications that one might wish to relax in a more general model. First, one should allow for an economy with many goods; second, one should allow for agents to have more complicated preferences than the subsistence preferences they have in this model. And it is necessary to consider how to define exploitation when people have more complicated preferences. Nevertheless, when the model is generalized in this way, Theorem 6.2 remains true.

Suppose people have various preferences over goods and leisure, they engage in economic activity to earn income, and they purchase goods. In this case the general definition of exploitation is as follows: an agent is exploited if the labor he expends in economic activity is greater than the labor that is embodied in *any bundle of goods he could purchase with his revenues,* that is, if any commodity bundle within his budget embodies less labor than he expended. Similarly, an agent is defined as an exploiter if all bundles of goods that can be purchased with his total revenues from production embody more labor than he expended. This definition allows for the possibility of a significant group of agents who are neither exploited nor exploiters, because the revenues they earn from production enable them to buy a commodity bundle embodying just the amount of labor they expended (although they will not necessarily purchase just that bundle). The Class–Exploitation Correspondence theorem states that any agent who optimizes by being in a labor-hiring class is an exploiter and any agent who optimizes by being in a labor-selling class is exploited. This is the generalization of Theorem 6.2, and it remains true in the framework of arbitrary preferences and many goods.

Does the Class–Wealth Correspondence remain true with general preferences and many goods? Not always. If preferences of agents are bizarre in a certain way (see Chapter 9), then the relationship between class and wealth can fail. This happens only for preferences that are quite unusual. When it happens, the relationship between wealth and exploitation fails as well, for wealth is related to exploitation status by virtue of the class–wealth and class–exploitation correspondences. The consequences will be discussed in Chapter 9.

6.5 The Significance of Class

Classes are important in the Marxist theory of historical materialism; class struggle is the midwife of social revolution, the instrument by which property relations are transformed in radical ways—from feudalism to capitalism, from capitalism to socialism. Now that a theory of class formation has been formulated, it is possible to comment briefly on why classes might be interesting and why class struggle is apparently so prevalent, at least in the Marxist theory of history.

Theorems 6.1 and 6.2 immediately suggest two answers to the question, "Why is there class struggle?" First, the fight of the working classes against the capitalist class may just be a fight of poor against rich, a fight against the consequences of unequal initial distribution. This position is suggested by the Class–Wealth Correspondence. Or perhaps there is some underlying reason why the exploited should fight the exploiters—this position is associated with the Class–Exploitation Correspondence. There is a third factor that might motivate class struggle: conflict between the dominated and those who dominate. I refer to the domination by the employer of the worker at the point of production, the social relations in the workplace, in which the worker's subservience to the boss is enforced by various extraeconomic means, which I referred to earlier. These three explanations can be labeled, respectively, the *wealth, exploitation,* and *domination* accounts of class struggle.

How sensible is the explanation that class struggle arises by virtue of the association of class with exploitation as such? That is, do the exploited classes fight the exploiting classes because they can only purchase consumption bundles embodying less labor then they expended in production? I find this account unconvincing. One of the central points of Chapter 4 was that relations of exploitation are obscured by commodity relations and the social division of labor under capitalism. Workers are not so conscious of their exploitation under capitalist property relations. They may feel unfairly taken advantage of, but not by virtue of comparing the socially necessary labor time they consume in goods with the labor they expend. Theorem 6.1 says that class is a good statistic for exploitation, but one cannot use *exploitation* as an explanation of class struggle unless it is perceived by the workers as an injustice they wish to erase. It is hard to make this case, when one simultaneously wishes to claim that capitalist relations obscure relations of exploitation.

Of course, to the extent that workers fight for a higher wage, or for a shorter length of the working day for the same wage, they are de facto fighting against exploitation, for victories in those struggles will lower the rate of exploitation (at least in the short run). But in those cases workers are fighting not against their exploitation as such, but because they want a higher real income or more humane conditions of work.

It is much more likely that workers struggle against capitalists in part because of the methods of control that are used against them in the workplace, to extract their labor. This struggle takes the form of fighting about the conditions of work. Fights against speedup and the methods used to implement it are an example. The fight against domination has been institutionalized in the American trade union movement, with careful delineation of job rules that prevent the employer from having the freedom to use workers in arbitrary ways; these rules are the consequence of an attempt to limit the arbitrary power of employers to extract labor from labor power on the job. I do not claim that all struggles for better conditions on the job are struggles against domination; but capitalists do use extraeconomic coercion of workers to squeeze more labor out of a day's labor power, a squeezing that often has exhausting and harrowing consequences for the worker.

Why is there extraeconomic coercion, or domination, by foremen over workers on the job? The ultra-neoclassical explanation is similar to the North-Thomas explanation for feudal coercion. Recall that the serf was said to have implicitly agreed to a contract with the lord under which he was forced to work, and public goods that otherwise would not have been available were provided. A weaker version of the explanation claims that even if the serf did not so agree, provision of otherwise unavailable public goods was the upshot of feudal coercion. Similarly, if the worker does not work on the job, then profits fall and workers are fired. Thus, the story goes, workers implicitly contract with employers to have themselves coerced on the job, because otherwise in their myopia they would not work as hard as is necessary to produce the revenues sufficient to pay the wages they want.

I do not think the implicit contract explanation of job-site domination is credible. Rather, such domination exists because of the impossibility of writing and enforcing a perfect contract for the exchange of labor for the wage. What the capitalist buys is the worker's capacity to work for a day. But it is not easy to delineate his tasks precisely nor to enforce their execution. This difficulty gives rise to a range of acceptable performances: naturally, the capitalist tries to get workers to perform at one end of this range, and if that involves pain and tension, the worker resists.

There is also another explanation offered by Marxists for job-site domination, in which its place is more central in the maintenance of capitalist property relations. Such domination is said to be a method by which the capitalist exerts power over the worker and demoralizes her, keeping her in a subservient position from which it becomes difficult to challenge either the individual boss through collective action on the job or the capitalist system more generally. Domination breaks down the worker's ability and will to resist (a claim that I do not find compelling), and because of that its role is much more central in the maintenance of capitalism than the one assigned to it in the imperfect-contract argument just presented.

Is it plausible to argue that class struggle is a direct attack on the wealth differential of capitalists and workers? Certainly the most revolutionary struggles are just that—the working class supporting a call for a massive redistribution of private property or an end to the institution of private property. In our times, this call is typical of the great socialist revolutions. One Soviet slogan of 1917 was "Bread, Land, and Peace." "Land" meant redistribution of land to the peasants. A Chinese slogan was "Land to the tiller." Indeed, socialist revolutions have gone much further than redistributing private property; they have abolished private property in the means of production.

In less generalized struggles, such as strikes, it is not plausible to argue that class struggle attacks the wealth differential of capitalists and workers. Trade union struggles do not call for such a redistribution, they only call for better wages and working conditions. Indeed, Marxists have often characterized trade union class struggle as "economist," because it is limited to relatively parochial economic demands instead of taking on the basis of the inequality, the system of private property in the means of production. This is not to say that Marxists oppose trade union struggles, but that they do not view them as necessarily leading to the revolutionary transformation that would be necessary to end the class system and the inequality that lies at its foundation.

The working class may sometimes become an important historical actor by virtue of the consciousness created among workers of their power, consciousness that arises as a result of the conditions of capitalist production. The factory system brings together many workers and teaches them to work in a disciplined, coordinated fashion in one place. It creates both relations of cooperation among workers and a conception of their power that were lacking in the small-scale private production characteristic of the putting-out system or of artisan work. Having this consciousness, workers see the possibility of changing their conditions through collective action. According to this explanation of class struggle, the combination of having "nothing to lose but one's chains" and being educated with respect to the potential collective power of the class is a by-product of the nature of capitalist production and enables the working class to fight. Thus, although capitalists may dominate workers in order to demoralize them, the demoralization does not always succeed because of the nature of the industrial (or capitalist?) labor process, which reveals to workers their power and potential.

Class struggle takes place only when the members of the working class see a potential for victory. The costs of fighting are too great for an individual, even in a collective mass where he is relatively anonymous, unless there is some expectation of victory. (I do not refer here to the free-rider problem of collective action, in which it is maintained that even if conditions are very bad it is not in the interest of any individual to join a collective struggle. That is a distinct theoretical issue.) It is a classic observation that the absolutely poorest—the unemployed and completely marginalized members of society—are not the most revolutionary. People must have some vision of their power, and this is provided, in the Marxist account, by their class relation to one another, the discipline and cooperation that is a by-product of capitalist production. Marginalized individuals do not achieve this vision because of their isolation from the cooperative enterprise of capitalist production.

There are, then, a variety of sociological and psychological reasons, as well as economic ones, for believing that classes, as I have defined them, are important social actors. The economic reason is chiefly the relation of class to wealth. The sociological and psychological reasons are the relations of class to domination, power, discipline, and consciousness. Consciousness, in turn, is determined by the common experiences that members of the same class have, both in production and in consumption.

6.6 Exploitation Deemphasized

Two characteristics of agents have emerged as important to positive and normative concerns: wealth and class. What is surprising is that exploitation, in the technical sense, seems to have fallen out of the picture. Differential initial wealth is of normative interest, as Chapter 5 emphasized, because it may well be the central injustice of a capitalist system, by virtue of the unequal opportunities that it creates. Differential wealth is also of positive significance, to the extent that it explains social rebellion and the transformation of systems of property. But it is more likely that differential wealth works indirectly through the formation of classes. Class is of interest as a positive statistic of class struggle, and hence of social transformation; the reasons for class struggle may not be directly related to the wealth associated with class position but with the consciousness that comes about by virtue of common class membership. But although exploitation is related to both class and wealth, it does not appear to be of direct interest from either the positive or the normative viewpoint. If workers are unfairly taken advantage of, it is not because they are exploited (in the technical sense) but because an unfair wealth distribution produces that exploitation as a by-product; and if workers unite in class struggle, it is not because they are exploited as such, but for the other reasons I have given. Exploitation, in the technical Marxist sense, appears to be an unnecessary appendage to our basic concerns, both ethical and positive.

To put this bluntly, some central concepts of classical Marxist economics—the labor theory of value and exploitation—seem not to be of fundamental interest. Analysis with economic tools reveals that much work remains for Marxist ethics and for sociology and history, the first to study the moral legitimacy of private property in the means of production, the second to study the usefulness of class as an explanation for the formation of attitudes and preferences and, ultimately, for the collective action that transforms society. What the economic analysis shows is that class position can be explained endogenously, as the consequence of initial differentiation in wealth, and that the technical notion of exploitation is closely related to the two more fundamental measures, class and wealth. In Section 9.2 further evidence will be presented for the position that exploitation (always in the technical Marxist sense) does not provide the best measure of the injustice associated with differential ownership of the means of production.

7

Exploitation without a Labor Market

In Chapter 6 I demonstrated that the initial unequal distribution of wealth is the common ancestor of both exploitation and class. Whereas the wealth distribution is pertinent to an ethical evaluation of capitalism and the class structure may have much to do with the formation of preferences and class consciousness leading to collective action, exploitation appears to be a subsidiary concept of little direct importance, for either positive or normative concerns. Therefore, I suggest that Marxists (and others) should focus their analysis directly on property relations and on the class relations that the distribution of property entails, bypassing the circuitous route to those concerns through the technical concept of exploitation.

Even if exploitation is dispensable as a statistic for phenomena of social and political interest, class position, defined by an agent's relation to the act of hiring and selling labor, is still important. Indeed, as I mentioned, much original Marxist social science has been directed to the study of the labor process. The evolution of the labor process under capitalism has been determined by, among other things, the confrontation of workers and capitalists at the point of production. Stephen Marglin argues in his article entitled "What Do Bosses Do?" that capitalists adopt technologies and ways of organizing production with a purpose of maintaining control of workers in the labor process. Technological development, in this view, would take significantly different directions were property relations not capitalist, for the class power of capitalists is dependent upon their monopolizing the knowledge of production. I will not evaluate this argument, but I do want to point out the central role it ascribes to the relationship between the capitalist and the worker at the point of production.

I claim that the labor market is, perhaps surprisingly, not central to an understanding of the emergence of class and exploitation. Indeed, a class structure just like the one of Chapter 6 can be produced using only a capital market (Section 7.2). Instead of the hiring and selling of labor, only the borrowing and lending of capital need occur. In actual capitalist societies, both capital and labor markets exist; and labor markets seem to be much more important in the relations between capitalists and workers. But I believe that capitalism's apparent dependence on labor markets must have some explanation beyond the traditional Marxist one that capitalism thrives on exploitation, because the phenomena of exploitation and class can be reproduced in their entirety in the absence of labor markets.

I must reiterate that I am not claiming that capitalism can dispense with labor markets. Rather I am arguing that the labor market should not be the focus of Marxist concerns, to the extent that those concerns are property relations, exploitation, and class. The Marxist concern with the labor process should focus on issues that differentiate capital markets from labor markets, issues that are not those directly related to property relations. I will amplify this point after I have shown how a class structure can emerge when only capital markets operate.

7.1 The Corn Economy with a Capital Market

Suppose the economy in Chapter 2 exists on Labor Market Island, where a labor market exists and agents trade in labor. Suppose there is another place, Capital Market Island, which is identical to Labor Market Island in its technology, agents, and initial endowments; but on Capital Market Island the agents have not discovered the labor market, or perhaps for some reason they have social norms against the hiring of labor. They do, however, allow the borrowing and lending of capital. I begin, then, with 1,000 agents and an aggregate capital stock of 500 units of seed corn; each of 10 wealthy agents (capitalists) owns 50 units of corn, and the other 990 (peasants) own nothing but their labor power. The technologies are, as before,

Farm	3 days labor	→ 1 unit of corn
Factory	1 day labor + 1 unit of corn	→ 1 corn, net, or 2 corn, gross

Agents can borrow and lend seed corn to each other, but each agent must work only for himself. Subsistence preferences are as in Chapter 2: each agent desires only to reproduce his initial capital stock and in addition to consume 1 unit of corn. After that, leisure is preferred to more corn; but if more corn can be forthcoming with no labor cost to the individual, so much the better.

What is the equilibrium? The 10 rich agents will offer to lend seed corn to the peasants. The equilibrium rate of interest is 66⅔% per week. At this rate, what does a typical peasant do? If she borrows 3 units of corn from some rich agent, she can produce 6 units of corn, gross, with 3 days of labor. Of that product, she must repay 3 units of corn as principal plus 2 units of corn as interest, leaving her 1 unit of corn to consume. She is indifferent between this arrangement and working for 3 days on the Farm. The lender, on the other hand, earns 2 units of corn from this transaction without expending any labor, so he is clearly satisfied. Note that at this interest rate there is not enough seed corn to lend to all the peasants; so assume that 500/3 peasants each borrow 3 units of seed corn, and the other 823-odd peasants stay on the Farm, an alternative that satisfies them just as much at this rate of interest.

Could the interest rate be any lower? No, for if it were, then every peasant would want to borrow capital, because she could then get a strictly better deal in terms of corn and leisure consumption than she can on the Farm—but there is not enough seed capital to employ all the peasants in the Factory. So competition among the peasants will bid the rate of interest up to 66⅔%.

Could the rate of interest be any higher? No, for then no peasant would want to borrow corn, and the capitalists also would have to work. Hence, in an effort to reduce their labor time, the capitalists will propose an interest rate no higher than 66⅔%. Thus, the only interest rate capable of equilibrating the demand and supply of loans is 66⅔%.

Note that the equilibrium interest rate is the same as the rate of profit on Labor Market Island in Chapter 2. This would be the case even if the model were more complicated (Section 7.2). The equality of the interest rate and the profit rate has led to a confusion in terminology among Marxist and neoclassical economists. In neoclassical terminology interest is a factor return and profit is a surplus beyond the returns to factors that are explicitly taken into account in the production process. (Sometimes in neoclassical analysis profits are viewed as a return to some hidden factor, such as entrepreneurial talent, which is not mentioned in the model.) Thus, a neoclassical account would hold that there are zero profits in the models of this book—the gross product is partitioned into replacement of seed (depreciation), corn consumption, and interest, the last being a return to capital, or perhaps, more precisely, to the attribute of the budding capitalist that gave rise to his original accumulation, for example, his low rate of time preference, his risk propensity, or the special capacity he had to plunder his neighbor. In the Marxist account, interest is viewed as a surplus whose distribution must be decided by social convention; and private ownership of the seed corn stock, in conjunction with competitive markets, determines one convention.

To return to the model, note that there are, at equilibrium, three classes, just as in Chapter 2: a class of capitalists, who do not work and live off interest; a class of proletarians, who work on borrowed capital in the Factory; and a class of peasants, who work on the Farm in circumstances identical to those of their peasant cousins on Labor Market Island. In terms of the definition of class, borrowing capital takes the place of selling labor and lending capital, of hiring labor. Now it may be the case that classes defined in terms of an agent's relation to the capital market produce social consequences considerably different from those produced by the classes defined by an agent's relation to the labor market. The proletarians on Capital Market Island might work in factories that they control, whereas on Labor Market Island they might work under the malevolent gaze of the capitalist's foreman. But these differences do not exist in the models under discussion. They enter at a more concrete level of the description of labor and capital markets. If classes are important, as I claim they are from a positive viewpoint in Marxist analysis, the question remains whether it is only *labor* classes that are important, or capital market classes as well. So far as exploitation is concerned, Labor Market Island and Capital Market Island are identical: each agent is exploited precisely as much on one island as is his twin on the other. Either the labor market as such is tangential to the concerns of Marxism or its importance derives from phenomena other than its relation to property and exploitation, for example, domination (Section 7.2).

7.2 Capital Market Island: The Five-Class Model

The more highly articulated five-class model of Chapter 6 also can be reproduced on Capital Market Island. Agents borrow and lend on this island but do not engage in relations of labor exchange. The two islands are otherwise identical: each agent on Labor Market Island has a twin on Capital Market Island with exactly the same endowment, ω^i units of seed corn. The technologies on both islands are $\{a,L\}$. On Capital Market Island, each agent wants to maintain his capital stock and to consume an amount of corn b per period. Agent i has three choice variables: x^i, the amount of corn he will produce (gross) using his own capital; z^i, the amount of corn he will produce using borrowed seed corn; and y^i, the amount of corn he will lend to others. Facing a price of corn–interest rate pair (p,r), an agent has an optimal plan $\langle x^i,y^i,z^i \rangle$ that earns him at least the revenue required to buy corn in amount b, does not commit him to lending out and using more capital than he has, and minimizes the labor he expends subject to these constraints.

A pair (p,r) that allows all agents to realize their plans is called a *reproducible equilibrium*, as before. The markets that must clear are the consumption corn market at the end and the seed corn capital market at the beginning. To say that the capital market clears means that at the going interest rate the demand for borrowed capital equals the supply of capital that agents desire to lend. To say that the corn market clears at the end means that at least Nb units of corn are produced, net, so each can buy his desired consumption bundle and society replaces its capital stock. In addition, it must be the case that enough corn is available in the society at the beginning to realize the production plan. These conditions, formally, are analogous to conditions (6.4), (6.5), and (6.6); and, of course, the agent's labor-minimizing program is similar to program (P_i) in Chapter 6.

To be explicit, the agent's labor-minimizing (or utility-maximizing) program on Capital Market Island, facing a price–interest pair (p,r), is to choose a vector of numbers $\langle x^i,y^i,z^i \rangle$ to

minimize $Lx^i + Lz^i$
subject to $(p - pa)x^i + [p - (1 + r)a]z^i + rpy^i \geq pb$
$ax^i + y^i \leq \omega^i$
$Lx^i + Lz^i \leq 1.$

The first constraint guarantees that his net revenues derived from using borrowed seed corn, that is, revenues remaining after paying back the principal and interest on the borrowed corn (middle term), plus his revenues from production on his own corn (first term), plus the interest income from the corn he lends out (third term) are sufficient to purchase his subsistence amount of corn, b. The second constraint says that the amount of corn he uses in his own production plus what he lends out does not exceed his stock. The third constraint is the agent's labor constraint.

The relevant class positions into which society can be partitioned at equilibrium are summarized in Table 7.1. As in Chapter 6, a "+" in a particular spot means that the agent does engage in that kind of activity, and a "0" means he does not, at the equilibrium. The agricultural descriptions are the same as those on Labor Market Island; motivation for those descriptions may be found in the quotations from Mao and Lenin in Chapter 6.

The main theorem states that at a reproducible equilibrium on Capital Market Island, conditions of class and exploitation of each agent are identical to the conditions of his twin on Labor Market Island.

Theorem 7.1 Capital Market–Labor Market Isomorphism Suppose there is a reproducible equilibrium (p,π) on Labor Market Island. Then there is a reproducible solution (p,r) on Capital Market Island in which the interest rate, r, on the latter island equals the profit rate, π, on the former. Furthermore, each agent on Capital Market Island has the same class and exploitation status as his twin on Labor Market Island at this solution. Each agent works precisely as long as his twin on the other island.

For example, if an agent with corn wealth ω^i is in the class $\langle+,0,0\rangle$ on Labor Market Island—he neither hires nor sells labor to optimize—then on Capital Market Island his twin (with the same wealth) will be in the capital-market class $\langle+,0,0\rangle$—he neither borrows nor lends to optimize. Because of Theorem 7.1, I can state, precisely, that the capital market and the labor market perform the same function and that the hiring of labor is identified with the lending of capital and the selling of labor is identified with the borrowing of capital.

Table 7.1 Class positions on Capital Market Island

Class position $\langle x^i, y^i, z^i \rangle$	Class name with credit market	Class name in an agricultural economy
$\langle 0,\ +,\ 0 \rangle$	Pure lender	Landlord
$\langle +,\ +,\ 0 \rangle$	Mixed lender	Rich peasant
$\langle +,\ 0,\ 0 \rangle$	Independent producer	Middle peasant
$\langle +,\ 0,\ + \rangle$	Mixed borrower	Small peasant
$\langle 0,\ 0,\ + \rangle$	Pure borrower	Landless laborer

Furthermore, what on one island appears as profit, on the other appears as interest.

The early-twentieth-century Swedish economist Knut Wicksell was perhaps the first explicitly to remark upon this isomorphism (although in a different guise) when he observed that it does not matter whether capital hires labor or labor hires capital in a perfectly competitive system. (Wicksell's observation was later popularized by Paul Samuelson.) On Labor Market Island capital (or, rather, capitalists) are hiring labor, whereas on Capital Market Island labor (or, rather, workers) hire capital. The upshot is the same, with regard to income distribution, to the rate of profit, and to the exploitation status of every agent.

What conclusions can be drawn from the Isomorphism Theorem? Mainly, that whatever objection one may have to the hiring of labor on grounds related to exploitation, it is not intrinsically connected with the labor market. For, with respect to income distribution and exploitation, exactly the same results are produced by banning the labor market and replacing it with a capital market. The agent who is exploited at a rate of .5, for example, when he is hired by a capitalist on Labor Market Island will be exploited at a rate of .5 when, on Capital Market Island, he borrows capital at the equilibrium rate of interest.

Other objections to the hiring of labor, objections that do not apply to the borrowing of capital can be made, but they cannot be made on grounds of exploitation, or on account of the relation of the class structure to the initial distribution of wealth. For, according to the Isomorphism theorem, it follows from the Class–Wealth Correspondence (Theorem 6.1) and the Class–Exploitation Correspondence (Theorem 6.2) that exactly the same relations hold among class, exploitation, and wealth on Capital Market Island as hold on Labor Market Island. The class an agent belongs to on Capital Market Island is a proxy for his wealth and his status as exploited or exploiting.

What might be some special objections to the hiring of labor that do not apply to the borrowing of capital? Perhaps working for someone else involves a relation of subservience that does not exist if one borrows capital from someone else. The former may be associated with slave- or serflike relations. There may be a domination effect associated with labor markets that does not exist with capital markets. Perhaps the lender does not supervise and dominate the borrower the way the hirer dominates the seller of labor power. It is not altogether clear whether this distinction exists in reality. There are places, chiefly small-scale agricultural economies, where the capital market is important. Poor peasants borrow corn or land from rich ones, paying back interest. Share-cropping is a complex example of such an institution; it is, in fact, not exactly like a capital market, for the rate of interest is not fixed but is a percentage of the crop. Where capital markets are used, there is either some collateral that the borrower will forfeit if he does not pay back, or there is direct supervision by the lender to make sure the principal is being well used. So domination exists in practice in actual capital market economies, too.

If neither domination nor collateral exists, but capital markets still operate, it may be because the borrower wants to borrow again next year, and the necessity of maintaining a good reputation minimizes the amount of supervision necessary. When labor markets operate in small economies, such as villages, where the reputations of individuals are well known, then the supervision of workers is probably not necessary either. In fact, what may be empirically the case is that labor markets are used when reputation and the repeated nature of trade between the same pair of agents cannot be relied on to ensure performance, and capital markets are used when reputation can be relied on, or the borrowers have some collateral.

If the domination effect does, to some extent, differentiate in historical fact the experiences of those who participate in labor and capital markets, then the class consciousness developed by those participants may consequently differ. Members of the proletarian class $\langle 0,0,+ \rangle$ on Labor Market Island may hate their bosses (because of the domination by the bosses) more than members of the borrowing class $\langle 0,0,+ \rangle$ on Capital Market Island hate their creditors, because the borrowers have a less proximate and nondominated relation to creditors. Hence, the class struggle between classes on Capital Market Island may differ from that on Labor Market Island—if domination is an important determinant of class struggle.

If wealth is really the determinant of class struggle, then there will be no differences between the nature of that struggle on the two islands, for the Class–Wealth Correspondence is true on both islands. But there is a third possible cause for a distinction between the class consciousness that might be associated with what are otherwise the "same" class structures on the two islands. There are technological factors that appear to be associated with the choice between labor and capital markets as the main markets for arranging production: labor markets are used when economies of scale are prevalent and large-scale, cooperative production by many workers is required; and capital markets (at least to mediate relations between the poor and the rich) are used in small-scale production (such as certain kinds of agriculture) where cooperation is not necessary. I remarked in Chapter 6 that the discipline and cooperation of industrial production may in large part be responsible for developing the class consciousness of workers and for enabling them to recognize their potential power and ability to act collectively. If this is the case, and the technological determination of the distinction between the use of labor and capital markets holds, then one would not expect the same class consciousness to develop among pure borrowers as develops among proletarians.

In small-scale agricultural economies, such as peasant economies in India, both capital and labor markets are used. The landlord who hires the poor peasant to work on his land is often the same person who lends money to the peasant, who in turn uses it to buy fertilizer and inputs for his small plot. (Sometimes the loan is used for consumption and not investment. One of the causes of class struggle between poor peasants and landlords in prerevolutionary China was that the interest rates that money-lenders, often landlords, charged to peasants who had to borrow rice to survive through the winter were exorbitant.) Indeed, capital and labor markets are linked in peasant economies in which the relations between a peasant and a landlord with respect to the loans they transact play a role in determining the relations between them on the labor market. For example, if reliable labor is relatively scarce in a region, then a landlord may establish a money-lending relationship to certain peasants in exchange for the guarantee, from them, that they will sell their labor power to him at harvest time. It is by studying these actual economies that one learns more about the characteristics of labor and capital markets that may differentiate them.

7.3 Capital Markets and Workers' Cooperatives

Why are labor markets rather than capital markets the main conduit through which capitalism organizes the union of labor and capital that is necessary for production? Why do modern capitalist societies look more like Labor Market Island than like Capital Market Island? A first response is that increasing returns to scale make it necessary to join many producers together in one place; one individual, property-less agent cannot borrow capital and produce effectively. But why, then, are there not more workers' cooperatives under capitalism, institutions in which many workers get together, borrow capital, and set themselves up as firms? Under such an arrangement, increasing returns to scale could be effectively exploited.

There are significant difficulties in organizing such coalitions. It may be that diseconomies of scale in organization prevent workers' cooperatives from taking advantage of economies of scale in production. Cooperatives do exist in firms that were originally set up as privately owned enterprises and were then sold by the owners to the workers. Besides the difficulty inherent in organizing a large group to begin a firm, workers do not have the necessary access to capital markets. Those who run the institutions that mediate between borrowers and lenders are not willing to lend to workers, because cooperatives do not have a reputation for being able to make a profit. If a firm has been operated for some time under capitalist ownership, the banks may be more convinced that the workers can run it themselves, which would explain the relative prevalence of worker-owned firms formed as takeovers of capitalist firms.

It is sometimes argued that worker-owned firms are rare because workers will not work hard enough to survive in the market, where they must compete with capitalist firms. Supervision and discipline are required, it is said, to get workers to work hard enough to produce competitively. As noted previously, certain neoclassical writers maintain that workers enter into an implicit contract with capitalists, under which workers implicitly agree to be supervised by capitalists—in order to be forced to produce the revenues funding their high wages. To this there are several replies. First, worker-owned firms are often successful even though previously, as capitalist firms, they were not. Second, nothing prevents workers from hiring their own supervisors. Third, if workers do prefer to work less hard than they would under capitalist ownership, they can trade off a high intensity of work against a lower wage, thereby keeping the price of their product competitive.

7.4 Exploitation without Labor or Capital Markets

I have claimed that the exchange of labor power for the wage on a labor market is not an essential part of the Marxist story of exploitation and class, for those phenomena can be reproduced with a capital market instead. If labor markets are necessary for a private property system, as they certainly appear to be from the historical instances of capitalism, the reason must lie in the attributes that differentiate labor markets from capital markets. But these differences are not part of the traditional Marxist story. They have, indeed, been a topic of research mainly in the industrial organization literature, Marxist and non-Marxist, of only the last 20 years. The conclusion I have derived from this discussion is that Marxism's preeminent concern is not with the institution of labor exchange as such but with the underlying property relations: the unequal and private ownership of the means of production. The labor market is just one way that the private ownership of the means of production can be turned into unequal final incomes and welfares, which one would judge to be unjust if the initial distribution of wealth were judged to be so.

Consider again the point that the inequality of outcome associated with exploitation is not fundamentally related to the existence of the labor market. Suppose there is a third island, where there are neither capital markets nor labor markets. In this economy exploitation and unequal outcomes will still emerge as a result of the private ownership of the means of production. One cannot place the blame for this exploitation on either the labor market or the capital market. It lies more directly on the original unequal wealth distribution and on the existence of trade in ordinary commodities.

On Primitive Island, whose name derives from the lack of discovery of either labor or capital markets, two goods are produced: corn and flax. For simplicity, suppose that both goods are in the subsistence bundle that each agent must consume each week; call the bundle b. Both corn and flax may be inputs into production of both goods, and labor is also an input. Suppose that there are many agents in this economy and that they begin with different endowments of corn and flax; the initial endowment of corn and flax of agent i is the vector ω^i. Although there are no labor and capital markets on Primitive Island, agents do trade corn and flax with each other and they do so at two times—at the beginning of the period, to acquire the inputs they need for production in the right proportions, and at the end of the period, to trade what they produce (which might be all flax or all corn) for the proper bundle b of corn and flax each wants to consume. Traders in this economy are motivated by the same preferences as previously described. Each wishes to minimize the time she works subject to two constraints: that she be able to earn enough with her produced output to purchase the bundle b and that she choose a production plan that is feasible for her, given the initial value of her holdings ω^i. A *reproducible equilibrium* in this economy is a vector of prices $p = (p_c, p_f)$ that clears the corn and flax markets when each agent engages in her optimal production plan.

Formally, the problem is stated as follows (I will use the matrix and vector notation introduced in Section 4.4.) The problem can easily be represented as one with many goods, not just corn and flax. Let there be n goods, a technology input matrix A, and a row vector of labor input coefficients L. Agent i has endowment ω^i of the n goods at the beginning of the period. Each agent desires to consume a subsistence vector b of goods. Suppose there is a price vector p (a row vector) for the n goods. Then agent i chooses to produce a vector x^i of goods—or to run the n production processes at levels x^i—to solve this program: choose x^i to

minimize Lx^i
subject to $\quad p(I - A)x^i \geq pb$
$\qquad\qquad pAx^i \leq p\omega^i$
$\qquad\qquad Lx^i \leq 1.$

The first constraint states that the value of the net output the agent produces is sufficient to purchase the consumption bundle b at the going prices; the second constraint says that the inputs for the production plan x^i can be paid for at the beginning of the period given i's finance capital, which is $p\omega^i$. The third constraint states that the plan x^i does not involve the expending of more labor than i has, which is 1 unit. If x^i satisfies the three constraints, then i will not run down the value of his capital stock (because the revenues reported in the first constraint are net revenues, enabling him to replace his original capital stock as well as to eat), and his needs will be satisfied. Subject to these constraints, agent i chooses that plan that minimizes the labor he must expend.

A price vector p equilibrates the economy if, when every agent pursues his optimal plan, markets clear; that is,

$$Ax \leq \omega, \tag{7.1}$$

$$(I - A)x \geq Nb, \tag{7.2}$$

where $x \equiv \Sigma x^i$ and $\omega \equiv \Sigma \omega^i$. Inequality (7.1) says that the inputs required at the beginning of the period by society's aggregate production plan are available in aggregate, and hence agents can trade with one another to get the inputs they require for their individual plans; and inequality (7.2) states that the aggregate net output of society is sufficient for each of the N producers to consume b. Thus, society meets consumption needs and replaces the capital stock used.

The important property of a reproducible equilibrium on Primitive Island is stated in the following theorem.

Theorem 7.2 At a reproducible equilibrium, $Lx = N\Lambda b$, where Λ is the vector of embodied labor values and N is the number of agents.

Socially necessary labor time is Λb, the amount of labor embodied in the production of the consumption bundle b. Theorem 7.2 states that the total labor expended at a reproducible solution is just socially necessary labor time for the society as a whole. This statement means that if some individual works more than socially necessary labor time $(Lx^i > \Lambda b)$, then some other individual must work less than socially necessary labor time. Now it will generally be the case, as can be seen from examining the programs of the individual agents, that they will work different amounts of time—the richer one is, the less one works. Thus, at the equilibrium, agents are divided into two groups—exploiters and exploited—who work, respectively, less than and more than socially necessary labor time.

The key observation is that this partition of society into exploiters and exploited agents occurs without the mediation of either a labor or a capital market. It is simply the consequence of unequal initial assets and trade. The intuitive explanation for what happens is that those agents with small amounts of initial capital choose more labor-intensive activities to operate—they substitute their labor for the capital they do not have—whereas wealthy agents can choose labor-saving activities to operate.

This phenomenon cannot occur in a one-good corn economy. At least two goods are required, for there must be some reason for agents to trade with one another, because they are not trading either labor or capital. In this model trade allows a social division of labor to unfold—the wealthy agents operate "capital-intensive" activities and the poor ones operate "labor-intensive" ones—and at the end they trade the outputs with one another so that each gets the subsistence bundle he needs. At the equilibrium prices, this social division of labor is implemented.

I do not propose this model as a representation of any actual economy but as a thought experiment to illustrate that property rights should be the focus of those concerned with exploitation or with inequality of final outcome (in this case, welfare as measured by the amount of leisure a person has in the workweek), rather than the particular markets that mediate that outcome. If one had to name the one site that accounts for the inequality Marxists call exploitation, one should choose neither the labor process nor the capital market, but the initial determination of unequal capital stocks. Notice that the economy on Primitive Island does not have classes as defined earlier. Agents do specialize in different activities—in that sense, agents have somewhat different relations to the production process—but there are no relations of hiring or lending among them. Primitive Island does not have a market structure rich enough to exhibit classes; what it illustrates is that in an economic sense exploitation is a concept that can be thought of as logically prior to class.

7.5 International Capitalism: Imperialism and Labor Migration

The models of this chapter also are applicable to countries. Each agent can be thought of as a country, with an endowment of labor and capital. There is a common technology available to all countries, and each country tries to maximize national income. A country can borrow capital from or lend capital to other countries and hire labor from or sell labor to other countries (that is, workers and capital can migrate across borders). Facing the international prices for goods, labor, and a rate of interest, each country decides on its optimal program of borrowing capital, hiring "guest workers," and operating its own capital stock with its own workers. Of course, there are many assumptions of these models that are not realistic; for example, neither the wage rate nor the technology really are uniform internationally. Nevertheless, some basic observations that do conform in a broad way to reality can be made.

An equilibrium is a set of prices, a wage, and an interest rate that allow all markets to clear; the markets in this model are the commodity markets for consumption, the markets for initial productive inputs, the international labor market, and the international capital market. At equilibrium, countries fall into different "classes." The index that determines a country's class is not its initial wealth (as in the Class–Wealth Correspondence) but its initial capital–labor ratio. Thus, countries with high per capita wealth lend capital to other countries and hire workers from other countries. They are imperialist, in the classic sense that they export capital and import labor. Countries with low per capita wealth do the opposite: they optimize by importing capital or exporting their labor or both. Indeed, the five class positions listed in Table 7.1 are all represented by countries of various capital–labor ratios.

For example, let $\langle x^i, y^i, z^i \rangle$ be the levels at which country i uses its own workers on its own capital stock to produce goods (x^i), hires workers from other countries to work on its capital stock (y^i), and sends workers abroad to work (z^i). Then the class decomposition of countries becomes that shown in Table 7.2. One does not observe countries of the first class—such a country would be one with no domestic labor force, but with some capital stock. In reality, all countries use some of their own labor force at home, because countries are not trying to subsist but are trying to maximize national income. If this is the case, they must use their own labor, either at home or abroad. Nor does one observe purely "proletarian" countries, because in fact every country has some capital stock. But the middle three classes of countries do exist.

The Class–Exploitation Correspondence has its analogue in this international model as well. A country is said to be exploited if the labor embodied in its net national product is less than the amount of labor its labor force expends; a country is an exploiter if its national income can purchase goods embodying more labor than its nationals expended in production. It is simply a reinterpretation of the Class–

Table 7.2 Class decomposition of countries

Class position $\langle x^i, y^i, z^i \rangle$	Description of countries on the basis of their relation to the labor market
$\langle 0, +, 0 \rangle$	Countries that only hire foreign workers
$\langle +, +, 0 \rangle$	Countries that use their own workers and hire foreign workers
$\langle +, 0, 0 \rangle$	Countries that neither export nor import workers
$\langle +, 0, + \rangle$	Countries that use their own workers and export workers
$\langle 0, 0, + \rangle$	Countries that export all their own workers

Exploitation Correspondence that countries optimizing by exporting labor are exploited countries, and ones that optimize by importing labor are exploiting countries.

Indeed, according to the Isomorphism Theorem 7.1, the same relationship can be demonstrated between a country's exploitation status and its relationship to the international capital market. Let x^i be the level of industrial activity that a country finances with domestic capital; let y^i be the amount of capital that it exports to other countries; and let z^i be the level of domestic production that it finances on capital borrowed from abroad. The class decomposition of countries with respect to the international capital market, then, is shown in Table 7.3. One does not see countries of the first and fifth classes, but one does see the others.

The Isomorphism Theorem states that the relationship of exploitation to class is the same for countries with respect to the international capital market as it is for countries with respect to the international labor market. Thus, a relationship called economic imperialism can be demonstrated between capital-exporting and capital-importing countries, with the "exploitation" of some countries by others. An imperialist country is one that exports capital to others or imports their workers. The Class–Exploitation Correspondence states that imperialist countries are exploiters, and imperialized ones are exploited. Whether a country becomes imperialist is determined by how large its domestic capital-to-labor ratio is. Thus, the imperialist nature of countries with high per capita wealth can be demonstrated to be a predictable outcome in a world with international markets for labor and capital.

Table 7.3 Class decomposition of countries

Class position $\langle x^i, y^i, z^i \rangle$	Description of countries on the basis of their relation to the capital market
$\langle 0, +, 0 \rangle$	Countries that export all their capital and import none
$\langle +, +, 0 \rangle$	Countries that use domestic capital and export surplus capital
$\langle +, 0, 0 \rangle$	Countries that neither export nor import capital
$\langle +, 0, + \rangle$	Countries that use domestic capital and also import capital
$\langle 0, 0, + \rangle$	Countries that only import capital, having none of their own

Demonstrating that technical exploitation exists does not establish that the exploitation of one country by another is necessarily a bad thing. Recall that in Chapter 5 I concluded that the exploitation of one person by another is not ipso facto a bad thing. Similarly, one's opinion about international exploitation must be founded upon a judgment of the equity of the initial inequality of capital-to-labor ratios that drives the relations of exploitation. The common ancestor of the class and exploitation status of a country is its capital-to-labor ratio, or rather, where that ratio falls relative to other ratios in the international spectrum. There has been a debate in Marxist circles about "unequal exchange" between countries, which, roughly speaking, maintains that international exploitation takes place and is the source of the wealth of the rich, imperialist countries. I would prefer to say that the source of wealth is their high initial capital-to-labor ratio—the exploitation that exists is just a symptom of that initial distribution.

There are many imperfections in international markets that allow powerful countries to take unfair advantage of poor countries in noncompetitive ways (because of various kinds of monopoly power or colonial relationships) and in politically imperialist ways, which inhibit competition. Poor countries may tend to trade with their former colonial masters, not seeking out better deals. That, in fact, may be the kind of unequal exchange that is more significant than the phenomenon I have referred to as international exploitation. The point of this section is that, even in a world of perfect, frictionless markets, countries will be in different classes—borrower countries, lender countries, labor-importing countries, and so on—and class status will have a predictable relationship to each country's per capita wealth, and to its exploitation status, which is defined as the relation between the labor its population expends and the labor socially embodied in its net national product.

7.6 Domination versus Exploitation versus Property Relations

I have argued that the existence of a labor market is inessential for exploitation; both the exploitation and class structure associated with a labor market can be reproduced with only a capital market (Sections 7.1 and 7.2), and exploitation alone can exist, without either a capital or a labor market (Section 7.4). The determining factor is the initial distribution of wealth, and, more generally, the institution of private ownership of the means of production, which allows a distribution of wealth to be parlayed into substantial inequality that lasts for generations. Neither the labor market, nor even exploitation, are the sources of the inequality and injustice with which Marxism is concerned.

Sometimes Marxists argue that the source of capitalism's injustice is the domination of capitalists over workers—and, they would claim, chiefly that domination existing in the factory, at the point of production. I think that that kind of domination is of second- or third-order importance in maintaining capitalism and its injustices; to my mind it is essentially a technique that is necessary because of the impossibility of writing and enforcing a perfect contract for the exchange of labor power for the wage. Of first-order importance is the maintenance of capitalist property relations; and that is accomplished chiefly through ideological means in modern capitalist societies. There are, of course, an army and a police force that will protect capitalist property relations in the last instance, but that force would be of little value if the working class as a whole were of a mind to abolish private ownership of the means of production. They do not do so because they do not believe the system is unjust, or because it is too difficult for them to organize to do so, or because they perceive the costs of transition to socialist forms of property as being too high, or because they see socialism as an alternative that is not worthwhile. To discuss these four causes would take me beyond my present purpose; my point now is a smaller one, namely, that domination at the point of production, so often a concern of Marxism, is quite distantly related to the concern with exploitation. I think the essential injustice of capitalism is located not in what happens at the point of production, but, prior to that, in the property relations that determine class, income, and welfare.

This distinction is not a hollow one in its political application. Those who focus upon the labor market and domination at the point of production as the nasty characteristics of capitalism advocate industrial democracy and worker-owned firms as the appropriate redress. But if property relations are the fundamental source of nastiness, then a policy of socialization of the means of production, whatever that may mean (see Chapter 10), is dictated. Socialization does not necessarily involve the democratic running of firms by their workers, because industrial democracy is neither clearly necessary nor sufficient for public ownership of means of production.

8

Historical Materialism

Historical materialism is a theory of history that has received much attention in the past decade. Although I cannot review that work in depth here, I will show how the formal theory of class and exploitation that has been developed has its intellectual ancestry in the Marxist view of history. My summary of historical materialism relies almost entirely on the works of G. A. Cohen, which have, more than any others, rejuvenated historical materialism as a serious candidate in social and political theory. In Section 8.4 I will review a competing Marxist variant of historical transformation found in the work of Brenner.

8.1 Economic Structure, Productive Forces, and Superstructure

Although historical materialism is central to Marxism, Marx wrote very little about the theory as such. The main statement, a brief one, appears in the preface to *A Contribution to the Critique of Political Economy*, published in 1859:

> In the social production of their existence, men inevitably enter into definite relations, which are independent of their will, namely *relations of production* appropriate to a given stage in the development of their material forces of production. The totality of these relations of production constitutes the *economic structure* of society, the real foundation, on which arises a *legal and political superstructure* and to which correspond definite forms of social consciousness. The mode of production of material life conditions the general process of social, politi-

cal and intellectual life. It is not the consciousness of men that determines their existence, but their social existence that determines their consciousness. At a certain stage of development, the material productive forces of society come into conflict with the existing relations of production or—this merely expresses the same thing in legal terms—with the property relations within the framework of which they have operated hitherto. From forms of development of the productive forces these relations turn into their fetters. Then begins an era of social revolution. The changes in the economic foundation lead sooner or later to the transformation of the whole immense superstructure. In studying such transformations it is always necessary to distinguish between the material transformation of the economic conditions of production, which can be determined with the precision of natural science, and the legal, political, religious, artistic or philosophic—in short, ideological forms in which men become conscious of this conflict and fight it out. Just as one does not judge an individual by what he thinks of himself, so one cannot judge such a period of transformation by its consciousness, but, on the contrary, this consciousness must be explained from the contradictions of material life, from the conflict existing between the social forces of production and the relations of production. No social order is ever destroyed before all the productive forces for which it is sufficient have been developed, and new superior relations of production never replace older ones before the material conditions for their existence have matured within the framework of the old society. Mankind thus inevitably sets itself only such tasks as it is able to solve, since closer examination will always show that the problem itself arises only when the material conditions for its solution are already present or at least in the course of formation. In broad outline, the Asiatic, ancient, feudal and modern bourgeois modes of production may be designated as epochs marking progress in the economic development of society. The bourgeois mode of production is the last antagonistic form of the social process of production—antagonistic not in the sense of individual antagonism but of an antagonism that emanates from the individuals' social conditions of existence—but the productive forces developing within bourgeois society create also the material conditions for a solution of this antagonism. The prehistory of human society accordingly closes with this social formation. (Marx, 1859 [1981, pp. 21–23])

I have italicized some key phrases in the passage. Relations of production are relations of economic power; people have or do not have economic power over the means of production, which include the physical means of production and their own labor power. Thus, feudal relations of production involve only partial control by the serf over his own labor power (because the lord also has some control of it), and only partial control by the lord over the serf's plot (because the serf cannot be excluded from the use of it). In other words, both the serf and the lord have some economic power over both the serf's labor power and the land. Under capitalism, in contrast, the proletarian has complete control over his labor power, in the sense that he can decide whether or not to sell it, and he has no control over the nonlabor means of production. (This statement would be challenged by some, who argue that the proletarian is forced to sell his labor power in order to survive and that, once having sold it, he no longer is in control of it because the capitalist dominates him at the point of production. On the other hand, at the point of production the worker does exert some control over the means of production, which explains the necessity for supervision and the systematic disenfranchisement of workers from knowledge of the production process [see, for example, the work of Marglin discussed in the Bibliographic Notes to Chapter 5].) The slave has no power over either his labor power or the means of production. The ideal vision of communism has the producer having complete control over both his labor power and the means of production, although many would regard that vision as unacceptably utopian.

The economic structure is defined as the total of all the relations of production. The form of the economic structure—that is, whether society organizes itself as feudal, capitalist, slave, or communist—is the consequence of the level of development of the productive forces, which includes the level of development of technical knowledge and the skill of the producers. The first claim of historical materialism is that the existing economic structure is not the consequence of ideas people have, or of their religious notions. Instead, each economic structure is fitted to the level of technological development of the time. At one time Western European society was feudal in its organization because feudalism was the most efficient way of organizing production in an economy with the productive forces of that era. When the productive forces developed further, feudal relations of production were no longer an efficient way of organizing the economy, but capitalist relations of production were. The feudal economic structure became a fetter on the further development of the productive forces and were successfully challenged by a capitalist economic structure, which eventually won out. Historical materialism also claims that eventually the forces of production will be so advanced that capitalist relations will no longer be optimal for harnessing them. When capitalist relations become a fetter on the further development of the productive forces, then (Marx and Engels predicted) socialism (or communism) will win out as the optimal economic structure for organizing productive activity. Marx refers to the period up to the end of capitalist society as the prehistory of human society, because after that (in his estimation) there will be no further exploitative class relations and a full flowering of human potential can be realized.

The key point of this analysis is that the underlying motive force is the development of the forces of production, to which the economic structure adapts (in some fashion yet to be explained). Associated with any given level of the development of the productive forces are, presumably, one or several feasible economic structures. If there is only one, then it must exist at that level of productive forces; if there are several, there will be some kind of competition for the realization of one economic structure. The economic structure adapts to the level of technological development, which, according to this theory, has a more or less exogenous tendency to develop.

The second major claim of historical materialism concerns the relationship between the economic structure and the legal and political superstructure, which is the political form of the state and the laws that enforce property rights. The superstructure is corollary to the economic structure. Thus, laws and politics are what we observe after the dust from the brawl has cleared and an economic structure has been established. Laws reinforce the set of economic powers that constitute the economic structure, but the primary relation of causation is held to be from the economic structure to the legal superstructure. Law and politics implement what the economic structure requires, and the economic structure is, in turn, required by the underlying productive forces. Thus, legal and political developments are determined two steps back by material economic developments.

The three main theses of historical materialism, then, are (1) that the productive forces tend to develop independently of the will of people, but surely somehow because of actions people perform in striving to improve their situation; (2) that the social relations of production (or economic structure) are explained by their efficacy with regard to organizing economic activity, given that the productive forces are at their particular level; and (3) that the legal and political superstructure of a society is explained by its effect in stabilizing and legitimizing the existing economic structure.

All three positions have been vigorously challenged and debated by social theorists, Marxist and otherwise. They maintain, first of all, that the claim that the productive forces tend to develop is a Europocentric observation. In Asia there were long periods with essentially no development of the productive forces, because the economic structure successfully fettered that development, contrary to the claim of Marx's Preface. Second, they claim that the way the technology and technical knowledge of the producers develop is determined in large part by the relations of production, rather than the other way around. Not only can the productive forces be successfully fettered by an economic structure, but also, when they develop, they do so with a strong imprint of the existing economic structure. These claims are put forward by Braverman, Marglin, and Brenner, to name only a few. A third challenge is made to the claim of the subordinate nature of the superstructure: many writers maintain that the political and legal superstructure has tremendous effect on the nature of property relations and that it is a mistake to view the primary causal relation as running the other way, as thesis (3) maintains. Theses (1) through (3) represent what is called economic determinism; and most contemporary writers, whether Marxist or not, do not think these claims emphasize sufficiently what historical materialism would consider to be merely "feedback effects," namely, the effects of ideology, religion, and nationalism on the way in which economic structures evolve. The virtue of historical materialism, whether or not it is a true theory, is that it is *a* theory of history, a sufficiently clear and simple statement of an economic theory of history with which any other theory must come to grips.

As an example of how an economic structure may come to fetter the development of the productive forces, consider Marx's statement: "The hand mill gives you society with the feudal lord; the steam mill, society with the industrial capitalist" (Marx, 1847 [1982, p. 109]). (Actually, Marx was wrong: he did not begin his historical research on feudalism until ten years after this was written. Had he done so, he would have substituted "water mill" for "hand mill." In sixteenth-century England, manorial lords often did not allow small hand mills to be used by serfs, but required them to use the lord's water mill, as a way of keeping account, for tax purposes, of the amount of grain harvested [Marglin, 1974, p. 105].) The milling of grain made possible by the water mill was useful on the scale of a manor, but it did not provide enough power to produce grain on a massive basis. With the advent of steam, it became possible to run machinery capable of producing an output much greater than the amount that could be consumed by the direct producers. That output could be traded for profit. Thus, possibilities for economic advantage came to exist with more productive technology, and a class arose to seize that advantage (capitalists). But such a class could not have existed were technology not sufficiently productive to yield far more than the producers themselves needed. In addition, a new technology of trade arose (transportation) and made available distant markets that could be supplied by an enterprise producing goods for exchange rather than for its own use. By elaborating on this theme, one can provide a historical materialist explanation of the emergence of capitalism and the eventual demise of feudalism. The argument that the development of trade was an aspect of the development of the forces of production that led to capitalism is called the commercialization argument for the transition from feudalism to capitalism.

The next example is not an instance of the historical materialist theory as I have presented it, although this example is often taken to be a Marxist argument. Consider the following explanation of the transition from capitalism to socialism: Capitalism develops the division of labor. It brings together large groups of producers in factories, teaches them to work in a coordinated and disciplined way, and educates them. (There is much discussion today about the increasing ignorance of the masses of people in capitalist society; but the overwhelming historical fact is that capitalism has urbanized the vast majority of people, and with urbanization comes facility of communication, literacy, and education.) By teaching workers such cooperation, however, capitalism sows the seeds of its own destruction, for workers then learn that capitalists are not themselves necessary for the process of production. The capitalist factory both shows workers their power and provides a place for them to organize and eventually expropriate the means of production for themselves. This explanation is not a historical materialist one, because capitalist relations of production are not said to act as fetters on the further development of the productive forces, rather they are said to become untenable given the *nature* of capitalist production.

An essential aspect of historical materialism is that it offers an economic explanation of the evolution of societies, an evolution that occurs "independently of the will of men." Institutions—of property, law, and politics—are seen to rise and fall insofar as they adapt well or poorly to exploiting the changing forces of production. According to thesis (1), productive forces tend to develop through history. As I noted, this thesis is challenged by examples of long-term stagnation in the productive forces. There does, however, seem to be a tendency for technological progress across time. Cohen argues that, because people are rational and face conditions of scarcity and are capable of alleviating scarcity by applying their rationality to improve the efficiency of the techniques by which they produce things, the forces of production therefore tend to develop. Cohen's presentation of this argument is more subtle, but suffice it to say that there are reasons to believe in the tendency for the development of the productive forces, as claimed by thesis (1). Thus, the three theses of historical materialism can be defended as reasonable ones, given certain suppositions about human rationality and the scarcity that characterizes the human situation. Even if the theory of historical materialism is logically consistent, the question remains whether it accurately depicts actual historical development.

8.2 The Role of Class Struggle

The Communist Manifesto opens with the line, "The history of all hitherto existing society is the history of class struggles," yet class struggle does not appear in Marx's statement that I quoted earlier. Some maintain that Marx was inconsistent in advocating two different theories of history; others have tried to reconcile the two positions. A reconciliation is not so difficult to propose, if class struggle is assigned the role of midwife at the birth of the new economic structure. Productive forces may have outgrown feudal property relations, which fetter their further development, but the bursting of those relations (making way for capitalist relations) comes about by virtue of class struggle—serfs against lords and lords against mercantile capitalists. Indeed, class struggle may be constantly happening, but the class of exploited producers is only successful in its rebellion when the existing relations of production are no longer able to deliver the goods. Only then does a revolution occur and a new kind of property relations becomes established. Even though it might appear that class struggle is responsible for the transformation, this reading of historical materialism claims that it is merely the facilitator, while the deeper cause of revolution is the dissonance between the level of development of the productive forces and the old economic structure.

This insertion of class struggle into historical materialism can be elaborated further. Imagine that there is a class of direct producers who are serfs in a feudal economy, but also imagine that a nascent capitalist economy is emerging alongside it, an economy based on possibilities for trade that have opened up with other areas. The capitalist sector, unlike the feudal sector, does not engage primarily in production for its own consumption but in production for trade. Even though the serfs have been rebelling for years, only the advent of the technology making possible the viability of the capitalist sector (which includes a mercantile technology) provides them with an alternative to the feudal economy on a mass scale. Now there is an option: capitalists and feudal lords can compete for control of the working population. If the technology or forces of production that the capitalists are using enable them to pay higher real wages than serfs earn, then there is an economic advantage to the liberation from serfdom that did not formerly exist. Thus, class struggle of serfs against lords is more likely to be successful, in the sense that serfs can cease being serfs as a consequence. They can succeed in becoming independent peasants and can participate in the trade that the capitalist sector has developed, or they can escape from the feudal estate and become artisans or proletarians in the towns. This competition between feudalism and capitalism now enables class struggle against feudalism to be successful even though formerly it was not.

In this account the class that emerges as the dominant one (capitalist as opposed to feudal) does so by virtue of its ability to develop the productive forces more effectively. The mechanism is this: the class best able to develop the productive forces will be able to offer the highest standard of living to the direct producers, and this higher standard of living will act as a magnet to draw the producers into its mode of production. The analogy to Darwinian evolution is clear. Natural selection "favors" the variant that is most suited to survive in the given environment. In historical materialism, the variants are different economic structures and the given environments are the different ways of producing things, including the use of different technologies. The variant that wins is the one that can provide the best conditions for the class of direct producers, who are constantly fighting for an improvement in their conditions and therefore constantly looking for alternatives. A capitalist class will eventually succeed in defeating a feudal class for control if it has knowledge of a technology sufficiently superior to feudal technology to act as a magnet, in the long run, for serfs and peasants. Such a change in control is effected through class struggle, but it is made possible only by the level of development of the productive forces.

Historical materialism works best as a theory of the transformation from feudalism to capitalism. But perhaps it is too closely tied to that one important historical episode to be a universal theory. The main purpose of this section has been to argue that it is possible to conclude both that class struggle is central to Marxism *and* that economic structures change to accommodate the developing forces of production. This is not to say that my account is historically correct, but that it appears to be logically possible. Some contemporary Marxists place class struggle in a less subservient role to economic determinism than does the account just given (see Section 8.4).

8.3 The Logic of the Theory

The logic of the theory of historical materialism has been attacked by opponents who claim that the explanation of the adaptation of the economic structure to the productive forces is a *functional* one. According to the theory the level of development of the productive forces explains the nature of the economic structure, and the economic structure promotes the development of the productive forces. Indeed, the economic structure associated with a given level of productive power obtains because it enhances the further development of that power. The explanation is functional, because the "cause" of the existence of this economic structure is said to be in an "effect" or a function that it has—to facilitate the development of productive power. How can the cause of a thing be the very effect that it has? This seems to reverse the temporal order of cause and effect that is part of the definition of the statement "A causes B."

Cohen argues that there are functional explanations that are logically valid and do not explain causes by their effects, and therefore he considers the argument against the functional explanation of historical materialism offered in the last paragraph to be wrong. Consider the case of an industry in which large factories replace small workshops over a period of time, and succeed in doing so because of economies of scale in the technology. It is reasonable to say that economies of scale explain the evolution of large firms in the industry, although the economies of scale are only realized after the large firms come into existence. The functional explanation is that the increase in scale occurred because the industry was of a sort in which increases of scale yield economies and hence lead to a competitive advantage. One can state this with fair assurance even without knowing the mechanism by which large firms were introduced: whether prescient managers saw that large firms were the way to go, or whether by accident some large firms were introduced and then drove out the small firms by virtue of the scale economies they could exploit (selective adaptation).

A second example illustrates that the functional nature of the historical materialist explanation may be valid. The analogy is again to evolution. Consider the statement, "Birds have hollow bones in their wings so that they can fly." It is sensible to say that birds have come to have hollow bones because hollow bones facilitate flying; the hollow bones may have been an adaptation from birds who were formerly poor flyers, lacking hollow bones. One can say that the hollow bones are explained by their function of enabling birds to fly without committing the logical error of putting the effect before the cause, because there is a process whereby the skeletal structure of birds adapted itself to flying animals, and the one most favorable to their survival involved hollow bones. The mechanism whereby the hollow bones came about may still be one of several: perhaps an Almighty Being gave the birds hollow bones, perhaps birds learned to eat foods that induced hollow bones, perhaps selective adaptation by chance mutation created birds that had hollow bones and therefore were more biologically successful. Similarly, although the mechanism by which the economic structure adapts to the productive forces is not understood, it may still be clear that there is an adaptation occurring by virtue of some mechanism; so a functional explanation is justified.

A major problem with many Marxist arguments is their uncritical reliance on functional explanation, in instances where the evidence is insufficient to support one. For example, acts of a state in a capitalist society are explained by their function of preserving the capitalist order, even when those acts seem to be in the interest of the workers. Consider the enactment of eight-hour-day laws. The functional explanation is that, had these laws not been enacted, workers would have revolted and the capitalist system would have fallen; hence, the state was acting in the interest of the capitalist class when it passed them. A more direct explanation of eight-hour-day laws is that the mass movement of workers fighting for the eight-hour day forced the state to enact them. It is not clear that they were required for capitalism's survival.

Consider the existence of racism in capitalist societies. Marxists argue that racism divides the working class, making it less able to organize against capital. If capitalists can pit one group of workers against another—by virtue of race, language, age, or gender—that strengthens their position. The functional explanation is that racism exists in capitalist society because it furthers the strength of capital. But this is not so clear, for there are economic arguments that competition should eliminate racism, or at least discriminatory pay differentials. If black and white workers are equally productive, the argument goes, then competition will eliminate a pay differential between the two groups. If a black worker is paid less than his value (say, the marginal product of his labor in the standard neoclassical model), then some profit-seeking capitalist will hire him at a higher wage; and this process will continue until wages reflect productivity. Thus, it does not appear to be in the interest of any individual capitalist to maintain a racist pay differential. If he wants to maximize profits he will seek out workers who are underpaid; and if many capitalists do this, wages will be bid up to the competitive level. Against this argument are arrayed many compelling examples of the tenacity of racist pay differentials, and they can be explained by models in which the capitalist realizes he can decrease the unity of the work force against him if he pits them against one another by maintaining, for example, pay differentials. (Hence, the phrase "divide and conquer" is descriptive of capitalist strategy.) There are clearly some countries, such as South Africa, where a concerted, centralized state policy maintains racism: that is an example of seeing clearly the mechanism whereby South African capitalism has promoted a racist policy, arguably in the interest of its capitalist class—although it is not obvious that apartheid exists because of its propensity to make capitalism more profitable. Indeed, apartheid may bring down South African capitalism, which might otherwise be able to maintain itself in a more liberal form. In the liberal capitalist democracies, racism may be functional for capitalism and racism may exist because of its propensity to increase the profits of firms and the stability of capitalism, but careful documentation is necessary to make the case for this mechanism convincing.

A third example of an insufficiently documented functional explanation concerns the education of working-class children in the United

States. The literacy rate of these children is low. Some Marxists maintain that capitalism requires an underclass of relatively poorly educated workers, who learn discipline and obedience to their boss but do not learn enough to read about the world and realize they have "nothing to lose but their chains." Because it is useful for capitalism to have such a semiliterate class of workers, the schools (organs of the state) therefore train working-class children in just those ways: to be obedient, but not to read. But, again, the functional explanation is not prima facie convincing, because most of those involved in the process—teachers, students, parents, many school board members—want students to learn to read. It is true that education in American schools is low quality, especially for working-class and minority students, but the functional explanation is too easy. One must display the set of incentives faced by all the parties concerned to explain why many working-class children do not learn to read.

Historical materialism has given theoreticians license to create facile and unconvincing explanations of all the evils of capitalist society. Even though the assertions may be true—that states in capitalist nations act in the interest of the capitalist class, that racism is greater under capitalism than it would be under socialism, that working-class children do not learn because they are in a capitalist society—their proofs require detailed historical documentation, not simply the invocation of the function these attributes of capitalist societies have for the maintenance of capitalism. These assertions must be documented on a case-by-case basis. Historical materialism is intended as a theory that explains certain massive historical transitions; if it is convincing, it is so because there is historical evidence attesting to its conclusions. But only for that reason may a functional explanation also be justified—as a kind of induction from many previously observed cases.

8.4 Challenges from Economic History

Robert Brenner has provided us with an interesting challenge to the theory of historical materialism. He claims, with respect to early modern Europe, that the relationship between the economic structure and the forces of production is quite different from the one put forth in thesis (2) (Section 8.1). He maintains that the realization of an economic structure of agricultural property relations as feudal or as capitalist (or as one characterized by an independent subsistence peasantry) depended, not on economic factors such as the level of development of productive forces, but directly on class struggle, on the "relative power of the combatants." Brenner wants to explain two historical phenomena: the general trends in income distribution between the direct producers and the exploiting classes in early modern Europe in various regions and the differential development of capitalist relations in agriculture, which were stronger in some areas than in others.

An important historical event at the center of Brenner's discussion is the Black Plague, which wiped out a significant fraction of the peasantry in the fourteenth century. Brenner is critical of the demographic model, which maintains that a large increase in the land-to-labor ratio, a consequence of the plague, should have improved the general conditions of the peasantry. The supply of labor became smaller, and so the wage should have risen. In this case the general economic conditions of the serfs and peasants are of interest, not just the wage. According to standard supply-and-demand analysis, the bargaining power of the peasantry vis-à-vis landlords improved as a consequence of the demographic catastrophe of the plague, hence enabling their liberation from or weakening of feudal bonds. After 1349 in England, and in Catalonia, Brenner says, the results accord with this standard explanation. There were attempts to control the peasantry and to exact harsher fees from them in the late fourteenth century, as landlords tried to recoup the losses they suffered from the loss of peasants by increasing their exploitation of the remaining peasantry. Landlords also attempted to limit peasant mobility, to legislate wage controls, and to increase rents. But the seignorial reaction failed; peasant revolt and flight dominated the fifteenth century, which marked the unambiguous end of serfdom in these areas. In Catalonia, peasant armies were organized and engaged in bloody confrontations with the lords, finally assuring peasant victory.

Apparently the opposite outcome occurred in Eastern Europe. In an effort to recover the revenues they had lost from the Black Death, the lords tried and succeeded in increasing their exploitation of the peasantry. This victory led to what is called the second serfdom, which occurred during the period 1400–1600 even though trade was increasing. The magnet of a commercial economy was not sufficiently powerful to draw the peasants away from feudal bondage. What was apparently lacking in Eastern Europe, according to Brenner's history, was a sufficiently well organized peasantry.

As a result of the second serfdom in the East, the productive forces did not develop. In the feudal economy competition was minimal, because feudal manors did not depend on trade for the reproduction of their economic life. Brenner writes that the newly emergent structure of class relations (of the second serfdom) had as its outcome the "development of underdevelopment," the preclusion of increased productivity in general and industrialization in particular.

Capitalist relations force upon capitalists the need to innovate in order to survive in a market. Others are trying to enter the market and are doing so with new and better techniques developed specifically to enable the developers to sell their products at lower prices, and this pressure forces all capitalists to innovate. But under feudalism the incentives are different; the feudal lord has very little incentive to innovate, and he is able to survive in a basically self-contained manorial economy. Trade may bring extra revenues, but it is not necessary for reproduction. Brenner argues, first, that the availability of forced labor from workers whose services could be almost arbitrarily intensified by the lord (due to the weakness of the peasant opposition) discouraged agricultural improvements. Second, the lords' surplus extraction from the peasantry limited the emergence of a home market for industrial goods, because the peasants had nothing left to trade. Third, direct controls over peasant mobility prevented the emergence of an industrial work force and suffocated industry, so the towns declined. In sum, then, the class power of Eastern European lords succeeded for some centuries in holding back the development of the productive forces, which is the opposite of what historical materialism would seem to claim.

In Western Europe the success of the peasantry against feudalism did not lead automatically to capitalism; rather it led to an economy based on small peasant units, with some land being used in common. Whether or not this independent peasant production was transformed into agricultural capitalism was determined, claims Brenner, not by the level of development of the productive forces but by the balance of class power between the peasantry and the class of nascent agricultural capitalists and landlords. In England the capitalist transformation occurred; the land was concentrated in relatively few hands during the enclosure movement, when the gentry expropriated the peasants' small holdings and land held in common. But, apart from the enclosures, the development of agricultural productivity in England was due to the type of class relations that emerged between landlords and peasants; unlike the peasants of Eastern Europe, the peasants in England were not squeezed so hard, and this less forceful treatment enabled the development of a peasant surplus and gave peasants the motivation for agricultural innovation. This innovation, in turn, provided the grain surplus that was a precondition for successful industrialization—to feed an industrial proletariat living in towns.

In France, by contrast, agricultural productivity did not develop, because of the type of class relations prevalent there. Unlike the subjugated peasantry of Eastern Europe or the English peasantry, who entered into capitalist relations with English landlords and agricultural capitalists, the peasantry of France remained independent. Brenner argues that the French peasants were able to maintain their independence because of the nature of the French state, which depended on an independent peasantry as its tax base (whereas in England this was not the case). The French state was interested in limiting the rents that landlords collected from peasants so that peasants could pay their taxes. The relevant point is that, fundamentally, a political variable explains why the forces of agricultural production developed in England and not in France. The relative stagnation in French economic growth is accounted for by the relative power of the French peasantry (backed up by the French state), whereas in England the landlord class was more powerful and succeeded in depriving the peasantry of control of their means of reproduction, thereby forcing them to enter into capitalist relations in the countryside. This development, in turn, brought about competition and innovation.

Brenner concludes: "In sum, it is not difficult to comprehend the dismal pattern of economic development imposed by this class structure in France. Not only was there a long-term failure of agricultural productivity, but a corresponding inability to develop the home market. Thus, ironically, the most complete freedom and property rights for the rural population meant poverty and a self-perpetuating cycle of backwardness. In England, it was precisely the absence of such rights that facilitated the onset of real economic development" (Brenner, 1986a, p. 62). This is a clear statement of a theory that turns classic historical materialism on its head. It is not the level of development of the productive forces that determines the economic structure, but class power that determines property relations, which in turn determine the speed of development of the productive forces. This is asserted both with respect to the emergence of the second serfdom in the East, which contrasts with a free peasantry in the West, and with respect to the development of industrialization in England, which contrasts with relative stagnation in France in the early modern period. Class struggle and the balance of class forces is the exogenous and driving element in Brenner's argument, to which economic factors such as supply and demand for labor are of subservient explanatory significance.

8.5 Evolving Property Relations

I have presented two different Marxist views concerning the cause of the transformation of property relations. The classic, historical materialist position asserts that the productive forces develop by virtue of the ceaseless effort of rational humans to alleviate their conditions of scarcity, and property relations must necessarily adjust to the productive forces as they are. Only certain kinds of economic structures can coexist with a given set of productive forces, and the determining factor is, in this account, the productive forces. Also, in this account, class struggle is the mechanism through which transformation of property relations occurs, but it is not the deep cause of that transformation. That cause resides in the fact, noted earlier, that only a certain economic structure (or set of such structures) can coexist with the productive forces as they are at a given time, and hence the structure in question comes about, with class struggle taking the role of midwife. In the second account, the balance of class forces is the exogenous datum, and the productive forces develop or stagnate as a consequence of existing property relations, which are in turn explained by class struggle. Both accounts agree that economic development is associated with capitalist relations of production and relative stagnation with feudal relations; they disagree on the centrality of class struggle in the transformation of class society from feudal to capitalist. In the second account, the economic structure need not adapt to ceaselessly developing productive forces; it can, indeed, hold back that development for significant periods. It might, however, be argued (against Brenner) that a few centuries' difference in the development of capitalism in different parts of Europe—the result of differing balances of class forces in regions—is not a significant period of time in human history and that his evidence therefore does not contradict Cohen's traditional reading of historical materialism. Sooner or later, and perhaps from a properly long-range historical point of view, more or less simultaneously all of Europe was transformed into a capitalist economic structure at the historical instant when the productive forces reached a certain level.

The point germane to the discussion of exploitation in the earlier chapters is that the causes of the transformation of property relations in both of these accounts are not the ideas about injustice and exploitation that the producers might have had. Ideas of injustice may, indeed, come about as a consequence of the kind of property relations that exist; but in the Marxist argument, at least, they are not causes of the transformation of those property relations. In Cohen's account of historical materialism, a new form of property relations emerges, because only it can fit with changes in the productive forces. In Brenner's account, the success of a revolutionary transformation is determined by the power and organization of the various classes. In these senses both of the variants discussed here offer materialist, as opposed to "idealist," explanations of revolutionary change. A materialist explanation is one in which the motive forces are competition, scarcity, supply, and demand; an idealist one emphasizes the role of ideas, usually of certain "great men," which are taken to be the exogenous driving element. In the Marxist view, the ideas of great men matter only when they fit with appropriate underlying economic structure. Just as class struggle may be the midwife of a change that is bound to come sooner or later, so a great idea is bound to come, sooner or later, when the underlying material and social conditions create the proper medium for it.

Although very few social scientists and historians today would endorse in a wholehearted way either of the two Marxist accounts given here of the evolution of property relations, it is probably the influence of historical materialism that accounts for the almost completely materialist approach to these questions now taken by social scientists and historians. An economic or materialist determination of historical and social change is now the ubiquitous research strategy, although class is not always the central concept, nor do the majority who take a materialist approach call themselves Marxist. Indeed, it is questionable what it means to take a specifically Marxist approach to history when the materialist axiom, the cornerstone of the Marxist approach, has become central to almost all contemporary social thought.

9

Evolving Forms of Exploitation

Marxists have generally defined exploitation in terms of surplus labor. In Section 9.2 I will argue that exploitation, so conceived, does not accurately capture the Marxist concern. I will redefine exploitation in terms of property relations and show that different forms of exploitation have emerged as property relations have changed.

9.1 Historical Materialism and Private Property

According to the theory of historical materialism, economic structures rise or fall as they become conducive or fettering to the further development of the productive forces. In particular, the nature of property changes as societies evolve. In slave societies, property can be held in other people. In feudal society, although property cannot be held in serfs as it is in slaves, lords do have some property rights in the labor of serfs. Capitalists, however, do not have similar property rights in the labor of proletarians. Under capitalism, all forms of property in other people are abolished. It is no longer legal to enter into voluntary contracts of slavery or indentured servitude. (The illegality of such contracts may in part account for the difficulty workers have in borrowing capital, for the only collateral they might otherwise have had is their future labor power, which capitalism forbids them to indenture.) In feudal society, forms of property that were legal in slave society no longer exist, and in capitalist society the same is true with respect to certain kinds of feudal property. Under socialism, a further kind of property is eliminated, namely, the alienable means of production. It is no longer legal to own factories and land for productive purposes, but people still maintain ownership of their labor power—in the sense that differential remuneration to differential skill is legitimate under socialism. Thus, according to the historical materialist description, an evolution in property rights takes place in which various kinds of property are progressively eliminated. The scope of private property diminishes.

It is important to note, however, that this claimed progressive socialization of property takes place not because of ethical views that the producing classes have but for reasons more related to efficiency. Only certain kinds of economic structures (including property relations) can support certain levels of the development of the productive forces. Why it should be that the kinds of economic structures associated with more advanced productive forces should involve the socialization of more types of property is a question that has not been addressed, nor is it addressed explicitly in the theory of historical materialism. An unsubstantiated and teleological view associated with Marxism is that society naturally progresses to more and more egalitarian forms, and hence, more types of property become socialized. In the end, if all productive factors (including skills) were socialized, no person would have a right to benefit by virtue of any skill. If, in addition, other attributes of people, such as their needs, were socialized, no person would suffer more than another on account of some special need she had—to do so would be to respect private property in needs. If needs are socialized, then the income distribution would have to be one that fulfilled the needs of all people equally. That is sometimes the view of communism (as opposed to socialism) that Marxists have put forth: "From each according to his ability, to each according to his needs." I shall have little to say about that. It is doubtless true that Marx held this teleological view to some extent; Elster (1985) comments that Marx's writing is imbued with "wishful thinking." Just as contemporary evolutionary biologists are critical of the notion that species are evolving to higher and higher forms, so contemporary Marxists must be wary of the view that societies necessarily evolve to be increasingly free and self-fulfilling.

What does seem clear is that in the last two millennia an evolution of property has occurred and that progressively fewer kinds of productive factors remain acceptable as property as time has passed. Associated with each economic structure, and its acceptable forms of property, are characteristic kinds of inequalities. The inequality associated with capitalist property forms Marx called exploitation: but one can also discuss feudal and socialist exploitation as the inequalities characteristically associated with those economic structures. How the several forms of exploitation evolve as property forms evolve and how each revolution in economic structure has the result (if not the purpose) of eliminating the form of exploitation characteristic of its predecessor structure will be the topics of discussion in the following sections.

9.2 The Failure of Surplus Value as a Measure of Exploitation

The inequality called exploitation that Marxist theory seeks to measure is that inequality of outcome due to the differential ownership of a certain kind of productive input, the alienable means of production. The models presented thus far have shown how exploitation is related directly to initial wealth and I have argued that exploitation, calculated by making the comparison between socially necessary labor time and labor expended, is an interesting statistic only insofar as it reflects the underlying inequality of distribution. Furthermore, I have argued that exploitation is only unethical if that initial distribution of wealth is judged to have come about through means that are not moral. In Chapter 5 I gave some examples of how exploitation might emerge in a moral way. If, for example, two people have different rates of time preference that can be judged to be their own responsibility, then an initial equal distribution of wealth can turn into an unequal one through the use of markets. The same is true if people have unequal skills, and the consequent inequality of income would be ethically protected if people were believed to legitimately own property in their own skills.

I will show that the Marxist concept of exploitation does not properly reflect, in all cases, the underlying inequality of productive assets that it purports to measure. This is a different point from the claim that exploitation, when it exists, is not necessarily bad unless the initial distribution of wealth is bad. I now claim that exploitation calculated in the Marxist way is a not the robust statistic for the inequality in the ownership of the means of production that would justify our interest in it.

Consider two examples. The first is taken from Chapter 2; in this model there were 1,000 agents, each of whom owned ½ unit of corn—the egalitarian initial distribution of capital. Recall that the technologies are

Farm	3 days labor	$\rightarrow$ 1 unit of corn
Factory	1 day labor + 1 unit of corn	$\rightarrow$ 1 unit of corn, net

Each agent has subsistence preferences: to consume just 1 unit of corn while expending as little labor as possible and reproducing his capital stock. One option for arranging an equilibrium involves a social division of labor in which agents divide themselves into the two classes H and S, hirers and sellers of labor. Each member of S first works up her own ½ unit of corn in the Factory, producing ½ unit of corn, net; she then sells her labor power at a wage rate of ⅓ unit of corn per day to three agents who hire her to work up their corn stock. She works as a seller of labor power for 1½ days, working up the corn stock of three members of H and earns as her total wages ½ unit of corn. Thus, she will have worked a total of 2 days and earned just 1 unit of corn, net. Each hirer makes a profit from the seller's labor, for the seller produces 1½ units of corn, net, in 1½ days and gets only ½ unit of corn as her wages: thus, hirers of labor make a profit of 66⅔% on their capital. Each hirer makes, indeed, ⅓ unit of corn net profit and then must go to the Farm himself to work for 2 days to make the other ⅔ units of corn he requires for consumption. Thus, members of the class H hire others to work up their capital stock, while they work only on the Farm, and members of the class S sell their labor only in Factories.

Now according to a property-relations view, and a welfare view, there is nothing morally wrong with this arrangement (assuming there is no particularly deleterious effect resulting from working for another person). Each person is working for 2 days and consuming 1 unit of corn. But depending on how the computation is made, one might conclude that there is Marxist exploitation in this arrangement. After all, the members of H are living off the labor of members of S; they are profiting from their labor in the normal sense of the word. A labor seller is paid at the rate of ⅓ unit of corn per day but produces, in the Factory, at a rate of 1 unit of corn per day. Her surplus labor is "expropriated" by the owner whose seed corn she works up.

Whether one calls this Marxist exploitation depends on how one measures socially necessary labor time. In Chapter 2, I concluded that the socially necessary labor time for 1 unit of corn in this model was 2 days (not 1 day), because I took account of the scarcity of corn and averaged in the time necessary to produce society's subsistence needs as a whole, which requires using the inefficient Farm technology. But a more classical view would claim that the labor sellers are exploited in the Marxist sense in the arrangement just outlined, because they produce a profit for the members of H who earn corn from members of S without working for it. The labor time embodied in a unit of corn produced in the Factory process is 1 day, but the producer is paid just ⅓ unit of corn for a day's labor. If one takes this classical view, then Marxist exploitation fails as an interesting statistic of inequality, for certainly the members of this society are indifferent between the social division of labor and the arrangement by which each works autarkically himself for 2 days, ½ day in his Factory and 1½ days on the Farm. Certainly there is nothing ethically wrong with the social division of labor in the arrangement described, so exploitation as a morally condemnable thing should not exist in the arrangement described.

In this example, exploitation calculated in terms of surplus labor exists when, from an ethical point of view, none exists. There is, however, some ambiguity in the calculation of exploitation based on whether one calculates socially necessary labor time using just the Factory technology or the Factory and Farm technologies. Consider a second example in which this ambiguity does not exist. Imagine that two agents, Karl and Adam, have the following preferences for corn and labor:

$$\text{Karl prefers } (\tfrac{2}{3}, 0) \text{ to } (1, 1) \tag{i}$$
$$\text{Adam prefers } (3\tfrac{1}{3}, 4) \text{ to } (3, 3) \tag{ii}$$

The commodity bundles are (corn, labor). Thus, the second line says "Adam prefers to work 4 days and consume 3⅓ units of corn than to work 3 days and consume 3 units of corn." Notice that both of these preference pairs are reasonable. Karl values leisure relatively highly—he would prefer to sacrifice a little corn so as not to have to work at all—whereas Adam values corn relatively highly—he will work an extra day beyond three for just a little more corn.

Now suppose that the technologies are the same: Farm and Factory; and suppose that the initial distribution is unequal: Adam owns 3 units of corn and Karl owns 1. Assume, as always, that neither is willing to run down his initial corn stock, so the preferences displayed above are for consumption of corn net of reproducing one's stock. What are the possibilities? Each could work autarkically; then Karl could achieve the bundle (1,1) by working up his 1 unit of corn in the Factory in 1 day, producing 1 unit of corn, net. Adam autarkically can achieve the bundle (3,3) in the same way. But they both can do better. Suppose Karl offers to hire Adam at the rate of ⅓ unit of corn per day; this is the competitive wage for Adam, whose next best opportunity is to go to the Farm and produce corn at that rate. Karl hires Adam to work up Karl's 1 unit of corn and pays Adam ⅓ unit of corn, keeping ⅔ for his profit. Adam has already worked 3 days on his own producing 3 units of corn, net. Then he works 1 day for Karl at the wage rate just announced, ending with the bundle (3⅓, 4), and Karl gets the bundle (⅔, 0). But the relations (i) and (ii) indicate that this is a Pareto improvement over the autarkic situation. By being more explicit about their preferences, this can be made into an equilibrium arrangement for Karl and Adam. At this equilibrium, notice that *Karl is exploiting Adam;* Karl does not work at all and lives off Adam's labor. He can do this week after week, as they repeat this process. But Karl is the poor one and Adam is the rich one. Thus, the measure of exploitation fails to reflect properly the initial inequality in ownership of the means of production.

Suppose the initial distribution of corn is unjust, in the usual direction; that is, the just distribution would be the equal one, and so Adam has unfairly advantageous opportunities compared to Karl. But Karl exploits Adam. With whom should our moral sympathies lie? Until now, exploitation has always been correlated with wealth, but in this example the Exploitation–Wealth Correspondence fails, because the Class–Wealth Correspondence fails. The poor one hires and exploits the rich one.

This example shows that exploitation (in the technical sense) is not a concept of fundamental ethical interest. We view exploitation as a bad thing only when it is the consequence of an *unjust* unequal distribution in the means of production. But in this case the direction of exploitation is wrong. I do not think this means our moral sympathies should lie with Adam because he is exploited by lazy Karl; rather, it means exploitation is not a good statistic for what it purports to measure. Of course, if exploitation is interesting for other reasons (as, for example, a measure of domination), then our moral sympathies might still lie with Adam. But I argued earlier against domination as the root of our interest in exploitation.

The correspondence between exploitation and wealth established in Theorem 6.1 here fails, because in this example agents do not have subsistence preferences. The Class–Exploitation Correspondence is true regardless of the preferences of the agents—notice that in this example it continues to hold, because Adam sells labor and is exploited whereas Karl hires and exploits—but the Class–Wealth Correspondence is only contingently true, for a broad but not universal class of preferences. The conditions under which the Class–Wealth Correspondence fails are quite rare, but not outlandish. The preferences of Karl and Adam in the preceding example are, after all, not outlandish.

I think, from a historical point of view, that the correspondence between exploitation and wealth is very good. The kind of preference pathology of the Karl–Adam example is not a likely historical phenomenon. What the example shows, however, is that no universal argument can be constructed to the effect that exploitation is a reflection of underlying inequality in wealth, because it is not always so. Only if one stipulates certain conditions on preferences will it be so. I argued in Chapter 6 that class and wealth emerged as the interesting attributes of a person and that his exploitation status faded into the background. Now I can go further and argue that exploitation is a misleading attribute if one's true interest is inequality in the distribution of wealth. There appears to be no reason for an interest in the technical measure of exploitation, calculated in the classical Marxist way.

9.3 A Property-Relations Approach to Capitalist Exploitation

As a general statistic of inequality, the surplus-value approach to exploitation fails. But the underlying Marxist idea still has power: we consider a distribution of income unjust if it stems from an unequal initial distribution of private property. The examples of the previous section indicate that exploitation should be defined directly in terms of property relations rather than through the circuitous and finally unsuccessful route of surplus value. In Chapter 4 I claimed that the labor theory of value fails as a theory of equilibrium prices. I now add that the theory of exploitation based on the comparison of labor expended to socially necessary labor time fails as well. Unlike the labor theory of value, the classical theory of exploitation still does quite well, because the aberration of preferences required to produce the pathology of the previous section is rare. But from a logical point of view it would be more convincing to base one's ethical criticism of capitalism directly on property relations than to filter it through the veil of exploitation theory.

It is not difficult to do this. I can redefine exploitation without using the concept of embodied labor value, by referring directly to the inequality in initial wealth that is the cause of my concern. Imagine a society with agents possessing initial wealths ω^i, and suppose that as a consequence of market activity there is an outcome by which agent i ends up with income y^i. Alternatively, ω^i and y^i can be viewed as some bundle of goods—as initial capital and final product, respectively. I define a person as exploited if he would have been better off had the initial distribution of wealth been egalitarian. This condition attempts to capture the notion of damage done by the actual distribution, by virtue of an inequality in the ownership of the means of production.

One way of representing this idea is as follows. Assume that there is some process called Π—in this book, it is the market process—that associates to any given initial set of alienable endowments for the population $\langle \omega^1, \omega^2, \ldots, \omega^n \rangle$ some final set of commodity bundles $\langle y^1, y^2, \ldots, y^n \rangle$. Schematically, we can indicate this as

$$\Pi(\langle \omega^1, \omega^2, \ldots, \omega^n \rangle) = \langle y^1, y^2, \ldots, y^n \rangle. \tag{9.1}$$

Incorporated in the process Π are many data—the given technology, the preferences of the agents, and the skills of the agents (which are the inalienable assets they possess)—whose explicit representation is represented in (9.1) for ease of exposition. Once these parameters are known, then the market (or some other process of organizing economic activity) implements a final allocation of goods from an initial distribution of wealth; this is the distribution process summarized by Π. Now suppose that the preference ordering of person i over the commodity bundles of final output is represented by the utility function u^i. What distribution of commodities would result under the market process in which the initial distribution of wealth in alienable assets is egalitarian but everything else remains the same (namely, the technology, skills, and preferences of the agents)? Call that final distribution $\langle z^1, z^2, \ldots, z^n \rangle$, which is given by

$$\Pi(\langle \omega/n, \omega/n, \ldots, \omega/n \rangle) = \langle z^1, z^2, \ldots, z^n \rangle, \tag{9.2}$$

where $\omega/n \equiv \Sigma_i \omega^i/n$ is the per capita amount of alienable endowment (means of production) in the economy.

We will say that *agent i is exploited at the distribution of (9.1) if $u^i(z^i) >$ $u^i(y^i)$*. Agent i is exploited if he would have been better off at the distribution of output associated with an egalitarian initial ownership of the means of production than he is at the actual distribution. Similarly, an exploiter is one for whom $u^i(z^i) < u^i(y^i)$—he is rendered worse off by the change to an egalitarian initial distribution. Note that the z^i's are generally not equal after the redistribution of alienable assets that occurs in the thought experiment (9.2), because people still have different skills and different preferences and so will produce differentially and will demand different goods to consume. This model is more general than the ones of earlier chapters, where agents were postulated to be identical with respect to skills and preferences.

This is a *property-relations* definition of exploitation, as opposed to one based on surplus value, because it makes no reference to embodied labor values but refers only to the root of our concerns—the effect of an inegalitarian distribution of property in alienable assets on the final distribution of income or commodities. It is also a *counterfactual* definition, because it judges the exploitative nature of an allocation by comparing it with some alternative that might have existed. Notice also that the stated definition of exploitation is explicitly *welfare oriented;* a person is exploited if he would have been better off (by his own conception of welfare) in a certain counterfactual situation. In previous chapters I also took a welfare-oriented approach when discussing the classical Marxist definition of exploitation; there, welfare was adequately represented by the amount of time a person worked or the amount of income he earned. This welfare-oriented approach to exploitation could be challenged, but I will not debate the issue here.

It is not hard to verify that the property-relations definition of exploitation corresponds to the classical definition in all the cases we have studied where it should do so—where, that is, the classical definition gives the right answer. Both definitions give the same verdict concerning the exploitation status of a person in every example except the two of the previous section. There, unlike the surplus-value definition, only the property-relations definition gives the right answer. In the first example of that section, no agent is exploited under the new definition. In the Karl–Adam example, Adam appears as the exploiter and Karl as exploited because Adam would lose and

Karl would gain, in terms of final welfare, by a redistribution of initial endowments so that each started off with 2 units of corn.

A number of possible problems and pathologies are associated with the property-relations definition of exploitation: the market process (more generally, the process Π) may not produce a unique allocation from a given initial distribution, so the comparison of the consequences of the egalitarian initial distribution and the actual one could be ambiguous. Also, because of interactions among individuals, the allocation may change in such a way under the egalitarian distribution of initial assets that some people whom we intuitively view as exploited in the present regime become even worse off in the egalitarian regime, and so the new definition will not give the right verdict. For example, suppose that an egalitarian redistribution of property in the alienable means of production will destroy incentives (as conservatives argue), thus decreasing the total pie substantially and leaving people who were proletarians under the new regime worse off than before. By this definition, one would have to conclude that they were exploiters in the old regime. I have generally ignored incentive issues in this book and will continue to do so here. There are, however, alternative possible property-relations definitions of exploitation that may not be vulnerable to this particular objection. (Imagine, for example, that to test whether the ith agent is exploited, the counterfactual situation does not involve distributing the alienable means of production equally but gives just agent i the average endowment ω/n; one then asks whether he becomes better or worse off. In this case the incentive effects that might accompany a massive change in property relations will not occur. There is also a game-theory approach to a property-relations definition, which I have pursued elsewhere.)

These are some of the costs associated with the property-relations approach (see Section 9.7 for elaboration). The benefit is that one can focus clearly on the notion that exploitation is the loss suffered by a person as a result of the unequal initial distribution of property. One views a person as unfairly treated because of his lack of equal access to the alienable means of production; whether he is taken advantage of is assessed by comparing what he gets in the present regime to what he would have gotten with an initial equal distribution of alienable assets.

Here are two more examples that contrast the surplus-value and property-relations approaches to exploitation. Consider the unemployed in a capitalist economy; these people receive some goods from the welfare state. According to the surplus-value definition, they would have to be considered exploiters, because the labor content of the goods they receive is greater than the labor they expend. According to the property-relations definition, they are exploited: for they would surely be better off with a redistribution of wealth in which they, along with all others, received their per capita share of the capital stock. The property-relations definition appears to fare better here, if one wants the verdict that the unemployed are exploited under capitalism. Consider, next, an economy with three classes: a very rich, urban, capitalist class, a class of reasonably well-off, urban proletarians who work for the capitalists but survive by consuming grain produced by the third class, an absolutely impoverished peasantry. The terms of trade between the city and the country are very much in favor of the city because of the excess rural population and barriers to mobility into the city, which prevent the urban wage from being bid down. In such a situation it may be that, according to the surplus-value definition, the proletarians are exploited—they expend more labor than is embodied in the goods (including grain) they consume—but that their conditions would deteriorate were there to be an egalitarian redistribution of initial assets. The peasants would gain, but at the expense of the proletarians. So the surplus-value definition says the proletarians are exploited whereas the property-relations definition says they are exploiters. Which is correct?

In these two examples the different judgments rendered by the definitions reflect the fact that these are hard cases: it is not clear whether, morally speaking, one should view the unemployed in the first example as unfairly taken advantage of or the proletarians in the second example as taking unfair of advantage of the peasantry. Nevertheless, I will declare a person as *capitalistically exploited* if he would gain by virtue of an egalitarian redistribution of society's alienable means of production, and a person as *capitalistically exploiting* if he would lose by such a redistribution.

9.4 Feudal Exploitation

In considering exploitation under capitalism, my focus has been on a certain kind of property: alienable productive assets. I have focused neither on property in other persons (which obtains in slavery and feudalism) nor on inalienable property (such as skills). The inequality characteristic of feudalism is due, not to the distribution of the alienable means of production, but to the rights some have in the labor of others. Thus, *feudal exploitation* can be thought of as that inequality associated with unequal distribution of rights in the labor of other people.

In parallel with the definition of capitalist exploitation proposed in Section 9.3, I can define a person in feudal society as feudally exploited if he would have been better off had the distribution of *feudal* property been egalitarian—that is, had there been no asymmetry in the labor rights some people (lords) had over others (serfs). The simplest way of accomplishing this symmetry is to abolish feudal property rights, so that no one has any property rights in another's labor. Then feudal property is abolished or, alternatively, each has complete property rights in his own labor. The test for feudal exploitation is to calculate whether a person would be better off under the distribution where no feudal property exists but capitalist property still exists. The only kind of property that is redistributed (or abolished) is feudal property.

Under this test, the serf appears to be feudally exploited and the lord to be a feudal exploiter. For, at least according to the Marxist account, the serf would have benefited if he did not owe the lord corvée and demesne labor, and the lord would have been worse off. Not all agree that according to this definition the serf was feudally exploited. Those who argue (such as North and Thomas, discussed in Chapter 3) that serfdom represents an implicit contract would say that both serfs and lords would have suffered by the abolition of feudal property. But according to the more prevalent view, feudal property rights represented an expropriation, not an implicit contract, and the test would conclude that serfs are feudally exploited and the lords are feudal exploiters.

Are proletarians *feudally* exploited? No. They already are the sole owners of their labor power and would not benefit by the redistribution of property according to the test for feudal exploitation. The view of exploitation that neoclassical economists often put forth is one similar to that of feudal exploitation. An economic agent is considered to be exploited (in neoclassical discussions) by virtue of some market failure or some fetter that prevents him from being able to take advantage of competition and to gain from trade. Sometimes it is said that an agent is exploited if he is paid less than the value of his marginal product; this underpayment is traced to something that prevents him from competing, for example, immobility or the absence of a market. These fetters to competition are similar in their effect to the feudal bond that prevents the serf from trading his labor. Because neoclassical economic theory takes *feudal* exploitation as the paradigm of exploitation, it does not comprehend the Marxist accusation that proletarians are exploited under capitalism: for proletarians are free to choose and trade and one may assume that they are paid the values of their marginal products.

The difference between neoclassical and Marxist views on exploitation can thus be viewed as due to the different counterfactuals that lie behind the moral judgments being made. Liberal theory views private property in alienable assets as morally legitimate and judges a person to be taken unfair advantage of economically only because he cannot take advantage of the opportunities that his property should make available to him. Such restricted opportunities may be due to direct coercion, of the slave or serf variety, or perhaps to barriers to mobility, which effectively render a person unfree to compete. The case of thin markets, where monopolies gain "unfair advantage" over buyers is a more subtle one, and some economists consider it to be an example of neoclassical exploitation. A thin market might be considered to be a special case of factor immobility—in many (but not all) cases, the monopoly is due to the buyer's lack of ability to communicate and to move around sufficiently to develop competition among sellers. More generally, neoclassical exploitation is associated with the imperfect development of competition, of which the immobility of the serf is a special case, whereas Marxist capitalist exploitation exists with perfect competition and is due to the differential opportunities that are the consequence of unequal access to the alienable means of production.

9.5 A Comparison of Revolutionary Transitions

Each revolution in an economic structure abolishes just that kind of property associated with its characteristic form of exploitation. Thus, the bourgeois revolution of 1789 in France abolished feudal property but not capitalist property, and the socialist revolutions of 1917 in Russia and of 1949 in China had as their aim the abolition of capitalist property but not property in skills.

When a form of property is abolished, some inefficiencies may result, for some opportunities for writing contracts are no longer available. Under socialism a person is, in principle, allowed to earn differential returns to differential skill and hard work, but it is illegal to capitalize that income, to purchase alienable means of production with it. Conservative critics of socialism argue that the incentive effects of this prohibition are bad, because people will not develop their skills if opportunities for capitalizing the income earned by their use do not exist. But the same kinds of prohibited opportunities exist when any form of property is abolished. Under capitalism a person can earn differential income based on differential ownership of alienable assets, but it is illegal to "feudalize" that income: a person cannot buy serfs or slaves with the income from capitalist property. This restriction, however, does not act as a disincentive to accumulate. I have already mentioned the case of the proletarian who cannot borrow because of the illegality of his conditionally indenturing his labor as collateral for the loan. But this outcome is not a reasonable argument for allowing voluntary servitude. Indeed, legalizing such "feudal acts" would not add to efficiency, all things considered, although opposition to them is not principally on efficiency grounds, but on moral ones.

Historical materialism takes a different position with respect to the efficiency of different property forms from the one just outlined; it claims that the evolution of property forms is necessary to harness the productive forces. The micro inefficiency due to the illegality of contracts of indentured servitude is washed out by the macro growth effect of a capitalist compared with a feudal economic structure. Capitalism derives its vitality from giving agents no alternative but to trade on markets, thereby abolishing subsistence arrangements and, hence, developing competition and innovation. Making those contracts illegal that would facilitate on-going feudal relations may in the small be inefficient, but in the large it creates an economic structure with much greater dynamism.

A similar argument may be made with respect to the abolition of the capitalist economic structure in a socialist transition. At the micro level incentives may be blunted, if people cannot capitalize their legitimately earned differential socialist incomes into private property. But at the macro level public ownership of the means of production may permit more rational development of large investment projects and the harnessing of increasing returns to scale. The secret behind the rapid development of the so-called NICs (newly industrialized countries) appears to be heavy state involvement in planning and production. To be sure, these countries do not call themselves social-ist, and they allow a substantial private sector; but that does not cancel the point. For example, Lester Thurow, claims that the only way the United States can compete with Japan and the NICs is by state involvement in directing economic activity in a way inimical to the free-market ideology continually spouted by the American mass media and by the Reagan administration. It is unclear exactly what public ownership of the means of production means—that will be a topic of discussion in the next chapter—but that is not the central point here. Rather I am claiming that changing property rights, al-though it may have micro disincentive effects, can have macro growth effects that are far more significant. In an egalitarian socialist society, the new property relations may additionally heighten the sense of self-worth of vast numbers of people, an effect that not only would be good in itself but also would have beneficial effects on productivity.

9.6 Socialist Exploitation

Under socialism certain kinds of productive assets remain as private property in the sense that agents earn differential returns with re-spect to their differential ownership of (or access to) them. These are mainly of two types: skills and status. If socialism is a system in which each "works according to his ability and is paid according to his work," then private ownership of skills is recognized. I will define socialist exploitation as that inequality attributable to differential skills after private property in the alienable means of production has been abolished.

Consider a thought experiment that tests for socialist exploitation of this type. Imagine that agent i has an endowment σ^i of skills and that all alienable productive assets have already been socialized. There is some allocation mechanism that characterizes the socialist economy, which I will continue to call Π, associating to any distribu-tion of skills $\langle \sigma^1, \sigma^2, \ldots, \sigma^n \rangle$ with which a population is endowed some final distribution of income $\langle y^1, y^2, \ldots, y^n \rangle$. As before, I can write

$$\Pi(\langle \sigma^1, \sigma^2, \ldots, \sigma^n \rangle) = \langle y^1, y^2, \ldots, y^n \rangle, \tag{9.3}$$

where y^i is the allocation of final output to the ith agent. The allocation mechanism Π now includes some description of the way in which society uses its publicly owned alienable means of production.

I must also construct a counterfactual distribution of skills in order to evaluate the existence of socialist exploitation. It is not necessary to actually redistribute the skills of agents, a feat that may be technologically impossible (even with state-of-the-art genetic engineering), but it is necessary to know how the process *would* allocate goods were skills to be equal. Thus, suppose that it is possible to define a notion of average skill:

$$\bar{\sigma} = \frac{1}{n} \sum_i \sigma^i$$

Then I can calculate

$$\Pi(\langle \bar{\sigma}, \bar{\sigma}, \ldots, \bar{\sigma} \rangle) = \langle z^1, z^2, \ldots, z^n \rangle. \tag{9.4}$$

In the actual socialist society agent i is socialistically exploited if he would be better off in a society with an egalitarian distribution of skills; that is, if $u^i(y^i) < u^i(z^i)$, where u^i is the utility function of the ith agent. Similarly, an agent who gains from socialist exploitation is one who would be rendered worse off in a society where each had the average skill.

But how could socialist exploitation be eliminated? Although it is desirable to eliminate feudal property, and perhaps even capitalist property, we do not wish to eliminate skills. And, in fact, that is not required in order to eliminate socialist exploitation. Eliminating property does not entail eliminating physical productive factors, because property in this context is a *legal* concept, not a physical entity. Just as eliminating capitalist property does not imply that the means of production themselves are destroyed, so eliminating "socialist property" does not entail the destruction of skills. Elimination of private property in skills just means that differential remunerations to skills is eliminated. It entails the redistribution of income in conformity with (9.4).

Accomplishing this redistribution might be a difficult task because of incentive problems, but it is certainly not a logically impossible one. As I argued above, ideologues of a given economic structure have always claimed that the elimination of the form of property characteristic of an economic structure would destroy economic productivity and ruin incentives. Social theorists of slave society argued that without slavery society would crumble, and this position has been repeated with respect to feudal and capitalist property in their associated societies as well.

There is another inequality in existing socialist societies that appears to be more pernicious than skill inequality, namely, inequality in the distribution of income due to differential status, or access to position. To the extent that occupying certain positions is a return to skill, then these status differentials are a reflection of skill differentials. But much status inequality of socialist societies seems to be due not to skill differentials but to the privileges that come with occupying certain positions. Political office often brings with it myriad material benefits, with respect to housing, automobiles, and consumer goods. Those of high status can shop in special stores and are not rationed with respect to the purchase of goods that are otherwise scarce. Status exploitation is the consequence of real income inequality due to differential status.

It can be argued, and proponents of central planning do, that status exploitation is the alternative to and a lesser evil than capitalist exploitation. If competitive markets and private property are used to organize economic activity, then inequalities arise as a result of wealth, but not as a result of position, for only dollars count in a market economy. Capitalism thus batters down the ramparts of feudal privilege and rewards only economic virtues. (One might note that status exploitation bears some resemblance to feudal exploitation; the resemblance is superficial, however, because lordly status is usually inherited whereas public offices are not.) In a centrally planned economy, bureaucracy replaces the market, and with bureaucracy comes position and status exploitation. People will naturally use their positions to economic advantage if other forms of property cannot be so exploited. A relevant quotation from Marx on the substitution of status for capitalist exploitation: "Rob the thing [money] of its social power, and you must give it persons to exercise over other persons" (Marx, 1857–58 [1973, p. 157]).

There is no question that status exploitation exists in socialist countries and that it is a kind of inequality one would like to eliminate. It is clear, however, that socialist economies are not unique in this regard. The income and perquisites of capitalist corporate executives are not entirely due to their skills, but are in large part a rent they collect by being the toll-takers on the bridge, the few who hold these scarce positions. Indeed, the living standard of American senators, relative to the rest of the U.S. population, is at least as lavish as the relative living standard of Soviet central committee members. Status exploitation is not so evident in advanced capitalist societies, because it is overshadowed in magnitude by capitalist exploitation. Where private property in the means of production does not exist, one sees only status exploitation. What makes status exploitation so apparently hypocritical in socialist societies is their stated commitment to equality of opportunity and to remuneration based strictly on merit. Capitalist society cannot be accused of such hypocrisy.

Some argue that status exploitation in existing socialist societies is as inegalitarian as capitalist exploitation; those of high status reap the rents, they say, coming from control of society's capital stock, just as capitalists reap those profits under a private ownership system. But this claim is not borne out by the facts. There are a small number of illegal capitalists in socialist societies (who actually skim the profits of socialist enterprises), but their wealth is not an instance of status exploitation. These capitalists are analogous to the leaders of criminal syndicates in capitalist countries. The inequalities due to the status exploitation are far less massive than those due to private ownership of wealth. Matthews (1978) estimates that a family in the Soviet elite stratum lives about as well as the average American middle-class family. There is, as well, a qualitative difference between the two forms of inequality: a socialist bureaucrat benefiting from status exploitation can be demoted, at which point he loses his status benefits, but this cannot happen to a capitalist. No committee can declare a capitalist's wealth to be unacceptable as coin of the realm. Closely related to this is the fact that capitalists can pass down property to their heirs, and hence capitalist inequality tends to be reproduced for generations through families; such is not the case with status exploitation. Although it is certainly true that the children of bureaucrats have access to better opportunities than the children of ordinary folk in existing socialist societies, status is not inheritable the way private property in alienable assets is.

Some, such as Charles Bettelheim, have argued that some existing socialist countries (in particular, the Soviet Union) are capitalist, by virtue of the class nature of the bureaucracy and the power attending to it. The bureaucracy, it is argued, controls the social capital stock in a manner similar to that in which capitalists control it in ordinary capitalist countries. But this argument confounds the nature of capitalist and status exploitation. A characteristic feature of status exploitation is that it has no prior determination: one achieves political power or status first, and *from* that flows material reward. Conversely, under capitalism, economic power is achieved first, and from that leading capitalists gain political influence. Because of this difference, the power of a socialist bureaucrat is more tenuous than that of a capitalist. The source of a capitalist's power cannot be rendered nugatory under the rules of the capitalist game, whereas a socialist bureaucrat can be replaced by a vote of a committee. As Walter Connor writes, "[In the Soviet Union] economic rewards of considerable size will flow *from* power; in the United States, the acquisition of behind-the-scenes power and the power that comes with public office both generally require substantial *prior* financial resources" (Connor, 1979, p. 321).

Whereas socialist exploitation, due to private ownership of skills, is supposed to exist under socialism, status exploitation is an unintended and undesirable form of inequality. If it is indeed associated with the excessive dependence of existing socialist countries on central planning, then perhaps it can be eliminated by the increased use of markets in socialist economies. Opponents of market socialism fear that markets will reintroduce capitalist exploitation. Proponents of market socialism believe that a judicious use of markets can increase efficiency, decrease the power inherent in bureaucratic office, and hence decrease status exploitation, while not giving rise to the accumulation of private property in the means of production, and hence capitalist exploitation.

9.7 Socially Necessary Exploitation

I have argued that each economic structure has associated with it a form of inequality, or exploitation, deriving from the kind of property that is characteristic of that economic structure—that is, a form of inequality that differentiates it from other economic structures. Feudal exploitation is that inequality associated specifically with property the lords own in serfs' labor, but it is not that inequality associated with the differential material wealths of the two classes. Capitalist exploitation is that inequality attributable to differential ownership of the alienable productive assets of an economy, but it is not attributable to the differential skills of agents. Socialist exploitation is that inequality associated with differential skills, after private ownership in alienable assets has been eliminated. There is also status exploitation in socialist societies (as there is in all societies).

Why should each of these forms of inequality become successively viewed as exploitative, as an unfair advantage enjoyed by one group over another? The bourgeois revolutionaries of 1789 viewed feudal inequality as unjust and inefficient and thought that the abolition of feudal privilege would bring about "liberté, égalité, fraternité." They were only right to some extent. The socialist revolutionaries of 1917 thought that the abolition of capitalist property would herald the "free development of each and the free development of all." Now, after some seven decades of socialism (which, after all, is not very long for an economic structure to prove itself), more emphasis is placed on inequalities of position and access to opportunities that continue to exist after other forms of private property are eliminated. (Another form of inequality that has been difficult to eliminate in socialist countries is that due to regional differences—urban versus rural in China, the southern versus the northern republics in Yugoslavia.) The explanation of why inequalities of various forms come to be viewed as unjust requires a sociology of injustice. It seems that people tend to concentrate on the forms of property that are the main causes of inequality of their historical period.

Another explanation of the emergence of a social awareness of exploitation involves the theory of historical materialism. Recall that this theory claims that an economic structure exists as long as it is useful for further development of the productive forces. One might propose that the inequality generated by a property form is perceived as exploitative only after that property form is no longer necessary. Although this position jibes nicely with historical materialism, I think it is wrong. For one would then have to say that the extreme inequality of early capitalist societies was not unjust, assuming that capitalism was an optimal economic structure for the development of the productive forces, and even for human welfare, at that time. This noncredible position would eliminate the concept of "necessary evils."

I suggest instead the concept of "socially necessary exploitation." Consider, for example, the capitalist exploitation existing during early capitalism. Suppose, as historical materialism maintains, that capitalism was the optimal economic structure for developing the productive forces at that time. In this case, it is reasonable to say that the exploitation is socially necessary. Had capitalism somehow been eliminated, stagnation in technological development would have occurred, and the workers soon would have been worse off than they were to become under the capitalist yoke, with its tendency for dynamic technical change. (An example of such an occurrence, according to Robert Brenner, was the stagnation of agricultural economic development in France, which was due to the control the small peasantry exercised. The retarded development in France contrasts with the dynamic agricultural development in England, which had pervasive capitalist agricultural class relations [see Chapter 8].)

There are two principal ways in which the redistribution of property might render those who are putatively exploited worse off. First, this might occur as a result of the incentive effects of the new, egalitarian distribution of property. Conservatives argue that an egalitarian distribution of the capital stock deprives potential entrepreneurs of incentive, and perhaps deprives the proletarians of the whip they require to be productive; so, according to the calculation of equation (9.2), the proletarians would be rendered worse off with an egalitarian distribution of wealth. This notion can be expressed formally by saying that the process Π, which associates to any initial distribution of wealth some final distribution of income changes as a result of (deleterious) incentive effects when the distribution of wealth is equalized. If this were to occur, then one might say that the capitalist exploitation is socially necessary from a static point of view. Second, a redistribution of property, while perhaps not affecting incentives immediately, might lead to a slower level of technological change, as I discussed above; if so, the exploitation can be viewed as socially necessary from a dynamic point of view. In either case, if exploitation is socially necessary, then there is an argument against eliminating it.

Historical materialism claims that each form of exploitation is socially necessary from a dynamic point of view for a certain period of time and then ceases to be so. Some say that the Soviet revolution in 1917 was premature because capitalism had not yet had a chance to perform its good deeds of developing the productive forces. Capitalist exploitation was, they say, socially necessary at that time. When Lenin introduced the New Economic Policy (NEP) in the early 1920s, it was to allow capitalist dynamism to develop the productive forces in a way which, at that time, socialism was unable to do.

One can argue that both socialist and status exploitation are socially necessary in the early stages of the transition to socialism. For socialist exploitation the argument goes as follows: if workers are not differentially remunerated for their skills and differential effort, those skills and effort will not be developed and expended, respectively. A policy for ending socialist exploitation, a policy involving paying people independently of their skills, would have deleterious incentive effects. An experiment to this effect was carried out as part of the Cultural Revolution in China, with results that are now generally viewed as disastrous. Differential remuneration to skills is increasing in Eastern European countries, a phenomenon indicating that socialist exploitation is socially necessary, at this time, from a static viewpoint. Conservatives argue that such differentials will always be necessary, because of an unmalleable human nature; but Marxists believe that to be a myopic view. At some point, it will be possible to eliminate property rights in skills (that is, the right to earn a high income because of high skill) without destroying incentives, just as slave and feudal property were eliminated without bringing economic development to a grinding halt.

There is much evidence that socialist exploitation is necessary at this stage of historical development; whether status exploitation is necessary is more questionable. Status exploitation exists because of the large degree of central planning and the consequent growth of a bureaucracy capable of creating privileges for itself. One can argue that such privileges can only be eliminated by the introduction of markets to organize economic activity, thereby replacing bureaucracy, and that with markets capitalist exploitation would soon develop, because the successful use of markets entails allowing economic agents to accumulate profits and to reinvest them. If a large segment of socialist society would be worse off with the ensuing capitalist exploitation than with status exploitation, then the latter could be viewed as socially necessary. I believe that this is probably not the case, because the increased efficiency that would be achieved by a judicious introduction of markets would compensate for the inequalities that might develop. It appears, that is, that the greater cost attributable to central planning in existing socialist societies is not the inequity associated with status exploitation but the inefficiency, which could be rectified by introducing markets for consumer goods.

It is not hard to imagine situations in which status exploitation would be a socially necessary form of inequality. Suppose that everyone in a population of producers, all of whom are equally skilled, is paid a wage of $1, and that each produces $2 worth of output. It is then announced that a lottery will be drawn from among the hardest working half of the population; the 1% chosen in this lottery will be paid a wage of $20, and everyone else will continue to be paid $1. Furthermore, the lottery will be drawn each year. It is likely that everyone will work much harder in the second regime—and perhaps equally hard—to qualify for the lottery. Then the national income will increase, and everyone could be made better off than in the first regime. The 1% of the population who win the lottery are status exploiters: their high-wage status is awarded, not because they work harder than anyone else, but to create incentive effects that render everyone better off. Perhaps internal wage hierarchies in capitalist firms exemplify this phenomenon. Artificial wage steps are created, not as a remuneration to differential skill, but to create loyalty among the workers to the firm, and to stimulate productivity.

9.8 Syndicalization versus Socialization

If inequality in the ownership of the means of production is the source of capitalist exploitation, why not remedy this with syndicalism, a system in which private property remains but is divided equally among all? Each person would have an equal share, but competition and private property would remain. This equal but private redistribution is the one implied by Equation (9.2), which was intended as the counterfactual thought experiment to diagnose capitalist exploitation. Socialist theory has long been antisyndicalist and has advocated, not the redistribution of private property in the means of production, but the abolition of that property form. The abolition of forms of property that is associated with the great transformations of economic structures is not captured by the formulas (9.2) and (9.4), which seem to imply that the remedy of a particular form of exploitation is an egalitarian redistribution of the property in question rather than its elimination as property. Indeed, I began Chapter 2 with an illustration of Marxist exploitation by comparing the allocation that ensued from an inegalitarian distribution of the productive assets with the welfare distribution associated with an egalitarian distribution of the capital stock. Thus far in this book, public ownership of the means of production, as opposed to equal private ownership, has not been discussed.

10

Public Ownership of the Means of Production

Capitalist exploitation is the consequence of private and unequal ownership of the means of production. It would seem that socialism could abolish exploitation by establishing an equal distribution of private property in the means of production. But Marxism advocates the abolition of private property (in the means of production) rather than the establishment of "people's capitalism," a system in which private property and markets are retained and each person begins his economic life with his per capita share of society's capital stock and resources. Such a redistribution of the capital stock might be just as difficult to achieve, politically, as socialization, for clearly the present owners of the capital stock would protest were this new order to be implemented. To some extent there has been a redistribution (to greater or lesser degrees) of the income flows from capital by taxation in various capitalist countries (but the topic of the modern welfare state is, unfortunately, beyond the scope of this book). Even syndicalism, which calls for cooperative ownership of property by small groups, does not endorse simple egalitarian private ownership, although the property relations of syndicalism are to be distinguished from public ownership as well.

The so-called second theorem of neoclassical welfare economics states that under appropriate conditions on the preferences of agents and the technology, *any* desired Pareto optimal allocation (for our purposes, any income distribution) can be achieved by *some* initial redistribution of society's assets, followed by the use of markets. Given this theorem, one is prompted to ask whether the socialist opposition to people's capitalism—by which I mean capitalism that starts after the state has monitored the appropriate redistribution of initial assets that will bring about the income distribution considered to be fair—is akin to Ludditism, in which the institution of private property is blamed for the inequality that is associated not with private property as such but with its initial distribution. I have not offered a definition of what public ownership of the means of production is, but whatever it is, the final distribution of income (or the allocation of goods and labor) under it should be Pareto optimal, so that distribution could be achieved using markets (according to the second theorem of welfare economics) by some appropriate redistribution of private property. If the socialist state has the power to socialize assets, should it not also have the power (achieved either by popular electoral mandate or by violent means) to redistribute the capital stock in any desired manner? Why abolish private property, why not redistribute it?

10.1 The Case for Public Ownership

One might contemplate two kinds of redistributions of initial property rights: (1) an equal initial distribution, in which each would begin with his per capita share of society's total wealth in alienable assets, or (2) some unequal initial distribution, designed to compensate people for other unequal opportunities that they face. I will center the discussion on the first option, which is, after all, the one indicated as the appropriate rectification of capitalist exploitation. Most of the arguments apply against the second option. But, in addition, the second option seems even less politically realistic than the first one.

The abolition of a form of property is not a historical innovation. As I pointed out in Chapter 8, forms of property typically are abolished when economic structures are transformed. Nevertheless, the question has some urgency today, because socialist countries are introducing markets and private property to cope with some of the inefficiencies associated with socialization as it has been implemented. This initiative is occurring in Hungary and in Yugoslavia, and more recently in the agricultural sector of China.

10.1.1 Efficiency of the Market System

Perhaps the main reason that Marxism has opposed private property as such is the view it maintains, in contrast with that of neoclassical economics, with regard to the efficiency of the market system. Thus far I have not discussed efficiency-oriented Marxist criticisms of capitalism, because my topic has been the ethical justification of private property, under the assumption that markets are Pareto efficient. But, in fact, Marxism does not endorse the view of the benevolent workings of the invisible hand claimed by the neoclassical theorem discussed above. Both neoclassical economics and Marxism view agents under capitalism as pursuing their material self-interest; but whereas neoclassical economics derives (under certain conditions) the unintended good consequences of such self-interested pursuits, Marxism characterizes the results as anarchical and inefficient. Capitalism is a system in which there is a vast misallocation of resources, the most obvious of which is unemployment on a sometimes massive scale. How can this be, given the neoclassical argument? Perhaps because some of the assumptions of neoclassical equilibrium theory fail to hold in reality. Indeed, many interpret the "invisible hand theorems" in a critical spirit. They say that, because so many conditions are required to guarantee the efficient working of the invisible hand, real market economies, which violate some of these necessary conditions, probably are inefficient.

Some of the premises of the invisible hand theorem are not borne out in real world capitalist economies. First of all, in the real world there are substantial nonconvexities, for example, instances of increasing returns to scale in production. One of the premises of the second theorem of welfare economics is that production exhibits constant or decreasing returns to scale. Given real-world indivisibilities and increasing returns to scale in production, one cannot assure that an initial distribution of ownership in the means of production deemed to be fair will bring about an equilibrium that is efficient.

Second, the invisible hand theorem assumes that there is a complete set of markets, including markets for all goods that might appear in the future contingent upon the various possible states of the world that may occur. People have to plan very far ahead and trade on these markets to assure that the desirable equilibrium, through time, is achieved. But these markets, in actuality, do not exist. There are very few futures markets—only for some commodities, and not for very far into the future.

Third, agents do not act as price-takers in the real world; there are monopolists and monopsonists who have the power to set prices. In the invisible hand theorem, every agent is assumed to be so small that he has no such power. The existence of monopoly destroys the optimality of the equilibrium. One might argue that such monopolies would not exist after the redistribution that implements people's capitalism, but this is not obvious. Various agents, or coalitions, might still be able to establish monopolies, perhaps because of their possession of scarce skills, or because of the luck of the draw in the distribution of some asset that is assigned by a lottery.

Fourth, uncertainty in the real world is so immense, and the set of markets that exist is so thin with respect to the necessity of coping with these uncertainties, that the achievement of a desired optimal allocation through the market system seems remote. Because of these uncertainties, socialists have advocated planning instead of markets as the solution when big investment projects are concerned. Indeed, huge investment projects are underwritten by the state in every capitalist country today, a fact that attests to the inability of the market to handle such investment. A related but different point is that, as cognitive psychologists have shown, people behave irrationally in the face of uncertainty. The assumption that agents are rational maximizers is almost surely false in a world of uncertainty. In such a world, what people choose will therefore not be in their interests, even as they conceive of them. (For example, people may not take out the correct amount of insurance.) This would be the case even were there a complete set of markets to deal with all possible contingencies.

Fifth, the invisible hand theorem refers to a property of the *equilibrium* of a market system, where all agents act as price-takers and there is a complete set of markets. No reference is made to how the system behaves out of equilibrium and how the system achieves an equilibrium from an initial position in which it is out of equilibrium. There is no guarantee, according to neoclassical theory, that trading on markets in a disequilibrium situation will bring about the market equilibrium with its efficiency properties. That is, there is no complete model of the dynamics of market economies, and if the prevalent state of market economies is not one of general equilibrium, then there is no reason to ascribe those efficiency properties to it.

Despite these criticisms, and there are others, I do not mean to attack the neoclassical model of equilibrium theory, which is one of the great contributions to social scientific method of the past century. It is, indeed, the model of all the examples of this book. But I do want to criticize the carelessness with which the theorems of that model are used to infer conclusions about actual market economies. The invisible hand theorems are statements about a model, not about reality; and I have already presented sufficient reason for skepticism concerning those inferences. Models are schematic simplifications of reality, and judgment must be exercised before boldly claiming that the simplifications are appropriate for the policy question at hand.

10.1.2 The Legacy of Capitalism

Suppose, now, that the market system is efficient, that the assumptions of the neoclassical model all hold in the real world, and that private ownership economies achieve the equilibrium described by the model. There are still reasons for socialist opposition to people's capitalism, because of the legacy of capitalism in the residue of preferences and skills with which people in the new society begin. Suppose that people's capitalism is implemented by giving each person her per capita share of the national wealth in alienable assets, but that each person retains ownership of her own skills and her preferences with respect to risk and saving. Doubtless, large inequalities will emerge within a generation. One might say that these inequalities are morally justified, except that the preferences, skills, and habits of people developed in and were determined by the old society. Some people have learned to save under capitalism and have trained themselves in ways conducive to getting ahead in any society based on private ownership and markets. Others have learned behavior and values that are dysfunctional for success in a private ownership economy; one might argue that their behavior is well adapted to surviving on the margins of such a society but not to succeeding in its mainstream. Because of education, some people will begin in the new regime with much better opportunities than others, opportunities that will surely be parlayed into greater wealth than the others acquire. Because the preferences and skills of people, which are themselves in large part the consequence of the prior unjust distribution of wealth, are not transformed by the redistribution postulated, it cannot be claimed that such a redistribution rights the wrongs of capitalism. And, one might conjecture, there will be a strong correlation between those who did well under the old system and those who do well under the new system.

From the ethical viewpoint, the goal of socialism is to annihilate the opportunities that are unequal as a consequence of unequal access to or ownership of the alienable means of production. Equal ownership rights in the means of production would go only part way toward rectifying those inequalities, because the skills and preferences of people are themselves a consequence of past unequal opportunities.

10.1.3 The Endogeneity of Preferences

The endogeneity of preferences—the fact that preferences and values are shaped by one's environment—was invoked in Section 10.1.2 to claim that an equal per capita redistribution of ownership rights in alienable assets would not right the wrongs of capitalism. But another kind of preference endogeneity is also invoked by Marxists, who oppose private property in the means of production. The preferences and values of people are a consequence not only of the class they are in, and the amount of wealth they have, but also of the very economic structure in which they live. A system based on private property and markets will induce in people certain values that, it can be argued, are not *good* values. Marxism speaks of commodity fetishism, which is the belief that things and people tend to be valued in a market system by their market value. For example, Marxists argue that women will be undervalued by societies using a market mechanism as long as the raising of children remains women's work and is unpaid.

This criticism of capitalism is nonliberal, because it passes judgment on what kinds of preferences are good for people, independent of what people themselves may think. Marxism has a tradition of arguing that capitalism is not conducive to self-realization—to creating people who are capable of fulfilling themselves in a meaningful sense. (Or, rather, capitalism allows this for only a small minority.) This is only partly because of the skewed distribution of wealth and the class system that markets bring about; it is also because the very process of organizing economic activity by use of private property, competition, and markets may instill in people values that stunt the development they otherwise could achieve.

10.1.4 Inequality of Talent

Suppose that none of the three criticisms discussed above applies: markets work efficiently, the slate is clean with respect to preferences and skills left by the old capitalist society, and no one wishes to pass judgment on the quality of values that the market system induces. It will still be the case that people differ in their internal talents, in the propensities that they are born with, or that emerge through luck, and that the market system enables them to benefit from. Some people will surely be born with handicaps, but many attributes that people have may be considered to be handicaps of a type, even if they are not such by any conventional definition. The market system allows people to transform those attributes they possess that are of value to others into wealth. If one views the distribution of these internal talents as morally arbitrary and itself an instance of luck, one may oppose a method of economic organization that enables people to benefit by virtue of their draw in the birth lottery.

Indeed, contemporary theories of justice expounded by political philosophers such as John Rawls and Ronald Dworkin argue against the right of people to benefit unconditionally by the morally arbitrary distribution of talents. Here, one must recall, talent is to be interpreted in a broad way. It may be the capacity to work harder than the next person, or to study longer, or to be more charming and thereby to acquire a desirable job. Such a talented person might do well in systems other than market ones, but surely well-organized markets will reward such people. On the other hand, some feel that such virtue is its own sufficient reward and should not be additionally compensated with the money that will accrue to its possessor under a market system.

10.1.5 Summary

The preceding four arguments against private property as an institution focus upon different sorts of consequences of the market institution. The first criticism makes no moral judgments but calls into question only the efficiency of the market system. This, it should be noted, is the main criticism of private property deriving from the theory of historical materialism—that, at some point, the economic structure of private property in alienable assets is no longer optimal for harnessing and further developing the productive forces. The second criticism holds even if the first does not. It says that equal redistribution of private property in the alienable means of production is not sufficient to right the wrongs ascribable to the previous unequal distribution. The third criticism calls into question not simply the effect of the previous distribution of wealth on preferences and behavior, but also the effect of the market system as such on preferences; it claims that the institution of private property is not conducive to self-realization.

The fourth criticism rejects the equal redistribution of private property as a sufficient remedy for inequality, because, even with equal ownership of private property, people would still benefit materially from inequalities in talents, whose distribution is morally arbitrary. The last two criticisms are nonliberal in that they invade the autonomy of individuals: as I said, the third criticism passes judgment on what values are good for people, and the fourth claims a person should not be the sole owner of his talents.

One need not argue that all of the four criticisms are compelling. Any one of them is sufficient to nullify the rectification of capitalist exploitation via the route of people's capitalism. This rejection underlies the socialist call to abolish property in the alienable means of production and to seek some other way of organizing economic activity, at least for some decisions—to implement public ownership of the alienable means of production. It is far from clear, however, what such public ownership means. Who shall decide how to employ publicly owned resources, and according to what criteria? Section 10.4 suggests a preliminary, and what I intend as cautious, approach to what public ownership entails.

10.2 Three Political Philosophies

Before discussing what public ownership of the alienable means of production might mean, I will outline three competing political philosophies that suggest different possible arrangements of property rights with respect to two kinds of assets: those external to the person (alienable means of production), and those that are internal (talents).

From an ethical point of view, how can one justify the degree of inequality (of income or of welfare) in contemporary capitalist societies, and, more generally, in societies whose economies rely substantially on private ownership of productive assets and markets? The clearest justification for that distribution is the liberal position, represented by libertarians such as Robert Nozick. (I use the term *liberal* here with its historical and philosophical meaning, to describe an advocacy of laissez-faire.) Nozick is viewed as an intellectual descendant of Locke (although that paternity has been contested). The liberal position justifies the inequalities that exist today by arguing that they could have come about in an ethically defensible way, from an initial state in which people owned themselves but the external world (land, natural resources) was unowned. By virtue of self-own-ership, a person is entitled (in this political theory) to appropriate objects in the external world as his own, so long as no one is rendered worse off after the appropriation than he was before. By virtue of my skills, which enable me to make use of that piece of land, I am entitled to establish property rights in it so long as others will not be rendered worse off than they were when the land remained in common use. According to this theory, private ownership of the external world, initially unowned, is established by virtue of the self-ownership of agents, subject to certain constraints on private appropriation whose intent is to prevent harm to others.

G. A. Cohen argues that Nozick's proviso for the appropriation of things in the external world is too weak; it does not offer sufficient protection to those who do not appropriate. He poses the following example. Two people, A and B, have common use of land, on which A gathers m bushels of wheat and B gathers n bushels. Then A appro-priates the land and designs a division of labor between himself and B, with the result that A ends up with $m + q$ bushels and B with $n + p$ bushels. Because A is the appropriator, one may assume that q is greater than p and that both p and q are positive. Call this the *actual situation*. Now B is better off in the actual situation than he was before the land was appropriated by A, if one assumes that all that matters to him is his consumption of wheat. Therefore, the appropriation passes Nozick's proviso, and is legitimate.

Suppose, however, that B could have appropriated the land as well and designed the same division of labor and the same distribution of the additional product, so that B received $n + q$ bushels and A re-ceived $m + p$ bushels. Call this the *hypothetical situation*. In the hypo-thetical situation, B is better off than in the actual situation (because q is greater than p). If one judges the actual situation by what could have occurred in the hypothetical situation, then A's appropriation giving rise to the actual situation is unjustified. Nozick does not per-mit this test. The legitimacy of an appropriation is judged, by him, by comparing the actual situation only to the counterfactual situation in which the appropriated resource remained in common use. But there are other counterfactual situations that are at least as relevant for judging the moral legitimacy of the appropriation of a previously unowned piece of land.

Locke's proviso for initial acquisition of resources is that the appro-priator must leave "enough and as good for others." By the examples

Locke gives, it is clear that he intends something much stricter than the arrangement Nozick proposes. In the example given earlier, A would not be allowed to appropriate land unless the appropriation made no difference to B; that is, the appropriation would be justified only if enough and as good land were left for B to use. This was not the case in the example. Locke's proviso for appropriation of private property is phrased in terms of the physical abundance of the appropriated resource, whereas Nozick's compares the welfare of those who did not appropriate before and after the appropriation. Locke's proviso, unlike Nozick's, is hard to satisfy.

If people begin with very different skills, or internal traits of various kinds, the Nozickian theory licenses a fairly rapid development of inequality of income or welfare. If, as Nozick believes, gift-giving is a legitimate means of transferring resources, then inheritance may assure that substantial inequality remains between families for generations, even though this inequality is based on the initial clean appropriations performed in a world whose resources were held in common. Thus far, I have called into question Nozick's legitimation of private property by pointing out that his criterion for appropriation has an arbitrary character, unacknowledged by Nozick, which may not provide sufficient protection to those who do not appropriate.

The most sustained argument against the liberal position is associated with John Rawls, and more recently with Ronald Dworkin. Their position is called, variously, a left-liberal or a social democratic one; it essentially denies that people should own themselves, or at least, that they should have unfettered rights over the income that their productive talents bring. For this reason, it is associated with the criticism against the private property system given in Section 10.1.4. Rawls has various complex arguments for deriving his "maximin primary goods" allocation as the just one. For our purposes, it is sufficient to describe his recommendation this way. The rich should be taxed as much as possible, in order to redistribute income to the least well off. Indeed, the just income distribution is the one among all possible ones that makes the worst off group as well off as it could possibly be. Under different income distributions, the worst off group might well change: the Rawlsian goal is to render the worst off (whoever they may be) as well off as possible, with regard to their endowment of what he calls primary goods. Hence, the Rawlsian maximin distribution can be thought of as an egalitarian distribution, except insofar as incentive problems render egalitarianism unachievable without harming all. The justification of Rawls's proposal is the assertion that the distribution of traits (skills, talents) is morally arbitrary; he argues that from a position appropriately anonymous for taking ethical positions, people would agree to tax, as I have described, the fruits of morally arbitrary endowments of internal traits.

Ronald Dworkin, in arguing for equality of resources as an appealing moral philosophy, maintains that among the resources to be "equalized" are the skills and talents of people. Thus, he does not distinguish, as does Nozick, between resources external and internal to the person. He advocates a particular allocation mechanism for implementing this kind of comprehensive resource egalitarianism. The purpose is to allocate goods in the external world in a manner that compensates people, somehow appropriately, for the morally arbitrary distribution of talents that occurs in the birth lottery. This approach constitutes a denial of self-ownership, and from that it derives a very different rule from the liberal one for distribution of assets in the external world. It would take me unnecessarily far afield to ask what distribution of income or welfare is associated with the equality of resources, in both the external world and in the talents of people, that Dworkin recommends. Suffice to say, if resources are interpreted sufficiently broadly, then outcomes can be shown to be as equal as you please. If, for example, a need is interpreted as the lack of a resource, as was suggested at one point in Chapter 9, then it can be shown that equality of resources implies an outcome in which everyone's needs are equally fulfilled.

The alternative to liberalism as represented by these theories does constrain outcomes to be quite equal. These theories take the radical step of denying self-ownership, a tenet that most would like to hold, at least to some degree. Even though I have offered some arguments against self-ownership based on the moral arbitrariness of the distribution of personal talents, it is nevertheless useful to ask whether there is an alternative to right-wing liberalism other than the left-wing denial of self-ownership, an alternative that might bring about more equality of outcome than is associated with capitalism. Even if one sympathizes with socializing talents (which does not mean cutting people up, but rather redistributing income), it would be compelling to demonstrate that arguments can be made against the inequalities that liberalism supports without challenging the cherished liberal tenet.

Recently, a third political philosophy has been enunciated by G. A. Cohen, whose intent is just that. Cohen's strategy is to attack the liberal position, not by denying self-ownership, but by denying that the external world should be considered ever to have been unowned. Instead of its having been initially unowned, why not conceive of it as having been jointly or publicly owned by its initial inhabitants? After all, there were, in fact, no legal rights held by people initially with regard to the external world, and it is up to us to propose an appropriate concept of what those rights should have been. Viewing the external world as jointly owned by its inhabitants—or, all inhabitants, present and future—is arguably a proposal as good as or better than the supposition that the external world was unowned. Joint ownership is to be distinguished from the common ownership of the external world, which, in Nozick's theory, holds before appropriations take place. In common ownership, the land is unowned, but each may use it as long as he does not interfere with others. With joint or public ownership, the land is owned collectively by all: no one may use it until all agree to the disposition of the product. In supposing that the morally appropriate original position is that people own themselves and their skills but are trustees in public ownership with regard to the external world, Cohen aims to keep what appears to be the more appealing premise of the neo-Lockean argument (self-ownership); but he points out that there is an alternative to both non-ownership and private ownership of the external world.

How much inequality in final outcomes is justified if one must respect these two kinds of property rights: public ownership of the external world and private ownership of self? In the next section, I will present a simple model to study this question. The somewhat surprising answer is that this apparently intermediate political position implies, when modeled as below, that commodities must be distributed in a way that equalizes the welfares of the agents. Thus, although I attempt to respect self-ownership, at least in a limited way, the conditions for public or joint ownership of the external world are sufficient to prevent the welfare differentials that one would expect to accrue to the talented agents. Public ownership of the external world leaves very little maneuverability for what self-ownership might seem to warrant. One might say that public ownership trumps self-ownership.

Cohen's philosophical position is the appropriate next step to take in pursuing the issue upon which my analysis has come to focus, the consequences of private ownership of the alienable means of production. For it suggests that one should study the consequences of nationalizing or socializing only assets in the external world, not skills and talents as well. While limitations on self-ownership are justified, in my opinion, the approach taken here is more conservative than the position of a priori denial of self-ownership, in that it asks how far toward equality of outcome one can get with public ownership of the external world only. Because of its more conservative premise, any egalitarian conclusion derived has more force.

10.3 The Story of Able and Infirm

The simplest parable illustrating the problem of respecting both public property rights in the external world and rights of self-ownership is a slight modification of one told by Cohen. Imagine that two people, called Able and Infirm after their abilities for work, jointly own the external world, which consists of land used to grow corn. Able and Infirm each derive utility from corn and disutility from labor. Land is of no consumption value but is useful only insofar as it produces corn when labor is applied to it. Able's labor is highly skilled, and Infirm is either completely incapacitated or, more generally, can work less efficiently than Able on the land. There is a given technology, a production function, which describes the conversion of labor and land into corn. The problem is to recommend an allocation of labor performed and corn consumed by Able and Infirm that respects both their joint property rights in the land and their self-ownership.

Because the land is jointly owned, Able is not allowed to farm it unless Infirm gives his consent, which will follow an agreement on how to distribute the corn produced. If Able keeps all the corn he produces (assume that Infirm cannot work at all), does that not violate the public property right Infirm has in the land? If Able has to give some of the corn he produces to Infirm, does that not violate his self-ownership? Not necessarily, for the corn was produced by using, as well as Able's skill, some of the jointly owned land.

This parable can be formalized as follows. There is an amount $\overline{W}$ of land in the world, a production function $f(W,L) = C$ that describes the conversion of land and labor into corn, and two agents with the same utility function over corn and labor, $u(C^i,L^i)$, where (C^i,L^i) is the amount of corn consumed and labor expended by agent i. Agent i

(where i is either 1 or 2) has skill level s^i, which means that if he works L^i hours that work translates into $s^i L^i$ units of *standard labor*. Hence, if the two agents operate the technology together using W acres of land, then the amount of corn produced will be $f(W, s^1 L^1 + s^2 L^2)$ where the second argument in the production function is the aggregate amount of standard labor that has been expended. A *feasible allocation* of corn and labor for this economy is a distribution of corn (C^1, C^2) to the two agents and amounts of labor expended by them (L^1, L^2), which together are feasible for the economy; that is,

$$C^1 + C^2 = f(W, s^1 L^1 + s^2 L^2). \tag{10.1}$$

I can summarize this description by reference to the *economic environment* $\mathscr{E} = \langle \overline{W}, f, s^1, s^2, u \rangle$. An economic environment is simply the list of all the relevant information that describes a possible world. The question I have posed is, What feasible allocation, or allocations, of corn and labor to the two agents will respect two kinds of property rights, their public or joint ownership of the external world, which here consists of the land and the technology, and their private ownership of their skills?

10.4 Characterization of an Economic Constitution

To answer this question is to provide an economic constitution that respects the various property rights of the two agents. My approach is suggested by methods used in a branch of economic theory called social choice theory. The provisions of an appropriate economic constitution should be applicable to a broad range of possible worlds, or possible economic environments, where the values of $\overline{W}$, s^1, and s^2 and the utility function u and the production function f can vary. The problem in defining such a constitution is that I do not know exactly what public ownership of the external world means. Nor do I know what self-ownership of skill means in a world with publicly owned assets. Despite this, I may be able to specify some necessary properties of these property rights that would imply some restrictions on the articles of the desired constitution.

The economic constitution I seek must render a judgment on the appropriate allocation of resources for any reasonable economic environment. I will call the class of "reasonable" economic environments X; it consists of every economic environment $\mathscr{E} = \langle \overline{W}, f, s^1, s^2, u \rangle$ where

f is any production function that is increasing in land and labor, u is any utility function that is increasing in the amount of corn consumed and decreasing in the amount of labor expended by the agent, and $\overline{W}$, s^1, and s^2 can be any nonnegative numbers. Class X represents a broad class of possible worlds, but these worlds are reasonable in the sense that the production function behaves as it should (it produces more corn if the amount of land or labor input is increased) and the utility function is appropriate (in the sense that corn is desired and labor is undesired). An economic constitution or *allocation mechanism* will be a rule, called F, that assigns to any economic environment $\mathscr{E}$ in X some feasible allocation of that environment. I can write this as

$$F(\langle \overline{W}, f, s^1, s^2, u \rangle) = F(\mathscr{E}) = ((C^1, L^1), (C^2, L^2)). \tag{10.2}$$

There are, of course, an infinity of possible rules, or functions, that associate to each economic environment some feasible allocation of labor expended by its members and corn produced. I will specify five conditions that are arguably necessary for an allocation mechanism F to be a satisfactory constitution in the sense I require. These conditions are to be viewed as restrictions on the behavior of the rule F, or axioms, that commit it to respecting the public ownership by agents of the external world and their self-ownership in the sense discussed.

Axiom 10.1 Pareto Optimality   In any environment $\mathscr{E}$, F should assign some Pareto optimal allocation.

That is, it should be impossible to find another feasible allocation of the given environment $\mathscr{E}$ that gives both of the agents greater utility than the allocation $F(\mathscr{E})$.

Axiom 10.2 Land Monotonicity   Let $F(\mathscr{E})$ be the allocation F assigns in an environment $\mathscr{E}$ in which the amount of land is $\overline{W}$, and now consider a new environment $\mathscr{E}^*$ in which the amount of land has increased to $\overline{W}^*$, but everything else remains the same as in $\mathscr{E}$. Then at the allocation $F(\mathscr{E}^*)$, both agents should be at least as well off in terms of welfare as they are at $F(\mathscr{E})$.

Formally, let $\mathscr{E} = \langle \overline{W}, f, s^1, s^2, u \rangle$ and $\mathscr{E}^* = \langle \overline{W}^*, f, s^1, s^2, u \rangle$ and $\overline{W}^* > \overline{W}$. Then $u(F^i(\mathscr{E}^*)) \geq u(F^i(\mathscr{E}))$, for $i = 1, 2$, where $F^i(\mathscr{E}) = (C^i, L^i)$ is the allocation under the mechanism F to agent i in the economic environment $\mathscr{E}$.

Land Monotonicity is intended as a necessary condition of public ownership of the land. We do not know precisely what such public ownership means, but it should at least require that no agent is harmed by an increase in the amount of a resource that is publicly owned. Axiom 10.2 commits the constitution to respecting this requirement.

Axiom 10.3 Technological Monotonicity   Let $\mathscr{E}$ be an environment with a production function f, and now consider a new environment $\mathscr{E}^*$ in which the technology has unambiguously improved to the production function g; that is, for the same inputs, at least as much corn can be produced with g as with f. (For all vectors (W,L), $g(W,L) \geq f(W,L)$.) Then each agent should be at least as well off in terms of welfare at $F(\mathscr{E}^*)$ as at $F(\mathscr{E})$.

Formally, let $\mathscr{E} = \langle \overline{W}, f, s^1, s^2, u \rangle$ and let $\mathscr{E}^* = \langle \overline{W}, g, s^1, s^2, u \rangle$ with $g \geq f$. Then for $i = 1, 2$, $u(F^i(\mathscr{E}^*)) \geq u(F^i(\mathscr{E}))$.

Technological Monotonicity represents the public property right that agents have in the technology, which is taken to be part of the external world. We do not know precisely what such public ownership means, but it should at least require that as the technology improves, neither agent should be rendered worse off. The motivation for this axiom is just the same as for Land Monotonicity.

Axiom 10.4 Limited Self-Ownership   Let $\mathscr{E} = \langle \overline{W}, f, s^1, s^2, u \rangle$ be an economic environment with $s^1 \geq s^2$. (The first agent is the relatively skilled one.) Then the first agent should be rendered at least as well off under F's action as the second agent. That is,

$$u(F^1(\mathscr{E})) \geq u(F^2(\mathscr{E})).$$

Limited Self-Ownership has an obvious motivation. Whatever self-ownership of skill means, it should at least imply that the more skilled agent fares at least as well in terms of welfare as the other one, because they are otherwise identical (that is, in terms of preferences). The self-ownership is modified as "limited" because self-ownership arguably could require much more than this. (For instance, it could require that an agent who is strictly more skilled than another should do strictly better under the constitution, which Axiom 10.4 does not say.) It is noteworthy that Limited Self-Ownership is, in fact, an axiom of self-ownership in a world in which external assets are publicly owned. The axiom implies that, if $s^1 = s^2$, then the agents be rendered equally well off at the allocation F assigns. The equal treatment of identical agents must come from their having equal rights in land and technology.

Axiom 10.5 Protection of Infirm Let $\mathscr{E} = \langle \overline{W}, f, s^1, s^2, u \rangle$ be an economic environment where the first agent is Able and the second is Infirm ($s^1 \geq s^2$). Then, under F's allocation, Infirm should not suffer by virtue of Able's ability. That is, Infirm should derive at least the welfare in $\mathscr{E}$ that he would derive in the environment $\mathscr{E}^* = \langle \overline{W}, f, s^2, s^2, u \rangle$ where the other agent is as unskilled as he is.

$$\text{Formally, } u(F^2(\mathscr{E})) \geq u(F^2(\mathscr{E}^*)). \tag{10.3}$$

Protection of Infirm can be summarized as requiring that Infirm should not suffer by virtue of Able's ability. That is precisely what it means to say that he should not be rendered worse off in the world $\mathscr{E}$ than he would have been had the other's skill level been reduced to his own. Alternatively, it can be said that the weaker agent should not suffer a negative externality from the skill differential that exists between the two of them.

I am not sure whether Axiom 10.5 represents a property right of public ownership of the external world or of self-ownership. It is, in any case, an axiom for an economic constitution that has independent appeal. The axiom does not commit Able to sharing the fruits of his relative advantage over Infirm; it only requires that Infirm not suffer by virtue of Able's superior skill. In addition, Limited Self-Ownership requires that the mechanism F assign an allocation giving rise to identical welfares for the two agents in the event they have the same skill—in a world $\mathscr{E}^* = \langle \overline{W}, f, s^2, s^2, u \rangle$. (Note that in $\mathscr{E}^*$, each agent has at least as much skill as the other, and by Limited Self-Ownership it follows that each must end up with at least as much welfare as the other, so they are assigned a welfare-equalizing allocation.) Thus, Limited Self-Ownership implies *symmetry*: that identical agents should be identically treated by the constitution in terms of welfare. Now Protection of Infirm says that in the world $\mathscr{E} = \langle \overline{W}, f, s^1, s^2, u \rangle$ where $s^1 \geq s^2$, the weaker agent should end up with at least the equal share of utility that he received in $\mathscr{E}^*$. Surely this is appealing, for $\mathscr{E}^*$ provides a symmetric baseline with which to compare $\mathscr{E}$.

These axioms can be illustrated by drawing the *utility possibilities sets* associated with economic environments (Figures 10.1, 10.2, and 10.3). The utility possibilities set is the locus of all utility pairs, for the two agents, that can be achieved by feasible allocations of corn and labor in an economic environment. The utility possibilities frontier is the boundary of the utility possibilities set; it is the locus of utility pairs associated with the Pareto optimal allocations that can be achieved in a given economic environment. Axiom 10.1 states that the constitution F must always choose an allocation associated with a point on the utility possibilities frontier, not a point in the interior of the utility possibilities set. Axiom 10.2 is illustrated in Figure 10.1. As the amount of land increases, the utility possibilities frontier moves outward, as it becomes possible to produce at least as much corn for the same amount of labor as before, because of the increased amount of land available. (Alternatively, one might think of an increase in land as an increase in the fertility of land—it makes no difference for the model.) In Figure 10.1 the notation $u(F(\mathscr{E}))$ means the utility pair associated with the allocation $F(\mathscr{E})$; and Axiom 10.2 requires that, in the environment with more (or more fertile) land, the utility allocation $u(F(\mathscr{E}^*))$ lie on the arc ab. Axiom 10.3 is illustrated by Figure 10.1 as well; the environment $\mathscr{E}^*$ and the larger utility possibilities set now refer to an environment in which not simply the land but also the technology has improved.

The effect of Axiom 10.4 is pictured in Figure 10.2, which shows that the allocation chosen by F must lie on or above the equal utility

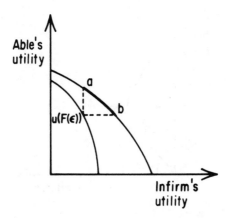

Figure 10.1 Utility possibilities set associated with resource allocation axioms 10.2 and 10.3 in the Able–Infirm world.

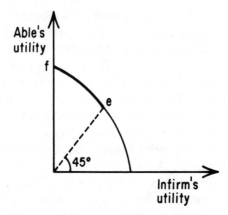

Figure 10.2 Utility possibilities set associated with resource allocation axiom 10.4 in the Able–Infirm world.

ray, on the arc *ef*. Finally, the effect of Axiom 10.5 is pictured in Figure 10.3. The larger utility possibilities frontier is associated with $\mathscr{E}$, and the smaller one is associated with $\mathscr{E}^*$ of Axiom 10.5. Limited Self-Ownership implies that in $\mathscr{E}^*$, F treats the agents identically, and so $u(F(\mathscr{E}^*))$ is the point *e* on the equal utility ray. Axiom 10.5 now requires that in $\mathscr{E}$ the allocation should induce some point on the arc *ab*, which renders the weak agent no worse off than he would be in $\mathscr{E}^*$.

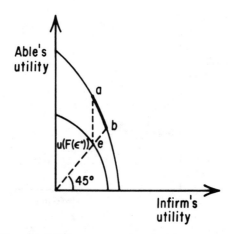

Figure 10.3 Utility possibilities set associated with resource allocation axiom 10.5 in the Able–Infirm world.

Although there are an infinity of possible constitutions F that satisfy any one of these five axioms, or even combinations of them, the remarkable fact is summarized as

Theorem 10.1 On the class of economic environments X, there is only one economic constitution F that satisfies the five axioms Pareto Optimality, Land Monotonicity, Technological Monotonicity, Limited Self-Ownership, and Protection of Infirm. That unique constitution assigns in any environment the Pareto optimal allocation of corn and labor that equalizes the utility levels of the agents.

Given any economic environment, the only constitution satisfying all five restrictions must pick out the allocation associated with the point on the utility possibility frontier that lies along the 45° ray in utility space. It is easy to verify that such a rule satisfies the five axioms; the fact of interest is the converse, that only that rule satisfies the five axioms.*

Theorem 10.1 is proved in the Appendix.

10.5 Evaluation

It is worth pausing here to review the approach that has been taken. The task has been to understand what distributions of income or welfare are consistent with various apparently competing property rights that members of a society may have, to wit, public property rights in the means of production and private rights in their own skills. Instead of trying to answer this question by looking at all possible income distributions in a given economy and deciding which ones would be acceptable given such property rights, I shifted the focus to a study of economic constitutions that lay out ground rules for how

---

* Economists will note that utility must be assumed to be interpersonally comparable for the conclusion of Theorem 10.1 to be meaningful. This is a departure from the treatment of exploitation, in which no interpersonal comparisons of utility were made. (The general definition of exploitation in Chapter 9 involves comparing a person's utility in the given state with what it would be in a counterfactual state, not comparing one person's utility with another's.) For the model of Theorem 10.1, it is assumed that utility is interpersonally comparable. Without this assumption, Axiom 10.4 would lack justification, for that axiom maintains that a necessary aspect of self-ownership is that a more skilled agent should be better off than a less skilled one, which is an interpersonal judgment. The other axioms of this model have a purely ordinal character.

labor and output should be allocated in any possible economy, consistent with the stipulated property rights. This shift of focus from economies to allocation mechanisms, or constitutions, that act on them, was crucial. Property rights were then modeled as guarantees provided by the economic constitution. The power of this method is evidenced by the theorem, which establishes that a small number of constitutional provisions suffices to determine completely the action of the allocation mechanism on any economic environment, thus establishing a unique allocation in each possible world that is consistent with the property rights postulated. The main question becomes whether the axioms of the constitution are, indeed, implied by the property rights one wishes to protect.

The theorem says that if one accepts the necessary conditions of public ownership of the external world and private ownership of self represented by the axioms, then the only permissible distribution of corn and labor is the welfare-equalizing one. Thus, public property rights in the external world trump private ownership of skills in the sense that the skilled agent never does strictly better than the weaker one. An outcome-egalitarian result is derived without recourse to the radical egalitarian premise of denying self-ownership. I make a limited effort to respect self-ownership with the Limited Self-Ownership axiom, but in the end that effort is ineffective. The axioms together allow no final inequality.

The chief defense of my method is that the axiomatic approach taken allows a characterization of an economic constitution without ever having to specify precisely what the property rights entail that one wishes the constitution to protect. One need mention only some necessary conditions of such property rights. Each of the axioms should be viewed as representing a right of one or both agents. Thus, Pareto optimality represents two rights, one for each agent: each has the right to propose a different allocation than one proposed, so long as the new allocation does not harm the other party. Likewise, Land Monotonicity and Technological Monotonicity each represent rights for both agents—each has a right to benefit by virtue of an improvement in a publicly owned resource. Limited Self-Ownership represents a right of the more skilled agent, and Protection of Infirm represents a right of the weaker one. The approach is minimalist, because it characterizes the constitution without further specification of the meaning of the property rights that one intends to represent.

Perhaps the most trenchant criticism of this approach is that it has what Nozick would call an "end-state" character. Property rights are described not by defining a process (such as use of a market or decision-making by a central committee) but by description of attributes of the final outcome. In his book Nozick is critical of end-state approaches to distributive justice and defends instead procedural approaches, which specify good procedures (such as clean markets operating from an initially clean distribution of private property) but place no a priori restrictions on outcomes. This is not the place to engage in that debate. But I note simply that it is not so easy to define a process that implements public ownership as it is to define one implementing private ownership. Does public ownership mean that everyone must agree on the disposition of the publicly owned asset before it can be used? That is surely too strong a condition, one that will almost never hold in any real world. Does it mean that people should vote for a central committee or a president who will decide how to use the publicly owned resource? But, in that case, what criteria do the central committee or its appointed planner use in deciding how to use the publicly owned asset? Is it not likely that the procedures they adopt are chosen on the basis of considerations of outcomes those procedures generate in usual cases? I am maintaining that the specification of a procedure implementing public ownership will take into account end-state considerations and that the end-state requirements of the axioms of Theorem 10.1 are ones that a procedure, whose purpose is to respect the property rights in question, should implement.

I remarked in Section 10.4 that the self-ownership represented by Axiom 10.4 is limited, and from the theorem it can be seen that this is necessarily so. A liberal might object and say that self-ownership requires that there be at least one world where the more skilled agent ends up strictly better off than the less skilled one in terms of welfare. Call this requirement Strong Self-Ownership. It follows immediately from Theorem 10.1 that there is no constitution that respects Strong Self-Ownership and the other axioms—for only welfare egalitarianism respects the other axioms. If Strong Self-Ownership is appended, there is an impossibility result: no allocation mechanism F exists that respects all the axioms including Strong Self-Ownership.

The theorem therefore cuts both ways. If one is strongly committed to public ownership of the external world, then one can argue that even though self-ownership is mildly protected (by Limited Self-Ownership) no outcome inequality can be defended. But a liberal committed to Strong Self-Ownership can use the theorem to argue against the moral appeal of public ownership of the external world, for it is incompatible with the Strong Self-Ownership to which he is committed.

I would like to return to the concept of people's capitalism (Section 10.1) for a final remark. Theorem 10.1 is true with any number of agents. The axioms have clear generalizations as requirements for an economic constitution operating on economic environments with many agents; and under those generalized axioms, the theorem remains true. Consider now the mechanism that implements people's capitalism. Each agent is given as private property her per capita share of the land and a per capita share in the ownership of a firm that runs the technology. (Thus, each agent shares equally in the profits or losses of that firm.) Agents then sell their labor power to the firm and rent their land to the firm, which operates the technology and sets a price for corn. An equilibrium is a set of wages (one for each degree of skill), a rental rate for the land, and a price of corn output, at which all markets (labor, land, and corn) clear. The firm demands amounts of labor of various skills and land, at these prices, to maximize its profits; and each agent supplies land and labor and demands an amount of corn, to maximize her utility given her budget, where her income is the sum of the wages, rents, and profits she receives (this last being her share of the firm's profits). Thus, the equilibrium set of wage rates, rental rate, and corn price equalizes the supplies and demands for types of labor, land, and corn. The mechanism of Equal Division Competitive Equilibrium or People's Capitalism assigns that allocation of corn and labor achieved by the market mechanism just described. Call this mechanism G.

Mechanism G violates some of the axioms, because G can easily be shown not to be welfare equalizing. In fact, G violates three axioms: Land Monotonicity, Technological Monotonicity, and Protection of Infirm. It respects Pareto Optimality and Limited Self-Ownership. We have, finally, another argument against people's capitalism as an implementation of Marxist concerns. If the restrictions on an economic constitution represented by Axioms 10.2, 10.3, and 10.5 are desirable, then people's capitalism is an undesirable procedure. If public ownership of the land and technology requires land and technological monotonicity, then people's capitalism is not a method for implementing public ownership.

Even if one does not agree that public ownership of the means of production is properly represented by these axioms, they might be endorsed by virtue of appeals to justice, where justice entails something other than public ownership. Perhaps the axioms represent what it means to have "equal opportunities in regard to external assets," a concept that may differ from public ownership. If so, and if such equal opportunities are a requisite of one's economic constitution, then people's capitalism is ruled out. In fact, in the model of the theorem, equal opportunities in that sense commit one to equality of outcome, as measured by welfare.

I have shifted course dramatically since my early discussions of labor exploitation. Early on, I concluded that the roots of exploitation lay in the distribution of property. It followed that the ethical evaluation of exploitation, as measured using labor accounts, depended on an evaluation of the system of private ownership of property in the means of production, and in particular, of the distribution of such property. Historical materialism takes the view that forms of property are not immutable, and that indeed they change dramatically as the development of the productive forces proceeds. This conclusion suggested that a more general approach be taken to exploitation, one that would permit an evaluation of the kinds of inequalities associated with various economic structures, or systems of property rights, not just capitalist ones. So a general property-relations approach to exploitation was outlined in Chapter 9; and the labor theory of exploitation disappeared. A particular distribution of property was evaluated (and declared exploitative or otherwise) by examining the distribution of welfare it gave rise to rather than the distribution of labor it effected. In discussing public ownership in this chapter, I have continued in this vein, making no mention of embodied labor time. Instead, I have moved property rights, and their effect on the distribution of welfare, to center stage.

11

Epilogue

A goal of this book has been to demonstrate that the central Marxist concepts of exploitation and class do not require a special logic for their construction. They can be studied in a model of a private property system, using standard tools of microeconomic analysis. I have been principally interested in exploitation as the route through which Marxism builds its critique of private ownership of the means of production, from an ethical point of view. This analysis required, first, the definition and exploration of the consequences of exploitation, which I did using a heterodox approach. The Marxist element of this hybrid approach involved the use of the notion (through Chapter 7) that a person is exploited if the labor he expends in production is greater than the labor embodied in the goods he can purchase with his revenues from production. The non-Marxist element in the development of Chapters 2, 4, and 6 involved establishing a relationship between exploitation and class without reliance on the labor theory of value. Neoclassical equilibrium theory was used to reconstruct Marxist concepts in a way that purges them of what I think is the principal weakness of the Marxist analysis, namely, the labor theory of value.

The crucial question remains: Why should exploitation, defined by calculating labor accounts, be considered a bad thing? My argument is that a person's attitude toward exploitation must derive from the moral status of the distribution of the alienable means of production, which is the cause of exploitation. In Chapter 5 I discussed the principal ways in which differential ownership of the alienable means of production can emerge and questioned their moral legitimacy. I must emphasize that for Marx the problem was much simpler than it is for us, for his approach was largely historical. He argued that the original or primitive accumulation of private property in the hands of a few, who then became capitalists, took place by various forms of robbery and plunder. He did not raise the more refined question of how one would view differential ownership if it came about by virtue of differential hard work, rates of time preference, risk-taking behavior, and the like.

In contemporary capitalist and socialist economies, however, these questions naturally arise, for in capitalist countries today, people differentiate themselves with respect to wealth in some part as a consequence of these different personal behaviors. And in many socialist countries, private property is being introduced on a limited scale, and will give rise to differential wealth, class, and welfare for the same reasons. One can argue, nevertheless, that the principal instances of inequality are due either directly or indirectly to robbery and plunder. The massive inequality in the capitalist, quasi-fascist dictatorships in many parts of the world is such an instance. And even in the democratic capitalist states, principally of Western Europe, North America, and Japan, it is probably the case that significant inequalities last in families for generations. The very poor in capitalist countries (often immigrants) are, for the most part, either the direct victims of robbery and plunder (perhaps of events that took place in fascist states) or the descendants of such victims. And the very rich are often the descendants of those who gained their wealth by reprehensible methods. Even when they are not, the question remains whether it is fair to inherit wealth from someone who earned it by the exercise of his own "talents." Because inheritance nullifies equality of opportunity for the new generation, a commitment to such equality would impugn even an originally clean multigenerational capitalism.

Some of the arguments I raised in Chapter 5 questioned whether self-ownership is ethically defensible. Should a person have a right to the income stream that will accrue, under a market system, to her inborn talents, which include propensities to take risks and saving behavior as well as more conventional skills? The principal liberal (or neoconservative) argument for capitalism is that she should. Although that claim is by no means obvious, I wish to emphasize that probably very little of the inequality one observes in capitalist society is attributable to self-ownership of that kind. There are certainly variations among individuals with respect to inborn talents, but the effect of the environment into which one is born is probably far more important for the development of one's talents than are one's genes.

And most of the relevant variation in environments (which gives rise to the behaviors differentiating economic success under capitalism) is directly linked to differences in wealth and class. Thus, differential opportunities that people face because of the existence of private property in the alienable means of production determine the largest part of their differential personal attributes, which partially account for their fortune in a capitalist system. Even if one does not wish to adopt a radical position against self-ownership, much of the inequality of capitalist societies can be attributed to robbery and plunder some generations back, or to luck, an instance of which is inheritance.

I propose that self-ownership of productive talents need not be denied to construct a convincing argument against the massive inequalities existing in the capitalist world today. People could be granted the right to returns on their natural gifts, and if the initial slate with respect to property and educational opportunity were clean enough, and wiped clean for each generation, there would be very little inequality of outcome. But it is necessary at least to put forth the point that the ownership of one's natural talents is not an obviously defensible notion, as liberal argument has it, because liberal political philosophy hangs so much on that premise. Indeed, even granting that premise, their conclusion hardly follows. So long as private property exists as an institution, it is for all practical purposes impossible to make and keep the slate clean.

In Chapters 8 and 9 I summarized several modern approaches to historical materialism; again, my goal was not a comprehensive account, but a highlighting of the notion of the transiency of property forms in the Marxist view of history. Whereas capitalist ideology views both private property in the alienable means of production and self-ownership as the natural institutions that have finally emerged as corollary to a rather immutable human nature, Marxism views property forms as much less stable, even if there is some constancy in human nature itself (a point I have not discussed). The classic historical materialist argument explains the evolution of property forms by an efficiency argument; I have not evaluated that argument but have presented it to remark on the transiency of the capitalist system and its associated ethics from the historical materialist viewpoint. If each economic structure develops a political and legal superstructure to support its property relations, then capitalist law and politics are in a subservient role to private property, and any independent morality one might ascribe to capitalism on the basis of the claimed morality of its law and politics is called into question. Another thesis of Marxism is that ideology, as opposed to law and politics, may be determined to a large extent by property relations. G. A. Cohen's version of historical materialism does not view that as an essential claim, whereas other versions do. Many have discussed the legitimation process, by which an ideology is developed in a capitalist system (for instance, through the media) that justifies capitalism and creates in people preferences for the attributes of capitalism.

Also in Chapter 9 I argued that the Marxist statistic of exploitation does not properly reflect the inequalities in the initial distribution of assets that, I claim, is its raison d'être. An alternative approach to exploitation entirely innocent of embodied labor calculations was proposed; this approach was based directly on property relations. The Marxist definition of exploitation is not the best tool for either positive or normative purposes. It is conceptually simpler, and more robust, to represent one's concerns with the consequences of an unequal distribution of property directly instead of taking the circuitous route through surplus labor.

I began Chapter 10 with a presentation of various reasons one might have for opposing a capitalist system, even if it began with a clean slate in which each owned exactly his per capita share of all alienable and natural resources. On the basis of those arguments, I claim that the antidote to the inequalities arising from differential ownership of assets in the external world is not equal ownership of those assets, but public ownership, which entails annihilation of private property of the appropriate kinds. It is not clear, though, what public ownership of the farms and factories means; and this is not surprising. History shows that property forms have evolved in ways far more complex than anyone, blinded by his own historical experience, can predict.

The last part of Chapter 10 was rather experimental. I took an agnostic approach to the meaning of public ownership, insisting only that it requires certain consequences for the welfare of the public. To wit, if the publicly owned means of production become more efficient or abundant, then everyone should benefit. I then claimed that, at least in one simple model of the problem, no inequality of final welfare could be sustained with that plank in an economic constitution, even if, a priori, some efforts were made to respect a person's right to benefit differentially by virtue of differential skill. It is important not to lose sight of the forest for the trees in this argument. Certainly the little model cannot provide a definitive answer to the question of what kinds of inequality are permissible with public ownership. It is intended merely to show that one need not necessarily take the radical view of denying self-ownership as a premise in order to show that the kinds of inequality which the liberal argument for capitalism attempts to justify are not justified. Public ownership of the external world, even granting some self-ownership, may be sufficient to constrain final outcomes to be quite equal. Someone who wishes to oppose the kinds of inequality associated with capitalism need not begin by countering the libertarian premise that we each have a right to our own kidneys. (Perhaps, as a conclusion, that right will be challenged, but it need not be as a premise. In any case, a great deal of inequality can be expunged before one needs to face the kidney question.)

The techniques I have used to explain the insights of Marxist economic philosophy have been quite circumscribed. I wish to offer an apology whose purpose is to assure the reader that Marxism has much more to offer to the analysis of capitalism than just what I have discussed. Marxism is concerned with analytic goals other than the demonstration of economic injustice; some of these concern the inefficiencies of capitalism (briefly referred to in Chapter 10) and some concern the type of societies and persons that capitalism creates, a type that may be undesirable for reasons other than injustice. The latter point relates to the theme of self-realization. Marxism argues that the people who are created by a private property system are by and large unfulfilled. There *is* a degree of immutability of human nature, and that nature is not well served by the behaviors and preferences that people adopt in capitalist society. This issue is not coextensive with considerations of economic justice: it is a shame if capitalism stunts human potential, even if it stunts it equally for everyone.

I offer this defense of my method: I have tried to show that one need not be annointed with special grace to view Marxist arguments in economic philosophy as cogent. The principal ideas can be explained simply, and with tools that were not built especially for the task. There is no special logic or language needed to make the main points, although I do think special language is valuable when it properly summarizes the insights of a theory. Marxism should be distinguished from other social thought, not by its tools, but by the questions it raises. Those questions, as I have said, come principally from its analysis of history, centrally organized around the categories of class and economic determinism. As I stated in Chapter 1, much of Marxist historical method has been absorbed by historians more generally, so it is hard to define what it means today to be a Marxist. There is little point to having a crisis about that identity.

This is not to say that the models I have used make the points in the strongest possible way. I close with an example. Contemporary economics has done little to develop a useful theory of endogenous preference formation. In standard models the story begins with a set of agents, each of whom is endowed with certain property (of the alienable and inalienable varieties) and preferences. For certain purposes, this is a good place to start; one can say that the endowments and preferences of the people were determined by history, before the present analysis starts. I have taken this viewpoint as well. Whereas I have spent considerable space discussing the history that might have determined the initial endowments of agents in these models, and how that might cause us to question the legitimacy of those endowments, hardly any space has been devoted to discussing where people's preferences come from. My topic has been the inequality of welfare produced by private ownership of the means of production, but I have taken as given and unanalyzed the utility functions—the conceptions of welfare—that people have. There is therefore a key dimension along which the autonomy of persons, in capitalist society, could be challenged; this I have not exploited. For, if people's conceptions of welfare are themselves determined by the economic structure in which they live, then a welfare distribution might stand condemned for the further reason that the structure has shaped those conceptions. Having a theory of how capitalism (or any economic structure) shapes preferences would add to the story.

Appendix: Statements and Proofs of Theorems

Statement and Proof of Theorem 4.2

Theorem 4.2 Let $\{A,L;b\}$ be a technology and real-wage vector. Let A be indecomposable. Then $\pi > 0$ if and only if $e > 0$, where π is the rate of profit at equilibrium and e is the rate of exploitation.

Proof. The rate of profit π and equilibrium price vector p are the solution of

$$p = (1 + \pi)p(A + bL) \tag{A.1}$$

(see Equation 4.23). Thus, p is a left-hand eigenvector of the matrix $A + bL$. By the Frobenius-Perron theorem, there is a right-hand eigenvector x for $A + bL$ associated with the same eigenvalue $1/(1 + \pi)$. That is,

$$x = (1 + \pi)(A + bL)x. \tag{A.2}$$

Premultiplying (A.2) by the vector Λ of labor values and rearranging yields

$$\Lambda x = \Lambda Ax + \Lambda bLx + \pi\Lambda(A + bL)x$$

$$= (\Lambda A + L)x - (1 - \Lambda b)Lx + \pi\Lambda(A + bL)x,$$

$$= \Lambda x - (1 - \Lambda b)Lx + \pi\Lambda(A + bL)x, \text{ from (4.18)}$$

which implies that

$$(1 - \Lambda b)Lx = \pi\Lambda(A + bL)x. \tag{A.3}$$

$(A + bL)x$ is a nonzero vector by (A.2), and $\Lambda > 0$ because A is indecomposable. Therefore, $\Lambda(A + bL)x > 0$ and the right-hand side of

(A.3) is a positive number if and only if π is positive. But the left-hand side of (A.3) is positive if and only if $(1 - \Lambda b) > 0$, which is the condition for $e > 0$ (see Equation 4.19). This proves that $\pi > 0$ if and only if $e > 0$. ∎

Statement and Proof of Theorem 10.1

Theorem 10.1 On the domain of economic environments X, there is a unique allocation mechanism F satisfying Pareto Optimality, Technological Monotonicity, Land Monotonicity, Limited Self-Ownership, and Protection of Infirm. F equalizes the utility of the agents.

Remark. Although economic environments have been specified as vectors of the form $\mathscr{E} = \langle \overline{W}, f, s^1, s^2, u \rangle$ in the text, we can dispense with listing $\overline{W}$ and instead view the land as subsumed in the specification of the production function. If $f(W,L)$ is a production function in $\mathscr{E}$, define $g(L) \equiv f(\overline{W},L)$. Then the economic environment $\mathscr{E}$ can be written more economically as

$$\mathscr{E}^* = \langle g, s^1, s^2, u \rangle.$$

Land Monotonicity now appears as a special case of Technological Monotonicity. The theorem will be proved for the domain of environments X^* consisting of all environments of the form of $\mathscr{E}^*$, where $g(L)$ can be any production function that is increasing in labor.

Definition The *induced utility mapping* associated with an allocation mechanism F is the function

$$u_F(\mathscr{E}) = (u(F^i(\mathscr{E})), u(F^2(\mathscr{E}))),$$

which assigns to each $\mathscr{E}$ the point in utility space associated with the allocation chosen by F. $F^i(\mathscr{E})$ is the corn–labor allocation assigned to the ith agent.

The proof of Theorem 10.1 follows from two lemmas.

Lemma A.1 Consider the class of economic environments

$$X^*_{s^1, s^2, u} = \{\langle g, s^1, s^2, u \rangle \in X^* \mid (s^1, s^2, u) \text{ is fixed}\}.$$

If F satisfies Pareto Optimality and Technological Monotonicity, then F is a monotone utility path mechanism on $X^*_{s^1, s^2, u}$.

Definition A *monotone utility path mechanism* assigns for any environment $\mathscr{E}$ the allocation associated with the intersection of some fixed monotonic path in utility space with the Pareto frontier of $\mathscr{E}$. It follows that F is a monotone utility path solution on X^* if and only if for any pair of environments $\mathscr{E}$ and $\mathscr{E}^*$ in X^*, either $u_F(\mathscr{E}) \geq u_F(\mathscr{E}^*)$ or $u_F(\mathscr{E}^*) \geq u_F(\mathscr{E})$.

Proof of Lemma A.1.

1. Let $\mathscr{E}^1 = \langle g^1, s^1, s^2, u \rangle$ and $\mathscr{E}^2 = \langle g^2, s^1, s^2, u \rangle$ be any two environments in $X^*_{s^1, s^2, u}$. Define the production function $g^*(L) \equiv \max[g^1(L), g^2(L)]$. g^* is an admissible production function, so the environment $\langle g^*, s^1, s^2, u \rangle = \mathscr{E}^*$ is in $X^*_{s^1, s^2, u}$.

2. By Technological Monotonicity $u_F(\mathscr{E}^*) \geq u_F(\mathscr{E}^1)$ and $u_F(\mathscr{E}^*) \geq u_F(\mathscr{E}^2)$, because $g^* \geq g^i$, $i = 1,2$. But note that $F(\mathscr{E}^*)$ must be a feasible allocation for one of $\mathscr{E}^1$ or $\mathscr{E}^2$ by the definition of g^*; say, for $\mathscr{E}^1$. Then, by Pareto Optimality, $u_F(\mathscr{E}^*) = u_F(\mathscr{E}^1)$, so $u_F(\mathscr{E}^1) \geq u_F(\mathscr{E}^2)$. This proves F is a monotone utility path mechanism on $X^*_{s^1, s^2, u}$. ∎

Lemma A.2 Consider the environment $\mathscr{E}_\alpha = \langle g_\alpha, s^1, s^2, u \rangle$ where g_α is the constant production function:

$$g_\alpha(L) \equiv \alpha, \text{ for some } \alpha \geq 0.$$

Pareto Optimality, Limited Self-Ownership, and Protection of Infirm imply that F equalizes utilities on $\mathscr{E}_\alpha$.

Proof.

1. By Pareto Optimality, no labor is expended at $F(\mathscr{E})$, because labor is pointless with the production function g_α.

2. Let $s^1 \geq s^2$. Limited Self-Ownership implies Symmetry: in an environment in which $s^1 = s^2$, both agents receive the same consumption–labor bundle. In particular,

$$F(\langle g_\alpha, s^2, s^2, u \rangle) = \left(\left(\frac{\alpha}{2}, 0 \right), \left(\frac{\alpha}{2}, 0 \right) \right) \quad \text{and}$$

$$u_F(\langle g_\alpha, s^2, s^2, u \rangle) = \left(u\left(\frac{\alpha}{2}, 0 \right), u\left(\frac{\alpha}{2}, 0 \right) \right).$$

3. By Protection of Infirm,

$$u(F^2(\mathscr{E})) \geq u(F^2(\langle g_\alpha, s^2, s^2, u \rangle)) = u\left(\frac{\alpha}{2}, 0 \right).$$

By Limited Self-Ownership,

$$u(F^1(\mathscr{E})) \geq u(F^2(\mathscr{E})) = u\left(\frac{\alpha}{2}, 0\right).$$

Therefore,

$$u_F(\mathscr{E}) \geq \left(u\left(\frac{\alpha}{2}, 0\right), u\left(\frac{\alpha}{2}, 0\right)\right).$$

But $(u(\alpha/2, 0), u(\alpha/2, 0))$ is Pareto optimal in $\mathscr{E}$, so $u_F(\mathscr{E}) = (u(\alpha/2, 0),$ $u(\alpha/2, 0))$, which proves the lemma. ∎

Proof of Theorem 10.1 By Lemma A.1, an allocation mechanism satisfying Pareto Optimality and Technological Monotonicity traces out some monotone utility path on the subdomain $X^*_{s1,s2,u}$. By Lemma A.2, the monotone path must be the 45° equal-utility ray, because any point on that ray can be generated from $F(\mathscr{E}_\alpha)$, for some α. (This is the case as long as $u(\alpha/2, 0)$ increases without bound as α increases.) Hence, on every subdomain $X^*_{s1,s2,u}$, F is the Pareto optimal, equal-utility mechanism, and the theorem is proved. ∎

The argument presented here can be refined considerably. In particular, the class of admissible production functions can be made smaller and the theorem remains true. For example, one may allow only production functions for which $g(0) = 0$ and which exhibit constant or decreasing returns to scale in labor. Details are presented in the paper by Moulin and Roemer cited in the notes to Chapter 10.

Bibliographical Notes

1. Introduction

For an accessible social history of Marxism that traces Marxism's influence and development over the past century through some key figures who tried to put it into practice in building socialism, see John Gurley's *Challengers to Capitalism: Marx, Lenin, Stalin, and Mao* (New York: W. W. Norton, 1979). The falseness of the theory of the falling rate of profit is discussed in my book *Analytical Foundations of Marxian Economic Theory* (Cambridge: Cambridge University Press, 1981), chaps. 4 and 5. The original contribution on this subject is due to N. Okishio, "Technical Changes and the Rate of Profit," *Kobe University Economic Review* 7 (1961), 113–114. Other contributors to the debate on that question are to be found in the relevant chapters of the book just referred to. The falseness of the labor theory of value is much discussed in Marxist literature; references are given in Chapter 4.

3. Feudalism and Capitalism

For a classic work on feudalism, see Marc Bloch's *Feudal Society*. A recent and controversial book proposing the "economic law" directing feudal economy is Guy Bois's, *The Crisis of Feudalism* (Cambridge: Cambridge University Press, 1984). Douglass North and Robert Thomas present the implicit contract view of feudalism in *The Rise of the Western World* (Cambridge: Cambridge University Press, 1973). North's more recent book, *Structure and Change in Economic History* (New York: W. W. Norton, 1982) presents a theory of feudalism much closer to the Marxist one. For a challenge to the implicit contract view of feudalism and an interesting contrast of feudalism and capitalism, see Robert Brenner's, "The Origins of Capitalist Development: A Critique of Neo-Smithian Marxism," *New Left Review* 104 (1977). S. F. C. Milsom's *Historical Foundations of the Common Law* (Toronto: Butterworths,

1981) displays the complexity of feudal property relations. Rodney H. Hilton has written much on the topic of the transition from feudalism to capitalism and on feudal revolts such as the Wat Tyler rebellion. See, for example, his *Bond Men Made Free* (London: Temple Smith, 1977). For a discussion of whether proletarians are forced to sell their labor power under capitalism, see G. A. Cohen's, "The Structure of Proletarian Unfreedom," *Philosophy and Public Affairs* (Winter 1983), pp. 3–33. Jon Elster, in *Ulysses and the Sirens* (Cambridge: Cambridge University Press, 1979), discusses the general problem of binding oneself to constrain one's future behavior, an issue that comes up in the implicit contract interpretation of feudalism. For a discussion of the role of financial institutions in corporate control in modern capitalism, see David Kotz's, *Bank Control of Large Corporations in the United States* (Berkeley: University of California Press, 1978).

4. Exploitation and Profits

Although the concepts of socially necessary labor time and exploitation were developed by Marx in *Capital*, vol. 1, the first mathematical statement of the ideas in book form in the English language along the lines of this chapter is in Michio Morishima's *Marx's Economics* (Cambridge: Cambridge University Press, 1973). Prior to that, various authors, notably Nobuko Okishio and Francis Seton as well as Morishima, had developed these methods in articles written in the early 1960s. (References to these works are available in Morishima's book.) The notion of embodied labor time goes back much further than Marx, at least to David Ricardo and Adam Smith. The modern formulation of it is based in large part on the Leontief input–output model, although the concept can be formulated in more general economic models (see, for example, J. Roemer, *Analytical Foundations of Marxian Economic Theory* [Cambridge: Cambridge University Press, 1981]).

The "fundamental Marxian theorem" is the formulation of Okishio and Morishima; their innovation was to note that the necessity of exploitation for profits could be demonstrated without insisting on the labor theory of value, the claim that prices are determined by or proportional to embodied labor values. Price are determined in the market and have no intrinsic relation to labor values; they are set by the equilibrium condition that the rate of profit must be equal across all sectors if all goods are to be produced by profit-maximizing capitalists. By this demonstration, Marxist economics was liberated from the need to press the false labor theory of value, for the essential feature of the exploitation of workers by capitalists was shown not to depend on it. Nevertheless, many writers believe that the labor theory of value is essential to Marxist insights, and they object to the modern reconstruction. These arguments are summarized in I. Steedman (ed.), *The Value Controversy* (London: New Left Books, 1981).

Associated with the belief in the importance of the labor theory of value is an interest in the "transformation problem"—the problem of how, precisely, to formulate the relationship of equilibrium prices to embodied labor values. Marx realized there was a problem, because prices would not be proportional to labor values in economies in which the "organic composition of capital" differed across sectors. The labor theory of value became ramified as the claim that labor values *determined* prices—that, although labor values were not proportional to prices, they could be shown to be more fundamental in an economic sense than prices. Many writers over the past century have spilled ink on the transformation problem. An influential argument against the labor theory of value and against the importance of the transformation problem is put forward by Paul Samuelson in "Understanding the Marxian Notion of Exploitation: A Summary of the So-Called Transformation Problem between Marxian Values and Competitive Prices," *Journal of Economic Literature* IX (1971). Samuelson's article initiated a debate between Samuelson and William Baumol in the pages of that journal. Ian Steedman, in *Marx after Sraffa* (London: New Left Books, 1977) presented further arguments against the cogency of the transformation problem; and in *A General Theory of Exploitation and Class* (Cambridge: Harvard University Press, 1982), I showed that to preserve classic Marxist insights concerning the relationship of exploitation to class, one has no choice but to adopt the position that embodied labor values are determined by equilibrium prices, not the other way around. (The relationship of exploitation to class is presented in Chapter 6.)

An excellent summary and discussion of the modern Marxist economic models is in Jon Elster's, *Making Sense of Marx* (Cambridge: Cambridge University Press, 1985), chap. 3.

5. The Morality of Exploitation

The Generalized Commodity Exploitation Theorem, which shows that each produced commodity that is an input into production is "exploited" if it is chosen as the numeraire commodity, has been discussed by various authors, including Samuel Bowles and Herbert Gintis, "Structure and Practice in the Labor Theory of Value," *Review of Radical Political Economics* 12, no. 4 (Winter 1981) and J. Roemer, *A General Theory of Exploitation and Class* (Cambridge, Mass.: Harvard University Press, 1982), p. 186. Marxists have argued that the commodity labor power differs from other productive inputs in that there is a struggle over the extraction of the use value, labor, from the input of labor power that is purchased by the capitalist, a struggle that does not take place in extracting the energy from coal. The voluminous literature on the evolution of the capitalist labor process discusses the ways that capitalism has designed to extract labor efficiently. Important books in this area are by Harry Braverman, *Labor and Monopoly Capital: The Degradation of Work in the*

Twentieth Century (New York: Monthly Review Press, 1974) and by Richard Edwards, *Contested Terrain: The Transformation of the Workplace in the Twentieth Century* (New York: Basic Books, 1979). See also the article by Stephen Marglin, "What Do Bosses Do? The Origins and Functions of Hierarchy in Capitalist Production," *Review of Radical Political Economics* (Summer 1974).

The most influential statement justifying laissez-faire capitalism in recent years is the work of the libertarian philosopher Robert Nozick, *Anarchy, State, and Utopia* (New York: Basic Books, 1974). In chap. 8, Nozick attacks the basis for condemning capitalism on grounds of exploitation. Much of Nozick's argument is aimed at justifying capitalist inequality by showing that highly differential ownership of property can come about in morally clean ways. For a challenge to Nozick, see the writings of G. A. Cohen on private property, especially "Nozick on Appropriation," *New Left Review* 150 (1984) and "Self-Ownership, World-Ownership, and Equality, Part II," *Social Philosophy and Policy* (Spring 1986). For further discussion of differential rates of time preference and exploitation, see J. Roemer, "Are Socialist Ethics Consistent with Efficiency?" *Philosophical Forum* XIV (Spring–Summer 1983).

The view that interest and profits are rewards to waiting is almost ubiquitous in neoclassical economics. The related idea that profits are a return to the scarce factor capital was challenged in a formal way in the 1960s in a debate that became known as the Cambridge controversy in capital theory. In the end, the formal points made in this debate were not so fundamental with regard to the basic issues I have discussed. The debate is summarized by G. C. Harcourt in *Some Cambridge Controversies in the Theory of Capital* (Cambridge: Cambridge University Press, 1972) and by Christopher Bliss in *Capital Theory and the Distribution of Income* (New York: American Elsevier, 1975).

There are many studies by historians and sociologists showing how capitalism proletarianizes populations through technological change, the development of markets, and other advances. This position is developed systematically by Immanuel Wallerstein, *The Modern World System I: Capitalist Agriculture and the Origins of the European World-Economy* (New York: Academic Press, 1974). Wallerstein has written voluminously, and there are many writers who work along similar lines. The history of the effect of the Green Revolution on proletarianization of the Mexican peasantry is told by Cynthia Hewitt de Alcantara, *Modernizing Mexican Agriculture: Socioeconomic Implications of Technological Change 1940–1970* (Geneva: United Nations Research Institute for Social Development, 1976).

There is a long history of writers who have claimed that intelligence differs across races. The history of this debate, and the current scientifically accurate position that there is no evidence for this claim, are related by Stephen J. Gould in *The Mismeasure of Man* (New York: W. W. Norton, 1981). The most prominent of the writers who resuscitated this view in the 1960s was Arthur Jensen in "How Much Can we Boost IQ and Scholastic Achievement?" *Har-*

vard Educational Review 33 (1969), 1–33. Richard Herrnstein, "IQ," *Atlantic Monthly* (September 1971), 43–64, maintained that nature has color-coded people so that a person can make instant inferences about the intelligence of another with whom he is dealing. In *The Science and Politics of IQ* (Potomac, Md.: Lawrence Erlbaum Associates, 1974), Leon Kamin reported his discovery that the data supposedly reporting "twin experiments," upon which the claims of a racial intelligence differential were based, were fabricated. The argument of James Q. Wilson and Richard J. Herrnstein's *Crime and Human Nature* (1985), that criminal behavior is the consequence of brain damage suffered by black infants in utero as a result of the bad habits of their mothers, is challenged, once again, by Leon Kamin in his book review of Wilson and Herrnstein in *Scientific American* (February 1986), pp. 22–27.

The data on wealth and inheritance are taken from D. W. Haslett, "Is Inheritance Justified?" *Philosophy and Public Affairs* 15 (1986), 122–155. Haslett argues against inheritance and for capitalism. For an empirical study of inheritance in the United States, see John Brittain's, *Inheritance and the Inequality of National Wealth* (Washington, D.C.: Brookings Institution, 1978). The facts on effective tax rates on inherited wealth are presented by Lester Thurow, *The Impact of Taxes on the American Economy* (New York: Praeger, 1971).

Joseph Schumpeter's views on entrepreneurial ability and capitalism are presented in his *Capitalism, Socialism and Democracy*, Part III, reprinted as *Can Capitalism Survive?* (New York: Harper & Row, 1978).

6. The Emergence of Class

The models in this chapter are simplified versions of those analyzed in my book, *A General Theory of Exploitation and Class* (Cambridge, Mass.: Harvard University Press, 1982). In that book, the economies have many goods and so the analysis is more difficult, but the Class–Exploitation Correspondence and the Class–Wealth Correspondence are still true as discussed (the latter being true if preferences are well-behaved in a certain sense). Lenin (*The Development of Capitalism in Russia*, 1895) and Mao Zedong ("Analysis of the Classes in the Chinese Countryside," 1925) wrote their sociological analyses of the class structures of the countries prior to the revolutions and early in their careers. There are many historical studies of class struggle. Of special note is the recent careful work by G. E. M. de Ste Croix, *The Class Struggle in the Ancient Greek World* (London: Duckworth, 1981), which maintains that the transformation of Greek society is best understood by the analysis of class, not status or interest group. The locus classicus arguing for the role of class struggle in history is Marx's and Engels's *The Communist Manifesto*, written when the revolutions of 1848 were sweeping Europe.

An important issue not dealt with in this chapter is how members of a class overcome the "collective action problem" and join in class struggles, the outcome of which may be in the interest of the members of a group, even though a self-interested calculation reveals to each individual that he should not participate; the costs to him of participating may be larger than the marginal benefit he will derive, if the group is already strong enough to win without him. For a discussion of this problem, see Jon Elster, *Making Sense of Marx* (Cambridge: Cambridge University Press, 1985), chap. 6 on classes. Erik Olin Wright has done empirical work demonstrating the relationship between the ownership of private property of various kinds and class consciousness: see his *Classes* (London: New Left Books, 1985), and his article "What is Middle about the Middle Class?" in J. Roemer (ed.) *Analytical Marxism* (Cambridge: Cambridge University Press, 1986). Wright begins with models similar to the ones in this book. For a statistical analysis of the class composition of the modern Indian peasantry, using the five-class model described in this chapter, see Pranab Bardhan, "Class Formation in India," in his *Land, Labor and Rural Poverty: Essays in Development Economics* (New York: Columbia University Press, 1983).

The neoclassical position that workers implicitly contract to be dominated on the job so that they will produce sufficient revenues to pay high wages is maintained by Armen Alchian and Harold Demsetz in "Production, Information Costs, and Economic Organization," *American Economic Review* 62 (1972), 777–795.

7. Exploitation without a Labor Market

Much has been written on the ways in which the labor process has evolved under capitalism. Harry Braverman argues in *Labor and Monopoly Capital: The Degradation of Work in the Twentieth Century* (New York: Basic Books, 1974), using industrial histories as evidence, that the labor process did not evolve to maximize some abstract kind of production efficiency, but was molded by the necessities of capitalism: to economize on skilled labor and to keep control in the hands of capitalists. Stephen Marglin, in "What Do Bosses Do? The Origins and Functions of Hierarchy in Capitalist Production," *Review of Radical Political Economics* (Summer 1974), goes further, and maintains that, in the early history of capitalism, capitalists deliberately adopted technologies that were inferior from a productivity point of view to others, because they provided capitalists with more control over workers. For example, Marglin views the factory system, not as a technological improvement over earlier forms of production, but as a good technique for keeping workers under the watchful eye of the capitalist. Marglin's theory gives capitalists more control over history and technological change than they receive in the conventional theory of historical materialism (see Chapter 8), in which capitalists are pushed along by history with everyone else. For a contribution to the ongoing debate on this question, see David Landes, "What Do Bosses Really Do?" *Journal of Economic History* 46 (September 1986), 585–623.

On the linking of credit and labor markets in rural India, see the essays by Pranab Bardhan in *Land, Labor and Rural Poverty: Essays in Development Economics* (New York: Columbia University Press, 1984). For an interesting perspective on Marxist development economics, see by the same author "Marxist Ideas in Development Economics: An Evaluation," in J. Roemer (ed.), *Analytical Marxism* (Cambridge: Cambridge University Press, 1986). There is a substantial literature on the question of why capital hires labor instead of the other way around in modern capitalist societies. For examples, see David Miller, "Market Neutrality and the Failure of Cooperatives," *British Journal of Political Science* 11 (1981), 309–329; Louis Putterman, "On Some Recent Explanations of Why Capital Hires Labor," *Economic Inquiry* 22 (1984), 171–207; and Avner Ben-Ner, "Producer Cooperatives: Why Do They Exist in Capitalist Economies?" in Walter Powell, *The Non-Profit Sector: A Research Handbook* (New Haven: Yale University Press, 1987).

The exploitation of one country by another has been discussed by Marxists under the rubric of "unequal exchange." The initial contribution to that discussion was by Arghiri Emmanuel in *Unequal Exchange* (New York: Monthly Review Press, 1972). The ideas put forth in Section 7.6 of this chapter are developed more fully in my article "Unequal Exchange, Labor Migration and International Capital Flows: A Theoretical Synthesis," in Padma Desai (ed.), *Marxism, Central Planning and the Soviet Economy: Economic Essays in Honor of Alexander Erlich* (Cambridge, Mass.: MIT Press, 1983). On the reasons that workers might not make a revolution, even if they understand the exploitative nature of capitalism, see Adam Przeworski, "Material Interests, Class Compromise, and the Transition to Socialism," in Roemer, *Analytical Marxism*. For a debate on the centrality of domination at the point of production in the maintenance of capitalist power, see Erik Olin Wright, "The Status of the Political in the Concept of Class Structure," and J. Roemer, "Reply," both in *Politics and Society* 11 (1982), 321–342 and 375–394, respectively. A more general discussion of the loci of domination in capitalist societies is to be found in Herbert Gintis and Samuel Bowles, *Democracy and Capitalism: Property, Community, and the Contradictions of Modern Social Thought* (New York: Basic Books, 1986).

8. Historical Materialism

G. A. Cohen's *Karl Marx's Theory of History: A Defence* (Oxford: Oxford University Press, 1978) is arguably the most rigorous work of Marxist scholarship of this century. It has generated a literature of criticism and rejuvenated historical materialism as a serious idea in historical theory. Cohen's position is summarized briefly in his "Forces and Relations of Production," published in J. Roemer (ed.), *Analytical Marxism* (Cambridge: Cambridge University Press, 1986). Robert Brenner's paper, "Agrarian Class Structure and Economic Development in Pre-Industrial Europe" was originally published in

Past and Present in 1976. Brenner's argument has stimulated debate among historians concerning the causes of economic development and long-run trends in income distribution. Contributions to this debate have been collected by T. H. Ashton and C. H. E. Philpin (eds.) in *The Brenner Debate* (Cambridge: Cambridge University Press, 1985); this book also includes Brenner's reply to his critics. Another recent Brenner paper presenting his position on class struggle and the development of the productive forces is "The Social Basis of Economic Development," in Roemer, *Analytical Marxism.* Jon Elster, in chap. 5 of *Making Sense of Marx* (Cambridge: Cambridge University Press, 1985), discusses contemporary views of historical materialism, including his own criticisms of Cohen's position on functional explanation. In "The Theory of Combined and Uneven Development," published in Roemer, *Analytical Marxism,* Elster presents an argument for why the revolutionary transformation to socialism may never succeed. Other notable contributions to the debate on historical materialism are Philippe Van Parijs's paper, "Marxism's Central Puzzle," in T. Ball and J. Farr (eds.), *After Marx* (Cambridge: Cambridge University Press, 1984) and Joshua Cohen's review of G. A. Cohen's book in the *Journal of Philosophy* 79 (1982), 253–273.

9. Evolving Forms of Exploitation

Jon Elster in *Making Sense of Marx* (Cambridge: Cambridge University Press, 1985) takes Marx to task for wishful thinking concerning the evolution of societies; there was a teleological residue in Marx's historical materialism, from his Hegelian intellectual ancestry. G. A. Cohen, in *Karl Marx's Theory of History,* chap. 1 (Oxford: Oxford University Press, 1978), discusses the Hegelian roots of Marxist historical materialism. The paleobiologist Stephen J. Gould has challenged in many writings the claim that evolution necessarily leads to higher forms of life; he advocates a nonteleological evolutionary theory.

More detail on how the Marxist measure of exploitation fails to represent the phenomena for which it purports to be a statistic (such as inequality in the initial endowment of alienable assets) is presented in J. Roemer, "Should Marxists Be Interested in Exploitation?" *Philosophy and Public Affairs* (Winter 1985), reprinted in J. Roemer (ed.), *Analytical Marxism* (Cambridge: Cambridge University Press, 1986). A theorem characterizing when the Class–Wealth Correspondence fails as a result of bizarre preferences is presented in J. Roemer, *Value, Exploitation, and Class* (1986), a monograph issued in the series *Fundamentals of Pure and Applied Economics* (New York: Harwood Academic Publishers). The property-relations approach to exploitation is presented in a different, game-theoretic fashion in J. Roemer, *A General Theory of Exploitation and Class* (Cambridge, Mass.: Harvard University Press, 1982), and summarized in "New Directions in the Marxian Theory of Exploitation and Class," originally published in *Politics and Society*, no. 3, (1982) and reprinted in Roemer, *Analytical Marxism*. A further elaboration of the game-theoretic approach to property relations and exploitation is in J. Roemer, "Property Relations vs. Surplus Value in Marxian Exploitation," *Philosophy and Public Affairs* 11 (Fall 1982). Criticisms of the game-theoretic approach, and of counterfactual approaches to exploitation more generally, are put forth by Jon Elster, "Roemer versus Roemer" in that same issue of *Politics and Society*, which also contains other papers critical of this approach. The property-relations approach to exploitation has been applied to an empirical study of class consciousness and the different forms of exploitation discussed in this chapter by Erik Olin Wright in *Classes* (London: New Left Books, 1985), who analyzes Swedish and U.S. society with respect to the categories of capitalist, socialist, and status exploitation. (His nomenclature is somewhat different.)

A more detailed discussion of socialist and status exploitation as applied to existing socialist economies is provided in Roemer, *A General Theory of Exploitation and Class*, chap. 8. Charles Bettelheim lays the basis for his thesis that capitalism has been restored in the Soviet Union in his *Class Struggles in the USSR: First Period 1917–1923* and *Second Period 1923–1930* (New York: Monthly Review Press, 1976 and 1978). There is an abundant literature concerning class formation in socialist countries; for example, George Konrad and Ivan Szelenyi, in *The Intellectuals on the Road to Class Power* (New York: Harcourt Brace, Jovanovich, 1979), argue that those in possession of intellectual capital (skills of a certain type) form the new ruling class in existing socialist societies. There is a literature on income distribution and the returns to status in socialist countries too vast to summarize here, but the reader might begin with Mervyn Matthews's *Privilege in the Soviet Union* (London: Allen & Unwin, 1978) and Walter Connor's *Socialism, Politics, and Equality: Hierarchy and Change in Eastern Europe and the USSR* (New York: Columbia University Press, 1979). For a useful analysis of the economic problems of existing socialist countries and of the inefficiencies that have resulted from too literal an application of received Marxist theory to organizing these societies, see Alec Nove's *The Economics of Feasible Socialism* (London: Allen & Unwin, 1983). Nove advocates a good degree of market socialism.

10. Public Ownership of the Means of Production

The political philosophies discussed in this chapter are represented by those of John Rawls, *A Theory of Justice* (Cambridge, Mass.: Harvard University Press, 1971), Robert Nozick, *Anarchy, State, and Utopia* (New York: Basic Books, 1974), and Ronald Dworkin, "What is Equality? Equality of Welfare and Equality of Resources," in *Philosophy and Public Affairs* (Summer–Fall 1981). G. A. Cohen's proposals, which motivate the model of Able and Infirm, are summarized in "Nozick on Appropriation," *New Left Review* 150 (March/April 1985) and in "Self-Ownership, World Ownership and Equality, Part 2," *Social Philosophy and Policy* 3, no. 2 (Spring 1986).

For an interesting discussion of the history of market socialist proposals in the Eastern European countries, see Alec Nove's *An Economic Theory of Feasible Socialism* (London: Allen & Unwin, 1983). There is a large literature by Marxists who variously attack the market system; for Marx's views of communism and self-realization, see chap. 10 of Jon Elster's *Making Sense of Marx* (Cambridge: Cambridge University Press, 1985).

On the implication of Dworkin's resource egalitarianism, see John Roemer, "Equality of Talent," *Economics and Philosophy* 1 (Fall 1986) and the more technical article, "Equality of Resources Implies Equality of Welfare," *Quarterly Journal of Economics* 101 (November 1986), 751–784. These articles argue that a policy of resource egalitarianism, where resources include internal talents of people, implies equalizing the welfares of people. Variants of the model presented in Section 10.4 are developed by Hervé Moulin and John Roemer in "Public Ownership of the External World and Private Ownership of Self" (forthcoming).

People's capitalism, in which everyone initially is given an equal share in society's property and then economic activity proceeds through markets, is advocated by James Meade in *Efficiency, Equality and the Ownership of Property* (London: Allen & Unwin, 1954). Chapter 5 of his book is entitled "A Property-Owning Democracy." The allocation mechanism "equal division competitive equilibrium," in which free markets operate after an equal division of property to all, has been studied as a proposal for distributive justice in the economics literature. The outcome of that mechanism has a property called "envy-freeness," considered by many to be desirable. For discussion, see Hal Varian, "Distributive Justice, Welfare Economics and the Theory of Fairness," *Philosophy and Public Affairs* 4 (1975), 223–247.

References

Alchian, Armen, and Harold Demsetz. Production, information costs, and economic organization. *American Economic Review* 62: 777–795, 1972.

Ashton, T. H., and C. H. E. Philpin (eds.). *The Brenner Debate: Agrarian Class Structure and Economic Development in Pre-Industrial Europe.* Cambridge: Cambridge University Press, 1985.

Bardhan, Pranab. *Land, Labor and Rural Poverty: Essays in Development Economics.* New York: Columbia University Press, 1983.

—— Marxist ideas in development economics: an evaluation. In *Analytical Marxism*, ed. J. E. Roemer, pp. 64–78. Cambridge: Cambridge University Press, 1986.

Ben-Ner, Avner. Producer cooperatives: why do they exist in capitalist economies? In *The Non-Profit Sector: A Research Handbook*, ed. Walter Powell, pp. 434–449. New Haven: Yale University Press, 1987.

Bettelheim, Charles. *Class Struggles in the USSR: First Period 1917–1923.* New York: Monthly Review Press, 1976.

—— *Class Struggles in the USSR: Second Period 1923–1930.* New York: Monthly Review Press, 1978.

Bliss, Christopher. *Capital Theory and the Distribution of Income.* New York: American Elsevier, 1975.

Bloch, Marc. *Feudal Society.* Chicago: University of Chicago Press, 1961.

Bois, Guy. *The Crisis of Feudalism.* Cambridge: Cambridge University Press, 1984.

Bowles, Samuel, and Herbert Gintis. Structure and practice in the labor theory of value. *Review of Radical Political Economics* 12: 1–26, 1981.

—— *Democracy and Capitalism: Property, Community, and the Contradictions of Modern Social Thought.* New York: Basic Books, 1986.

Braverman, Harry. *Labor and Monopoly Capital: The Degradation of Work in the Twentieth Century.* New York: Monthly Review Press, 1974.

Brenner, Robert. The origins of capitalist development: a critique of neo-Smithian Marxism. *New Left Review* 104: 25–93, 1977.

—— Agrarian class structure and economic development in pre-industrial Europe. In *The Brenner Debate*, ed. T. H. Ashton and C. H. E. Philpin, pp. 10–63. Cambridge: Cambridge University Press, 1986a.

—— The social basis of economic development. In *Analytical Marxism*, ed. J. E. Roemer, pp. 23–53. Cambridge: Cambridge University Press, 1986b.

Brittain, John. *Inheritance and the Inequality of National Wealth*. Washington, D.C.: Brookings Institution, 1978.

Cheyney, Edward P. *An Introduction to the Industrial and Social History of England*. New York: Macmillan, 1923.

Cohen, G. A. *Karl Marx's Theory of History: A Defence*. Oxford: Oxford University Press, 1978.

—— The structure of proletarian unfreedom. *Philosophy and Public Affairs* 12: 3–33, 1983.

—— Nozick on Appropriation. *New Left Review* 150: 89–107, 1984.

—— Forces and relations of production. In *Analytical Marxism*, ed. J. E. Roemer, pp. 11–22. Cambridge: Cambridge University Press, 1986.

—— Self-ownership, world-ownership and equality, Part II. *Social Philosophy and Policy* 3: 77–96, 1986.

Cohen, Joshua. Karl Marx's theory of history: A defence. G. A. Cohen. *Journal of Philosophy* 79: 253–273, 1982.

Connor, Walter. *Socialism, Politics, and Equality: Hierarchy and Change in Eastern Europe and the USSR*. New York: Columbia University Press, 1979.

Dobson, R. B. *The Peasants' Revolt of 1381*. London: Macmillan, 1983.

Dworkin, Ronald. What is equality? Part 1: Equality of welfare. *Philosophy and Public Affairs* 10: 185–246, 1981.

—— What is equality? Part 2: Equality of resources. *Philosophy and Public Affairs* 10: 283–345, 1981.

Edwards, Richard. *Contested Terrain: The Transformation of the Workplace in the Twentieth Century*. New York: Basic Books, 1979.

Elster, Jon. *Ulysses and the Sirens*. Cambridge: Cambridge University Press, 1979.

—— Roemer versus Roemer. *Politics and Society* 11: 363–374, 1982.

—— *Making Sense of Marx*. Cambridge: Cambridge University Press, 1985.

—— The theory of combined and uneven development. In *Analytical Marxism*, ed. J. E. Roemer, pp. 54–63. Cambridge: Cambridge University Press, 1986.

Emmanuel, Arghiri. *Unequal Exchange*. New York: Monthly Review Press, 1972.

Gould, Stephen J. *The Mismeasure of Man*. New York: W. W. Norton, 1981.

Gurley, John. *Challengers to Capitalism: Marx, Lenin, Stalin, and Mao.* New York: W. W. Norton, 1979.

Harcourt, G. C. *Some Cambridge Controversies in the Theory of Capital.* Cambridge: Cambridge University Press, 1972.

Haslett, D. W. Is inheritance justified? *Philosophy and Public Affairs* 15: 122–155, 1986.

Herrnstein, Richard. IQ. *Atlantic Monthly,* September: 43–64, 1971.

Hewitt de Alcantara, Cynthia. *Modernizing Mexican Agriculture: Socioeconomic Implications of Technological Change 1940–1970.* Geneva: United Nations Research Institute for Social Development, 1976.

Hilton, Rodney H. *Bond Men Made Free: Medieval Peasant Movement and the English Rising of 1381.* London: Temple Smith, 1973.

Jensen, Arthur. How much can we boost IQ and scholastic achievement? *Harvard Educational Review* 33: 1–33, 1969.

Kamin, Leon J. *The Science and Politics of IQ.* Potomac, Md.: Lawrence Erlbaum Associates, 1974.

—— Is crime in the genes? The answer may depend on who chooses the evidence. *Scientific American,* February: 22–27, 1986.

Konrad, George, and Ivan Szelenyi. *The Intellectuals on the Road to Class Power.* New York: Harcourt Brace Jovanovich, 1979.

Kotz, David. *Bank Control of Large Corporations in the United States.* Berkeley: University of California Press, 1978.

Landes, David. "What do bosses really do?" *Journal of Economic History* 46: 585–623, 1986.

Lenin, V. I. *The Development of Capitalism in Russia* (1899), Moscow: Progress Publishers, 1974.

Mao Zedong. Analysis of classes in Chinese society (1926). In *Selected Works of Mao Tse-tung,* Peking: Foreign Language Press, 1974.

Marglin, Stephen. What do bosses do? The origins and functions of hierarchy in capitalist production. *Review of Radical Political Economics* 6: 60–112, 1974.

Marx, Karl. *The Poverty of Philosophy* (1847). Reprint. New York: International Publishers, 1982.

—— *The Grundrisse: Foundations of the Critique of Political Economy* (1857–58). Trans. M. Nicolaus. London: Allen Lane, 1973.

—— *A Contribution to the Critique of Political Economy* (1859). Trans. S. W. Ryazanskaya; ed. Maurice Dobb. London: Lawrence & Wishart, 1981.

—— *Capital: A Critique of Political Economy,* vol. 1, *The Process of Production of Capital* (1867). Trans. Samuel Moore and Edward Aveling. London: Swan Sonnenschein, Lowrey and Co., 1889. Reprint. New York: International Publishers, 1947.

Marx, Karl, and Friedrich Engels. *The Communist Manifesto* (1848). Trans. Samuel Moore (1888). Reprint. New York: Penguin, 1967.

Matthews, Mervyn. *Privilege in the Soviet Union.* London: Allen & Unwin, 1978.

Meade, James. *Efficiency, Equality and the Ownership of Property.* London: Allen & Unwin, 1954.

Miller, David. Market neutrality and the failure of cooperatives. *British Journal of Political Science* 11: 309–329, 1981.

Milsom, S. F. C. *Historical Foundations of the Common Law.* Toronto: Butterworths, 1981.

Morishima, Michio. *Marx's Economics.* Cambridge: Cambridge University Press, 1973.

Moulin, Hervé, and John E. Roemer. Public ownership of the external world and private ownership of self. Forthcoming.

North, Douglass. *Structure and Change in Economic History.* New York: W. W. Norton, 1982.

North, Douglass, and Robert Thomas. *The Rise of the Western World.* Cambridge: Cambridge University Press, 1973.

Nove, Alec. *The Economics of Feasible Socialism.* London: Allen & Unwin, 1983.

Nozick, Robert. *Anarchy, State, and Utopia.* New York: Basic Books, 1974.

Okishio, N. Technical changes and the rate of profit. *Kobe University Economic Review* 7: 85–99, 1961.

Przeworski, Adam. Material interests, class compromise, and the transition to socialism. In *Analytical Marxism,* ed. J. E. Roemer, pp. 162–188. Cambridge: Cambridge University Press, 1986.

Putterman, Louis. On some recent explanations of why capital hires labor. *Economic Inquiry* 22: 171–207, 1984.

Rawls, John. *A Theory of Justice.* Cambridge, Mass.: Harvard University Press, 1971.

Roemer, John E. *Analytical Foundations of Marxian Economic Theory.* Cambridge: Cambridge University Press, 1981.

—— *A General Theory of Exploitation and Class.* Cambridge, Mass.: Harvard University Press, 1982.

—— New directions in the Marxian theory of exploitation and class. *Politics and Society* 11: 253–287, 1982. Reprinted in *Analytical Marxism* ed. J. E. Roemer, pp. 81–113. Cambridge: Cambridge University Press, 1986.

—— Property relations vs. surplus value in Marxian exploitation. *Philosophy and Public Affairs* 11: 281–313, 1982.

—— Reply. *Politics and Society* 11: 375–394, 1982.

—— Are socialist ethics consistent with efficiency? *Philosophical Forum* XIV: 369–388, 1983.

—— Unequal exchange, labor migration and international capital flows: a theoretical synthesis. In *Marxism, Central Planning and the Soviet Economy: Economic Essays in Honor of Alexander Erlich,* ed. P. Desai, pp. 34–62. Cambridge, Mass.: MIT Press, 1983.

—— Should Marxists be interested in exploitation? *Philosophy and Public Affairs* 14: 30–65, 1985. Reprinted in *Analytical Marxism*, ed. J. E. Roemer, pp. 260–282. Cambridge: Cambridge University Press, 1986.

—— Equality of talent. *Economics and Philosophy* 1:151–187, 1985.

—— (ed.) *Analytical Marxism*. Cambridge: Cambridge University Press, 1986.

—— Equality of resources implies equality of welfare. *Quarterly Journal of Economics* 101: 751–784, 1986.

—— *Value, Exploitation, and Class*. New York: Harwood Academic Publishers, 1986.

Samuelson, Paul. Understanding the Marxian notion of exploitation: a summary of the so-called transformation problem between Marxian values and competitive prices. *Journal of Economic Literature* IX: 399–431, 1971.

Schumpeter, Joseph. *Can Capitalism Survive?* New York: Harper & Row, 1978.

Ste Croix, G. E. M. de. *The Class Struggle in the Ancient Greek World*. London: Duckworth, 1981.

Steedman, Ian. *Marx after Sraffa*. London: New Left Books, 1977.

—— (ed.). *The Value Controversy*. London: New Left Books, 1981.

Thurow, Lester. *The Impact of Taxes on the American Economy*. New York: Praeger, 1971.

Van Parijs, Philippe. Marxism's central puzzle. In *After Marx*, ed. T. Ball and J. Farr, pp. 88–104. Cambridge: Cambridge University Press, 1984.

Varian, Hal. Distributive justice, welfare economics and the theory of fairness. *Philosophy and Public Affairs* 4: 223–247, 1975.

Wallerstein, Immanuel. *The Modern World System vol. I: Capitalist Agriculture and the Origins of the European World-Economy*. New York: Academic Press, 1974.

Wilson, James Q., and Richard Herrnstein. *Crime and Human Nature*. New York: Simon and Schuster, 1985.

Wright, Erik Olin. The status of the political in the concept of class structure. *Politics and Society* 11: 321–342, 1982.

—— *Classes*. London: New Left Books, 1985.

—— What is middle about the middle class? In *Analytical Marxism*, ed. J. E. Roemer, pp. 114–140. Cambridge: Cambridge University Press, 1986.

Index